WOMEN IN POLISH SOCIETY

Edited by Rudolf Jaworski
and Bianka Pietrow-Ennker

EAST EUROPAN MONOGRAPHS, BOULDER
DISTRIBUTED BY COLUMBIA UNIVERSITY PRESS, NEW YORK
1992

EAST EUROPEAN MONOGRAPHS, NO. CCCXLIV

Printed in the United States of America

CONTENTS

Preface

Women's history is currently enjoying a boom in the United States and in Western Europe. It is well on the way to becoming a discipline in its own right with an independent approach. Within women's history, however, Eastern Europe has rarely attracted the attention of historians. The present anthology proposes to focus the attention of Western readers on an Eastern European country in which women played an especially important role during the last century: partitioned Poland. An examination of the situation and the self-perception of Polish women in the nineteenth century, a fascinating and many-sided subject, not only furnishes us with an important dimension of Polish social history but additionally provides the basis for valuable comparisons in international women's history.

Three factors primarily determined the situation of Polish women in the nineteenth century, irrespective of the district they lived in or of their social class. The first decisive factor was the traditional patriarchal structure, which was partly modified in the upper classes by a ritualized veneration of women and in lower class rural areas by the equal importance of female labour. Secondly, the repercussions resulting from statelessness and foreign rule must be taken into account. In many respects, these led to the stabilization of traditional women's roles within Poland which manifested itself in the fact that even for socially active Polish women the struggle for national independence and self-determination took priority over the demands for equal rights for women. Under these circumstances, the maternal role could, for example, acquire a special elevated status, as the family organization proved ultimately to be the only safe sphere in which

Polish national culture could be completely preserved and passed on to the next generation. On the other hand, the permanent state of emergency of Polish society throughout the whole period confronted Polish women with responsibilities which far exceeded their usual sphere of activities, forcing them to hold their own identity professionally, educationally, publicly in defence of Polish interests, conspiratively and even in the insurrections against foreign rule. The irritated reports of Prussian and Russian superintendents amply demonstrate the ability of Polish women to live up to these varied tasks. The last but not least important determining factor for Poland in the nineteenth century was the social change which the divided country experienced under extremely unfavourable conditions and which particularly affected the female population as the gradual industrialization and modernization of the economy was to a not inconsiderable extent carried out with the help of female labour. The rural migration to the towns, the general increase of working women, and their entrance into many professions could not but have an impact on their self-image and on their role within the family. Up to now, comparatively little was known about the course of these sometimes conflicting developments within the various social classes and territories in Poland.

This does not mean that no attention has been paid to Polish women's history. A glance at the footnotes of various articles in this volume and at the bibliographical essay on the Kingdom of Poland show the reader that this is far from being the case. Especially where the nineteenth century is concerned, a relatively large number of separate essays are available, most of which, however, are either biographical or are aimed at a non-specialized readership. In this context, the numerous studies by *Dioniza Wawrzykowska-Wierciochowa* deserve acknowledgement as they provide an important contribution towards a comprehensive representation of Polish women's history. Memoirs and biographical studies further enrich our historical knowledge of Polish women, although much of this material belongs more to the category of literature or cultural history. In addition, a whole range of biographies is extant, which are devoted to the role of outstanding female figures during the struggle for national independence or within the socialist movement.

What most of these studies lacked was a comprehensive treatment of the issue of women's rights, in spite of the fact that there is no lack of source material and that Polish studies of social and cultural history are generally of a high standard. Why the history of Polish women has hitherto not attracted the attention it deserves is a topic which must be studied separately.

In the meantime, however, increased interest in these questions has begun to emerge within Poland. The change of the political system with its corresponding movement towards democratization and the forced admission of Western tendencies has provided a not unimportant stimulus. An increasing number of theses on the subject of women's history are being assigned. Corresponding research projects and study groups are being formed, for example in Posen and Warsaw. From the 25th to the 26th September 1990, the Historical Institute of the University of Warsaw held a conference on the changing social situation of women in the Polish territories during the nineteenth century, which has already been published in book form. [Anna Żarnowska and Andrzej Szwarc (eds.): Kobieta i społeczeństwo na ziemiach polskich w XIX w. Warszawa 1990].

The basic topics and the general tone of this first presentation of the newly-emerging women's history in Poland differs characteristically from the general approach in the West. The starting point and the object of these Polish studies is not primarily distinguished by an attempt to incorporate a new female perspective into historical research or to extend it by including the autonomous category of gender relationships in accordance with the methodology of "Gender History". Nor does it appear that comparable research in Poland is linked to emancipatory or even feminist aims of improving the status of women in Polish society or gaining them greater public recognition. Instead, research is being directed towards general social and historical questions such as mobility, employment, family and the like, taking the specific situations of women within their particular social class as a starting point. It remains to be seen how far this perspective with its tendency to integrate rather than to segregate and which bears a remarkable resemblance to the way politically active Polish women in the nineteenth century saw themselves merely betokens a passing stage at the outset or whether it will turn out to be, in the long run, an independent approach most suited to Polish circumstances.

The idea of tackling the subject with an international cast and then publishing the results in an anthology goes back to a section prepared by the two editors for the IV. World Congress for Soviet and East European Studies in Harrogate (21-26 July 1990) under the general title "Women's Movement and Social Change in the 19th Century. The Polish Case". The first four articles in this anthology are also offshoots of the same project. They clearly testify to the effort made to take all three parts of Poland with their respective problems into consideration. The other articles, which were included subsequently and nevertheless comprise more than half of the book, concentrate geographically on the Russian part of Poland. The focus on this particular field is by no means arbitrary or accidental. In the first place, it corresponds to the historical circumstances, i.e. the fact that the debate concerning the women's question first arose within the Kingdom of Poland where it reached its most radical and intensive form and became a matter of much public discussion. So it is understandable that historical research has paid particular attention to this area.

In order to provide a general framework for the various articles of this anthology, *Bianka Pietrow-Ennker* has provided a synopsis of the historical dimensions of the women's question in all three areas of Poland, examining the social-historical background and considering in particular the external and internal opinions concerning the role of Polish women in the nineteenth century. Subsequently, in a collective portrait, *Bogna Lorence-Kot* characterizes the mentality of politically and socially active Polish women in the Russian part of Poland after the insurrection of 1863. Their outstanding characteristic, she underlines, was their radicalism and their readiness to engage in underground activities, which could be equally mobilized for patriotic goals or for socialist ideals.

The survey of *Rudolf Jaworski* is concerned with an entirely different environment. It deals with the chiefly legal activities of Polish women in the Prussian province of Posen, all of whom were influenced by the German-Polish antagonism, and governed by the principles of "organic work" and a predominantly conservative catholic social solidarity. The article by *Irena Homola-Skąpska* on the other hand makes it clear that in Galicia the efforts to improve the educational opportunities for women became in general especially pronounced after the autonomy of 1867/68. The authoress describes the laborious advance from the initial establishment of secondary and vocational schools for girls to the successful entry of women into the universities at the turn of the century. Subsequently, *Adam Winiarz* describes the opposite turn of events in the Russian part of Poland. At least as far as external circumstances were concerned, the initially favourable educational opportunities for girls became progressively worse during the nineteenth century due to increased interference and encroachment on the part of Russian administrative bodies. On the basis of four case studies, *Małgorzata Czyszkowska-Peschler* describes the extremely difficult professional and social situation of Polish authoresses in Warsaw and in their Parisian exile after the second half of the nineteenth century and examines their opportunities of publication as well as their self-reflections as literary personalities.

All the articles mentioned so far concern themselves in one way or another with the social or political activities of Polish women or women's groups stemming, for the most part, from aristocratic or intellectual circles. In contrast, the articles by *Maria Nietyksza* and *Anna Żarnowska,* both of which were taken from the aforementioned Polish volume, trace the social-historical background which provided the impetus for the increasing importance of the women's question in the Russian part of Poland and look more directly at the lower classes. In both articles, the enquiry into the increased mobility of women and their entrance into the professions around the end of the century is the main focus of interest. Maria Nietyksza concentrates on the many-sided labour market in the Warsaw metropolis, whereas Anna Żarnowska centers her attention on the consequences of female labour for the proletarian family. The final article in this volume, a detailed bibliographical essay by *Adam Winiarz* on the women's question in the Kingdom of Poland, not only documents the extent to which the subject found its way into contemporary journalism but also summarizes once again the relevant Polish scholarship.

All in all, the present volume aims at providing a colourful mixture of independent studies which differ widely from one another in their choice of approach, their field of research and even in their style. The scope of this anthology ranges from essays to statistical analysis. At the present stage of scholarship, the editors did not consider it to be advisable to interfere normatively in any way, prefering rather to offer the readers the widest possible range of research approaches and modes of representation within the given frame of reference.

The thematic gaps in this volume are already evident in the table of contents. Important aspects, for example rural areas, were almost entirely omitted, likewise the links between Polish women's initiatives in the three separate Polish sectors and many more such subjects. A whole row of areas requiring further work were touched on in the individual articles. However, under the present circumstances, it was neither the ambition nor the function of this book, the first anthology on this subject in a Western language, to provide a finished picture of Polish women's history in the nineteenth century. This volume should be considered more in the light of a series of experimental drillings intended to encourage further research.

Rudolf Jaworski
Bianka Pietrow-Ennker

Bianka Pietrow-Ennker

1

WOMEN IN POLISH SOCIETY
A HISTORICAL INTRODUCTION

Interpretations by Polish historiographers of the relationship between the sexes in Polish history have frequently invoked the existence of a "benign patriarchalism". Thus a picture has been painted of Polish womanhood as having been held in particularly high male esteem ever since the end of the middle ages on account of her role both inside the family and in society at large. It has been by and large accepted that a perusal of the literature turns up countless portraits of self-confident, resolute women from all social classes, who not only ran their family households capably but also exercized considerable influence on their husbands and families and even on public affairs. Society's readiness to revere women is even supposed to have increased during the time of partition. For, it is argued, it was the mothers who kept Polish culture alive during the years of lost freedom by raising their children in the spirit of Polish national traditions.[1] This readiness to accord recognition and respect to women is held to be expressed most clearly in the image of matka Polka, the holy mother of Poland: just as Mary–symbolized in the iconography of Częstochowa–had been appointed to watch over the Polish nation, so too women–as Mary's successors on earth–were seen as being entrusted with the task of caring for the smallest unit of the nation, the family, and seeing that it had Christian values instilled into it.

1

At the beginning of the 20th century, though, the prominent advocate of women's rights, Iza Moszczeńska, rejected this interpretation. She argued that, on the contrary, Polish popular opinion saw women as deriving their status entirely from their husbands: the good or the bad points of their personalities, the presence or absence of ambition and intellect, were of no importance whatsoever. In the social hierarchy females were ranged well below males. To make sense of women's low place in society, the authoress felt obliged to refer to the materialist philosophy of history. She argued that, with the exception of when exercizing their maternal functions, women in prehistoric times had inhabited the same value universe as men, meaning that both sexes had then shouldered the same responsibilities for earning a living. However, with the emergence of a division of labor in connection with the rise of private property, women's fate had been to be relegated to the sphere of the home. Ever since then, according to this authoress, their status has been pegged to that of their husbands, the "rulers and providers". This was tantamount to a bloodletting of their psychic and physical energies, the result being that women were downgraded to playing very much a secondary role in the civilizational process—while their menfolk were left to get on with the struggle against the outside world and to book ever new victories to their credit. Confined to a marital nest-building role, women finally became reduced to serving a focal interest alien to their own ends, namely that of providing conditions conducive to the development of the male personality. This deep role division opened up a deep rift between husband and wife. Even the step-by-step integration of women into the work process brought them no closer to personal independence—for the same reason that work alone does not free serfs from their bondage. Since women were now the property of their husbands, the institution of marriage was saddled with a treacherous double morality, which bound only women to the narrow path of virtue while curtailing none of their husband's freedoms. Thus, concluded Moszczeńska, the women's question was also very much the men's question. "The accession of women to full humanity"–a central platform of the international women's movement–called for a change in the role division between the sexes; it required the moral rebirth of men as well as the free, creative self-development of women.[2]

The essay of Moszczeńska's was published in 1903 in a volume of collected essays which itself represents one of the pinnacles of the women's rights movement in the partitioned province of Galicia. Such leading lights of the local women's movement as Marya Turzyma, Kazimiera Bujwidowa and Paulina Kuczalska-Reinschmit had already (in 1902/3) organized a celebrated series of lectures on the position of women. When these appeared shortly afterwards in book form, protagonists of women's rights found themselves supplied with a whole battery of arguments for use in their struggle to achieve an equal say for women in family, society and state.

How then can we characterize the position of women in Polish society? On the one hand, we encounter the concept of a "benign patriarchalism", which posits that women were left with a certain amount of personal freedom of manoeuvre and control over their own lives; on the other hand, though, we find Polish women even as late as at the beginning of the 20th century still regarding themselves as the slaves of their menfolk. Is Danuta Markowska right in maintaining that "benign patriarchalism" is nothing but a fiction that has caught on by overinterpreting the importance of a few exceptional personalities that happen to be biographically well-documented?[3]

But let us return once again to Moszczeńska's demand for a transformation in the relations between the sexes, for a renegotiation of the hoary gender role division. In truth, her position only makes sense when seen against the background of the history of Polish womanhood. We must ask what role understandings determined women's lives in traditional Polish society? And what were the factors that induced women to "emancipate" themselves, i.e. in the literal sense of disavowing the traditional patriarchal ties in an attempt to colonize new fields of activity and grow in human terms?

The poor state of present research permits us only to peer dimly into the worlds these women emerged from; furthermore, the manner in which they disentangled themselves from tradition and then went on to stake out brave new worlds of personal unfolding for themselves as women is just as poorly apprehended.[4]

However, historical scholarship is heavily indebted to Bogna Lorence-Kot who, in her dissertation on the family structure of the Polish nobility of the 18th century, has been able to provide basic new insights into the traditional place occupied by women before the modern age. In her study, Lorence-Kot first lays the groundwork by going back even further and tracing the premodern role of women in the 17th century. Just how complex women's existential situation at this time actually was is shown by the following passage:

"As a group, Polish women counted for less than men. As szlachta, they were equal to men. But the importance of individual women depended on their family's status. That factor transcended sexual inferiority as well as noble equality. In addition, women as wives bowed to the authority of their husbands, but as mothers they reaped all the benefits of the fourth commandment."[5]

If we are to resolve the apparent contradiction between the principles of equality and subordination here referred to, we must reflect on the importance attached to the family in the Polish nobility as a core socio-economic institution. The equality principle, as part of the szlachta ethos, certainly did prevail among noble families in their dealings with each other and, at the same time, served to mark them off from other social classes. Thus the importance of having the right blood was expressed in the way males from the nobility all felt themselves to be "brothers" in a single large "family"–the overarching aristocratic order as such. From the viewpoint of the married women's position, this ethos of equality did indeed offer some protection. When disagreements arose, the standing of the women's parental house vied with that of her husband's own household as contending forces. Parents had the right to intervene to protect their daughter from humiliation at her husband's hands. However, there was no similar right to protect children from parental cruelty. Sons and daughters were under an obligation of absolute obedience to their parents. Since the latter looked on marriage primarily as a political and economic transaction undertaken to serve the interests of the family, they naturally reserved for themselves the prerogative of selecting suitable brides or bridegrooms for their offspring.[6]

Although the injuction of faithfulness was equally incumbent on both marriage partners, only the woman was under an obligation to obey–a constant we find cutting across all class divides. In this respect, her position was decidedly that of a subordinate–an inequality reflected most transparently in the laws applying to inheritance. In the agrarian social order of the day, central importance resided in the male heir as far as preserving the family possessions was concerned. A woman could not inherit her husband's estate, although she could administer it in his absence or after his death. The control that a husband could exercize over his wife was, however, limited by her possessing a degree of financial independence. Both during and after her marriage, the woman was entitled to a fixed legacy for her own material support. Prenuptial contracts fixing the size of the dowry were customary among the nobility. It was the daughters' established right to receive a fourth part of their father's estate, though this was customarily paid out in monetary form. In cases where landed property was available for inclusion in the dowry, the relatives had prior right of purchase if they chose to exercize it–the overriding aim here being to keep the family lands intact.[7]

In this matter, the szlachta even succeeded in enlisting the Polish Catholic Church in their service. Marriages between minors were contracted–despite Vatican misgivings and in express contradiction to canonical law. The number of marriage annulments was always considerable and even increased in the 18th century–although, to be sure, these were mainly confined to the highest ranks of the nobility, which alone had access to sufficient wealth and social prestige to be able to weather such frowned-upon procedures unscathed.[8]

As Bogna Lorence-Kot's detailed treatment has brought to light, annulment petitions in the 18th century show two things: First, they testify to the strong position held within the family by the wife as mother. Depending on the family's status, so the wife's own status would rise considerably as soon as she had given birth to a (male) heir. Indeed, this furnished proof of the highest virtue on her part. Second, the records of annulment hearings point to a certain decline in morals during the 18th century. If under the Sarmatian aristocratic order it was still considered an integral part of the male code of honor, even right down to the 17th century, to extend respect and esteem to married women and to protect both her and the children from marital arbitrariness, we now find these documentary sources increasingly charging married women with grasping and cruel conduct. The allegation is made that they force their daughters under threat of violence to agree to marriages with rich men of dubious reputation, who then promptly make their daughters' lives into hell on earth.

These petitions and hearing protocols, however, also furnished proof that a change of attitude was then getting underway; a new sense of individuality, accompanied by a demand for personal happiness, came to be felt and, in due course, became so strong that some women felt driven to throw over all ties of obedience to parents and husbands. In so doing, they were rebelling against the prevailing aristocratic ideology of the times (Sarmatism). This weltanschauung, which was based on an idealization of landed property, the family and the Catholic faith, enjoined on women a fixed code of behavioral conduct. It was held to be the "nature of women" to be ruled over and sexually controlled by their husbands. Chastity before marriage, virtuous conduct at all times, aptitude in running a household, and unconditional loyalty to the family—these were considered to be the hallmarks of a "good" wife. Infidelity was frowned upon, so as not to prejudice the family's genealogical purity. Suitors had to be able to point to at least the same social standing to have any chance of gaining a lady's hand. Women of the nobility spent their daily lives exclusively in the precincts of their households–indeed they lived in a state of secludedness, without access to the round of amusements that formed such a large part of West European courtly life. Not surprisingly, a low value was placed on the education of girls, no matter how elevated their family background. It was seen as more to the point that they should acquire skills in running a household. Yet it would be far from true to say that female illiteracy counted as the accolade of perfection in all noble houses.[9]

To recapitulate the argument so far: "benign patriarchalism", to the extent there was such a thing, was mainly an offshoot of the aristocratic ethos. The aristocratic code of honor was equally binding on both sexes, for all that each sex had a different gender role assigned to it by society.

It is a moot point whether such writings on the history of Polish women as those by Rudolf Ottmann really do prove the existence of "emancipation" for the women of the nobility or whether they do not merely reproduce the Sarmatian-influenced image of women prevalent in these early times. To be sure, the author correctly reports that women would represent their husbands in the administration of their landed properties and in legal affairs; also, that they displayed considerable acumen in these roles, and knew how to stand their ground in disputes.[10] On the other hand, though, the satires on women quoted by Ottmann (e.g. those written by the 16th century chronicler, Marcin Bielski) show how quickly women could become the butt of male derision as soon as they dared to defend even their most immediate private interests from male encroachment, let alone make an appearance in the public sphere. With raised finger and in no uncertain fashion, women were banished by their menfolk back into the world of the home if ever they dared to speak out against such crying injustices as the large incidence of marriages contracted for low, material motives, the exclusion of married women from society, frivolous male conduct at women's expense, etc.[11]

Women-related historical scholarship is still far too patchy to throw much light on the question of just how much women participated in public life in the distant Polish past. Stanisław Kutrzeba has made the point that the Church was unsuccessful in remoulding the image of women along the lines it favored. It took no more than a slight contact with the Renaissance to touch off a positive reassessment of women's place in society. Indeed even earlier we find courtly culture being influenced by the Franco-Hungarian style introduced by Elżbieta, the mother of Louis of Hungary and Poland (1384-1399), who ruled in Poland as his appointed viceroy. From that time on, entertainments, education, enjoyment of social life and joie de vivre were no longer viewed as exclusively male preserves.[12] But the even more important flowering of courtly culture in the first half of the 16th century is inseparably connected with the name of Bona Sforza, who endeavored to transplant the Italian lifestyle of her parental house into distant Poland.[13] The keen interest of the day in cultural products of all kinds did not remain confined to the court alone, but spread down from there to the great houses of the local magnates, the patricians, and the more prosperous of the nobility. Women from these circles discovered for themselves the world of the Renaissance and its spiritual ideals, which strove to raise relations between the sexes to a new level of mutual appreciation and respect. Women were no longer excluded from the marvels of the world of books. But even though we find individual women taking up the study of philosophy and the sciences, and actually embarking on scholarly careers, Dionizja Wawrzykowska-Wierciochowa is no doubt right in cautioning us not to forget the unrepresentative and privileged character of such cases. Both she and Łucja Charewiczowa stress that right down to the 18th century it was very much the exception for women to attain to any form of social influence through educational distinction.[14]

The reason why noblewomen were partially successful in emerging from the familiar world of the home may well have been the frequent absence of their menfolk—necessitated by the imperatives of warfare or by official duties that required their presence far from the family estates. During these absences, noblemen would entrust to their wives the administration of their sometimes far-flung landed estates, with all the manifold duties this involved. Indeed there were cases of women who so excelled at running the economic affairs of their husbands' estates that, in the end, their husbands were reduced to the largely formal role of representing the family in its dealings with the outside world. We find cases of wives, sisters and mothers being vested with such extensive responsibilities that they could themselves conduct trials or appear before courts and speak on their own behalf. We find other cases of women founding manufactories, engaging in trade and, not least of all, intervening in political affairs.

This advance in women's fortunes can be dated to the latter half of the 18th century. The consequence of the adoption of French culture was that women abandoned the sequestered world of Sarmatian domesticity for the vibrant life of the aristocratic salon. The conversational exchanges that were standard fare in these milieus inspired in many a woman a thirst for education and self-improvement, so as not merely to have to shine through one's physical charms. The first time noblewomen spoke out in public appears to have been in connection with the Confederation of Bar (1768-1772). This oppositional movement mounted by conservative nobles against the reformist policies of King Stanisław II August (Poniatowski) managed on by the great powers, France and Austria–to plunge Poland into a four-year civil war. Noblewomen were prominent on both the reformist and conservative sides in such numbers that contemporaries even heaped derision on the Confederation of Bar as being a "squabble among women." Furthermore, reports have it that, during the sessions of the four-year (reformist) diet or sejm (6 Oct 1788-29 May 1792), noblewomen would even barricade the chamber entrances in order to heckle and jeer at the hapless delegates inside![15]

The celebrated Anna z Sapiehów Jabłonowska was one of those involved in such escapades, a magnate who has found a firm place in the scholarly literature as a quintessential example of emancipated Polish womanhood. Stefan Król writes about her, "It was not the babble of voices in the Rococo salons that attracted her, not the courtly intrigues in which beautiful ladies decked out in powdered wigs cut such a figure. Her interest was in politics and, above all, in the art of sagacious economic management. Eagerly she studied the latest economic theories. She was also passionately interested in zoology and mineralogy...."[16]

Anna Jabłonowska's family background was representative of the cosmopolitan, progressively minded Polish nobility of the times. The daughter received a first-rate education and, after her marriage, traveled throughout Europe at her husband's side. After her return, she devoted herself to the task of running an estate–initially in place of her husband, who had remained abroad, and then later after his death in her own right. Soon she belonged to the most influential spokespersons of the Confederation of Bar, picking up the nickname "Madame de Barez" in the process. After the downfall of the Confederation, she was prudent enough to seek a reconciliation with the unpopular king. However, it was not long before she drew new attention to herself. Between 1783 and 1785 she saw through the press (incidentally her own press) her eight-volume opus Ustawy powszechne dla dóbr moich rządców, which was accorded an enthusiastic reception in reformist party circles at the time of the Four-Year Diet (sejm). In these "Statutes" she sought to reform the bondsman status of the peasants on her own estates, embracing the theory that the only way to raise agricultural productivity was to improve working conditions on the land. But her concern was not merely to effect a reorganization of the peasant economy; she also strove to ameliorate peasant life as a whole by introducing schools, medical care and accident compensation. In another of her many writings she analyzed the position of women, proposing that family law be modified to extend more rights to mothers and widows. Finally, in 1784, she published a guidance manual for young wives on how to run a household.[17]

Space does not permit me to present other examples of active, spirited noblewomen of the time–women of the likes of Zofia Lubomirska, Franciszka Krasińska, Anna Raciborska, Elżbieta Drużbacka and Izabela Czartoryska. Thus this present portrait of Anna Jabłonowska must stand proxy for many.

Historiographers are unanimous that the series of partitions of Poland not only generally steered the historical development of the country into new channels, but that they also cast a long and lasting shadow over Polish women's lives. The great reform debate on the need to modernize the structure of the Polish state–which got underway as soon as the shock of the first partition had subsided and which culminated in the passage of the May Constitution of 1791–did not bypass the question of women's place in society. Indeed the latter became one of the leading issues of the day in connection with the general issue of educational reform, when such progressively minded reformers as Hugo Kołłątaj came out for extending an improved education to girls. In any case, the general question of children's education had an overtly political component injected into it as a result of the decision by the three powerful neighbors of Poland to divide that hapless country up among themselves. Since Poles were now excluded from all responsibility for running their own land, the inculcation of national awareness came to devolve entirely upon the family. The latter became the stronghold of national identity during the whole of the time when Polish public life was hamstrung by the dictates of the partition powers. Poles came to regard their children–the next generation–as held in sacred pledge against a future to be spent in national freedom. And the task of raising them in the spirit of Polish ideals fell to the woman. Thus, as a direct result of the partitions, the position of women in the family came to take on a new semi-political, semi-cultural significance. Women were no longer enjoined to be mothers in the traditional sense (which had had a fairly low value attached to it in the family pecking order); now her task was to consecrate her maternal functions to the cause of national responsibility, to ensuring that her children were brought up across sex lines as patriots, as the coming saviors of the Polish nation.[18]

Thus women's lives in partitioned Poland cannot be separated from this phenomenon of the revaluation of the family. Both the Church and society at large joined forces to commit women to setting an edifying moral and emotional example. In line with religious tradition, the qualities sought from women were self-sacrifice and self-abnegation; these were now invested with new prestige–as exemplified in the person of Matka Polka, the divine protectress and patron saint of the nation. This idealization of women was certainly, on the one hand, a source of strength for national resistance; yet, on the other hand, it bound together family and nation so tightly that any strivings by women for emancipation from family ties seemed tantamount to national and religious betrayal. Such attempts at emancipation were strictly taboo–as is shown by the pejorative use of the term, which came to be generally associated with the emergence of women of the likes of George Sand.

Apart from this new cultural phenomenon of commitment to a somewhat extended maternal role, women's lives in the aftermath of partition were influenced by the social effects touched off by two further factors: on the one hand, the abolition of serfdom and, on the other, the introduction of industrialization. In order to grasp the problems that confronted all women irrespective of class as a result of the transition to a bourgeois, capitalist economy, it is first necessary to cast a glance at the altered existential circumstances brought about by the final partition of the Polish state undertaken by Prussia, Russia and Austria in 1795.

From the economic perspective, all three partitioned Polish lands ceased to be part of a single, unified regional economic order. The social changes involved depended on the way each partitioned land was incorporated into the economy of its respective occupying power, as well as on the political strategy adopted towards the Polish population in that particular land. To recapitulate the essentials only briefly: Russia adopted the policy in its province of undermining the economic basis of the Polish nobility, the ulterior motive being to break their political power. Thus the economic strength of the Polish nobility in the Congress Kingdom was weakened not only by severance from traditional trading routes and the imposition of new tariff barriers. On top of this, thousands of aristocratic families were hard hit–especially in the wake of the abortive uprisings in 1831 and 1864–by confiscation of their goods, enforced contributions to the state, and the elimination of whole groups of them from economic and social life as a result of political persecution. A further factor was the imposition of restrictive taxation and credit policies. The upshot was that the social differentiation process on the land was speeded up–helped along by the Czar's decision in 1864 to abolish serfdom (a decision taken, to be sure, with his own interests in mind). Hardest hit of all were the lower ranks of the nobility, i.e. the gentry, who were so numerous in the first half of the 19th century as to make up virtually 50 percent of the nobility as a whole.[19]

The ruined members of this class gravitated into the cities, where they proved fertile soil for the slowly growing class of the intelligentsia. Spreading along with industrialization itself, they found employment in private enterprise, trade, transport and in public office. Many of them, however, fell victim to the Russification policy embarked on after 1864: they were removed from their positions or, alternatively, they boycotted themselves out of national pride.[20] The result was a chronic lack of employment; but also an increasingly professional engagement in underground activities–especially in connection with education, where women too found a rich field of expression for their talents. Certainly education was not the only field to attract women–yet, according to the Russian census conducted in 1897, the numbers of women employed in education in the Russian province of occupied Poland amounted to no less than approximately 39 percent.[21]

Uneducated women (coming mainly from the impoverished peasantry) who, as a result of the differentiation process on the land, had lost their means of support, either went into service as maids or, more commonly, streamed into the expanding industrial sector, most notably the textile branch, where employers on the look-out for cheap labor were only too happy to give them the preference over men. According to a report compiled by the first Russian inspector of factories in the Congress Kingdom, 41 percent of all industrial workers in 1885 were women (or, to express it in actual numbers, there were 29,565 women employed). Women were especially prominent in some industries–for instance, in 1885 they made up 49.59 percent of the work force in textile manufacturing, 45.62 percent in paper manufacturing, and 40.58 percent in the timber industry.[22] Just these data alone make clear the extent to which female labor had become a central force by the 1880s in the economic life of the Russian part of divided Poland.

By comparison with the situation in Russian-occupied Poland, social change in the Austrian and Prussian provinces proceeded under quite different constraints. Whereas the relative autonomy of the government of Congress Poland headed by Finance Minister Drucki-Lubecki enabled developments favorable to industry and agriculture to be set in motion in the years after 1815, it was the fate of the Austrian province of Galicia to be stifled right from the start by the crushing weight of Austrian bureaucracy, which saw no point in furthering the economic development of this peripheral region. A combination of rapid population growth, backward production methods on the land, and the practice of dividing up the father's property on his death so as to give each son an equal share, all conspired to plunge the Galician peasantry into an ever-deepening spiral of poverty. Only when autonomous status was achieved in 1867 did political conditions emerge that were somewhat more conducive to economic growth (although even then the economic preconditions for bringing about a rapid industrialization process were still absent).

In Galicia, women seeking work came largely from the impoverished country gentry and the ruined peasantry alike. Such was their striving for education and qualified employment that, once the statute of autonomy had been ratified, they were quickly able to take advantage of the chance to form societies and establish democratic movements. They formed professional bodies and, at the close of the century, launched a movement for educational reform which won the right of entry to grammar school and university-level education for women.[23]

A predilection for activity within societies also characterized the women's movement in the Prussian-ruled Polish province, despite the fact that this movement developed under completely different socio-economic and political conditions from those in Galicia. In the Prussian part of Poland, the strategy pursued by the occupying power followed the diametrically opposite path: after 1815 a tolerant atmosphere prevailed at first; but in the wake of the abortive insurrections (which were supported by a wide section of the Polish population in Prussian Poland) this gave way to a frigid confrontationalism and Kulturkampf between Poles and Germans. In contrast to the situation in Galicia, the setting-up of the Grand Duchy of Posen testified to a Prussian interest in encouraging an economic integration of the region. Both in agricultural production and in manufacturing we find a Polish middle class developing which, even during the height of the Germanization policies, was able to extend its position and even thrive–indeed was able to set up a thick network of nationally minded organizations which stiffly opposed the Germanization policies practiced by the Prussians.[24]

As Janina Leskiewiczowa has emphasized, the socio-economic processes briefly adumbrated above resulted in a weakening of family ties across all social class divides. With the evolution of the middle-class family and the concomitant separation between economic production and home life, family structure itself began to undergo a functional transformation. From now on, family became synonymous with the private sphere and a refuge from the outside world–ruled over by the woman, while the man concentrated all his efforts on making his mark in the outside world. The importance of the aristocratic family was also whittled away progressively as high birth ceased to be regarded the sine qua non for social standing. Along with the migration of the rural population into the urban centers now getting underway, old family-centered mores–such as the custom of marrying within one's own class–also gave way slowly to codes of conduct of a more strongly individualistic bent. Another factor of special relevance to women was that their first experiences of earning a living outside the home environment (for all that their hand was forced here by material hardship) nonetheless instilled a new feeling of independence in them–coupled with a growing irritation at social discrimination directed at one's own person.

To an extent, this process of change was counteracted by the increased cultural and political importance devolving on the family, though the latter could not stem the erosion of the traditional family ties à la longue. Politically aware women felt increasingly thwarted by the fact that in all three partitioned provinces (in the Congress Kingdom the Code Napoléon had been introduced along with the establishment of the Duchy of Warsaw) they occupied a subordinate position with respect to men.[25]

Women's post-partition struggle for emancipation–understood as the attempt to cast off traditional ties in a patriarchally structured social order and achieve a greater degree of control over their own lives–was mainly channeled as a historical fact into the 19th century movement for educational reform. Here the new mandate extended to Polish motherhood to instill into their children the right national sentiments was just as potent a factor as the phenomenon of social change per se. As the history of the emancipation movement in all three partitioned provinces shows, women's endeavors to improve their lot cannot be separated from the national struggle for freedom and both grew hand in hand–especially since women's growing involvement in public life outside the home was at one and the same time also an act of national self-affirmation. For the reality confronting women was that their emancipation in political and social life had to be extracted not only from their own menfolk, but from the occupying powers as well. It is the presence of this national component that makes the Polish women's movement such a unique historical manifestation and which also differentiates it so utterly from the emancipation movements of other countries.

After partition, reformist circles in Polish society were well aware that women, in their dual role as mothers and as citizens, would have to counteract the danger of lost national identity by a new focus on the way they raised their children. Nonetheless, the nobility held out against improvements in girls' education. Since education was, initially at least, a prerogative of the nobility, this meant that women's education as a whole got off to a very slow start.[26]

An important date in the history of the women's emancipation movement in Poland is 1808. This is the year in which the Chamber of Education (Izba Edukacyjna) of the Duchy of Warsaw–originally established a year earlier (1807) in the tradition of the National Educational Commission of 1773–set up a central supervisory board with a network of regional departments. Women of the highest social standing were recruited to sit on this board and supervise the kind of upbringing imparted to girls. This was the first time women were ever granted the right to engage in a public administrative activity. Here we encounter once again such adornments of cosmopolitan aristocratic circles as Zofia Lubomirska and Izabela Czartoryska, who in the debate over educational reform mobilized their social connections in the service of their fellow women.[27] The activity of these noble-women points up in exemplary fashion how the traditional aristocratic duty of philanthropy became "modernized", i.e. merged imperceptibly with political engagement on behalf of the divided nation.[28]

Above all it can be said of Izabela Czartoryska–as well as of countless later figures in the history of Polish feminism, by no means all of them of aristocratic origin–that she took an active part in the insurgent movements. For instance, this magnate placed large sums of money at the disposal of Tadeusz Kościuszko. But there were other women too who worked as nurses caring for wounded insurgents, or who delivered dispatches, or who took in widows, orphans and prisoners; there were even some–like Joanna Żubrowa, Emilia Plater, Antonina Tomaszewska and others–who donned a uniform and took up arms to fight for the freedom of their fatherland. At the time of the November Rising, the first women's organization, the Charitable Society of Women Patriots (Towarzystwo Dobroczynności Patriotycznej Kobiet), was founded to serve the patriotic cause. Initially, it engaged openly in charitable works, before taking its operations underground after the repression of the insurrection and caring mainly for the victims of the political repressions.[29]

Four outstanding personalities symbolize the four stages in which the 19th century-women's movement developed: Kle-

mentyna z Tańskich Hoffmanowa, Narcyza Żmichowska, Eliza
Orzeszkowa and Paulina Kuczalska-Reinschmit. The lives of
these women stand for the social and national misery of the
Polish people. At the same time they represent the women's fight
for new ideas and initiatives in order to improve the fate of their
sisters.[30]

At the turn of the 18th century our attention is attracted by
Klementyna z Tańskich Hoffmanowa. Her life history intersects
with the social upheavals of the times in almost exemplary
fashion. It testifies to the way in which numerous aristocratic
families had their existential basis hard hit by the abortive
Kościuszko uprising, the Napoleonic Wars, and by the economic
hardships inflicted by the partition policies. Thus the young girl
was faced not only with the ruin of her family's fortunes and the
occupation of her homeland, but also with the negative effects of
both on her own life prospects. She was, however, able to come
to react to these on terms of her own making, by becoming
Poland's first woman writer to live from her pen alone. Not only
was she active as one of the pioneering members of the Towarzystwo Dobroczynności Patriotycznej Kobiet; she was also
the first female literary figure to train a critical eye on the
contemporary state of gender relationships. At the same time,
she was concerned to counteract the impression being received
in established society that she had come out for
"emancipation"–and this she did by publishing at the age of only
21 years a guidebook on ethical matters for mothers and daughters.[31] Klementyna did not call in question the prevailing conviction that men were intellectually superior to women; rather she
drew a contrasting picture of women as the backbone of the
moral order, as creators of homelife and nurturers of Polish
national culture. The female sex, she declared provocatively,
had a right to the same respect as the male, since both sexes
discharged different, though socially speaking equally indispen-
sable functions.

Tańska Hoffmanowa's work on educational theory was revolutionary inasmuch as it offered no less than a critical reception
of the functional transformation of the family just then getting

underway. The authoress addressed herself to the emerging division of labor in middle-class households, where women were supposed to represent the inner sanctum and were expected to pass on to their children the socially sanctioned behavioral norms. On top of this, Hoffmanowa herself was the personification of a new kind of women's awareness, this time of distinctly middle class origins. Despite remaining unmarried, she took on the role of "spiritual motherhood" when she set about earning her own living in 1828. She became an instructress at the first state-run vocational school for women, the Instytut Rządowy Wychowania Płci Żeńskiej, the function of which was to train governesses.[32]

The next two phases in the struggle for women's emancipation are associated with the names of the writers Narcyza Żmichowska and Elżbieta (Eliza) z Pawłowskich Orzeszkowa. The first of these, Żmichowska, came from the ranks of the impoverished nobility. She had taken vocational training so as to be able to earn her own living–in fact she was one of the graduates of the Warsaw Governess Institute. An important influence in the intellectual formation of this revolutionary, democratic woman was her own brother, whom Narcyza visited in exile in France at the end of the 1830s (where he had fled to after actively participating in the November Rising). On her return to Poland, she became associated with the radical-democratic forces moving in the orbit of the Democratic Society (Towarzystwo Demokratyczne). Not only did she make their demands for equal treatment and freedom for the Polish people her own, but she also sought to have women's rights made part of the platform–a step seconded by the circle of "Enthusiasts" she had gathered around her (and to which e.g. the revolutionary Edward Dembowski also belonged, the members of this circle being no means only women). It was Żmichowska and her circle who demanded the liberation of the female sex from its traditional gender shackles. Under the influence of the French Romantic movement and inspired by the optimistic mood of the "Springtime of the Nations" in the run-up to 1848, they spoke out for the inclusion of women within the ambit of full humanity, for the actualization of their personalities, for their right to higher education, for granting them equal access to participation in public life–all of this infused with the ideal of placing any new freedoms gained in the service of the Polish people and fatherland.

The small collection of women intellectuals making up this movement was not able to influence public opinion over any lengthy period of time. They and it together fell victim to the repressions launched after the uprisings of 1846 and 1848 (in which Żmichowska herself played an active part). Nonetheless, this group was of fundamental importance for the cause of women's emancipation. The "Enthusiasts" championed the idea of equality for both sexes irrespective of class–just as had been proclaimed by the French Revolution, at least in Olympe des Gouges' interpretation extended to women. Furthermore, they were instrumental in helping women attain new freedom of movement, i.e. by simply brushing aside conventions and following in the footsteps of George Sand and other like-minded members of the feminist avant-garde.[33]

By the 1870s, when Eliza Orzeszkowa became active in support of the cause of women's emancipation,[34] the socio-economic circumstances in the Congress Kingdom had already undergone radical change. Women were streaming from the land in droves and seeking work in the newly established industrial centers. Impoverished women of aristocratic origin–who had already in the first half of the century been driven to accept positions as maids, governesses, heads of households or nurses in well-to-do houses, while discreetly trying to set themselves up in various handicrafts (despite the fact that this flew in the face of their class ethos)–were thrown onto the market more than ever before from the 1860s on. Thus, the phenomenon of women working for a living now assumed mass dimensions.[35] This in turn changed the terms in which the debate on women's rights was being conducted, introducing a new emphasis on economic issues and material hardship. Women's emancipation–in these years more or less identified with social and legal equality–developed into a major preoccupation of the Warsaw positivist school, which accepted the values of bourgeois society and was orientated towards the doctrines of Auguste Comte, John Stuart Mill and Herbert Spencer[36] Yet in taking a firm principled stand on women's issues no one outdid Eliza Orzeszkowa, who was by now the leading woman exponent of positivism and was destined to become something of a mythical figure within the Polish emancipation movement of the day. Her novel *Marta* (1873) touched off an unexpectedly deep resonance; indeed it became *the* Polish novel of the century written by a woman about a woman. In *Marta* Orzeszkowa describes the tragedy of a young widow whose fate it is to have to fend for both herself and her child, without having any vocational training to fall back on. Marta's life ends in poverty and death, but not before going through a series of bitter experiences with a society that previously accorded her the greatest respect as long as she had been married to a prosperous husband. But now that she was left alone to fight for survival, the suffering gone through by Marta in her eventually losing battle finally leads to the bitter insight that "by existing human rights and standards [a woman is]...not even a human being but just a thing."[37]

There are many points of contact between Eliza Orzeszkowa's own fate and that of the heroine of her novel. Her husband's entire possessions were confiscated by the Russian authorities as a reprisal for taking part in the 1863 insurrection and he himself was banished to Siberia. She was obliged to part with her own possessions on account of the crippling taxes imposed on them, meaning that from then on she had to earn her own keep. As a progressively minded positivist activist (who founded Polish schools along positivist lines) she soon found herself placed under Russian police surveillance; as a woman who when her marriage failed took steps to get an annulment and then entered into a liaison with a married man, she was long ostracized from polite society. Thus it is no wonder that Orzeszkowa's 52-volume complete works show her repeatedly returning to the position of women in the social order. We find her protesting against an obsolete gender role division that hardly left women with any time to cultivate their own highly contemporary individual needs. Within the framework of the positivist program, she dismissed the Romantically tinged mood of rebelliousness then prevalent, opposing to it her own rationally minded program of "organic work", which was rooted in the belief that tolerance, education, work and science are the basic motors of civilization. In this approach, we find the education of women once again playing the cornerstone role in lifting women's general intellectual level, degree of self-articulation, and capacity for work. Orzeszkowa won additional renown as a proponent of women's rights, expending much of her energies in the encouragement of women–e.g. in 1896 she turned her house into an underground cultural institute for girls.[38]

Thanks to her prodigious energies, this woman of letters became a leading light in the reform-minded national resistance movement mounted by Polish womanhood–which stood in place of an organized women's movement in the Congress Kingdom during the years of political repression after 1863.[39] On top of that, Orzeszkowa's activities in fact contributed much to the eventual formation of an organized women's movement in later years. Thus, when the first Polish Women's Congress met clandestinely in Warsaw, it was to honor her literary achievements.

In the Russian-administered province of Galicia where, by contrast, there existed more or less complete freedom of manoeuvre, this was made full use of by proponents of women's rights–by the likes of Kazimiera z Klimontowiczów Bujwidowa, for example, who came to Cracow together with her husband, a professor of bacteriology. In her Warsaw days Bujwidowa had already been an education-obsessed "student" sitting in on lectures at the "Underground University" (*Uniwersytet Latający*), which had been founded by the teacher and publicist Jadwiga Szczawińska-Dawidowa. Now, in the Cracow of the 1890s, she developed into a prominent spokesperson for granting women access to tertiary education.[40]

The drive for women's rights as an organized socio-political movement can be traced back to the 1880s–actually, in the Russian-ruled province its inception can even be assigned an exact date, 1883, when the Women's Circle for Popular Education (*Kobiece Koło Oświaty Ludowej*) was set up by around 70 Warsaw women under the leadership of Kasylda Kulikowska, the aim being to take the educational idea directly to "the people", i.e. the women on the land.[41] Three years later, at the instigation of the emigrant organization, *Liga Polska*, the Women's Circle of the Congress Kingdom and Lithuania (*Koło Kobiet Korony i Litwy*) was set up to engage in a political and patriotic program of activities. This organization worked in cultural and educational affairs in all three partitioned provinces, the overriding goal being to lay the basis for a new attempt by the Polish people to wrest their freedom from their oppressors. A large part of the female intellectual elite of the day became involved in its activities; women's congresses—some held underground, some in full public view—were organized and held; and, in general, an outburst of energy was unleashed that was in no sense diminished by its division in 1901 into two wings, one more sympathetic to the organized labor movement and the other more national–democratically inclined.

A further, more internationally orientated branch of the women's movement grew up around the person of Paulina Kuczalska-Reinschmit, and academically trained woman whose mother had belonged to "Enthusiast" circles and who had raised her daughter in the spirit of their ideals. After participating in the international women's conference held in Paris in 1889, Paulina returned to found *Unia,* a semi-illegal organization which saw itself as an outpost of the international middle-class women's movement.

In following years, the activities of Kuczalska-Reinschmit were so manifold that she won the reputation of being the "Cossack hetman of the women's movement" par excellence.[42] Writings of all kinds poured from her pen; she founded the radical women's journal *Ster*[43]; her pet projects included women's education, protective measures for working women, and women's vocational associations; on top of this, she was a tireless agitator who in 1905 initiated a movement petitioning for women's right to vote, etc. The efforts of Kuczalska-Reinschmit and her fellow activists finally led to the founding in 1907 of the Union for

Women's Equality (*Związek Równouprawnienia Kobiet*), modeled on the *Russian Sojuz Ravnopravija Ženščin*. From that time on, this new organ vehemently pursued the goal of equal treatment and opportunity for women before the law, in public affairs and economic life.[44]

Let us now return to the question we asked at the outset: was there such a thing in 19th-century Polish society as a "benign patriarchy"? We may now attempt an answer: as long as women took their place beside their menfolk in the struggle for freedom and were fired to raise their children in a Polish national spirit, the relationship between the sexes may well have merited this accolade; women were able to extend their activities into the public arena without encountering male opposition, but only if they did not challenge all too radically the prevailing consensus on women's place in the social order. Nonetheless, we should not forget that there were women like Orzeszkowa's Marta who would have indignantly rejected the thesis of a benign patriarchy. After all, it was Marta's name that was polemically invoked by Iza Moszczeńska when she demanded full equality for women on the basis of a new gender role division still to be worked out.

To this extent her contribution can be seen as part of a general trend in the international women's movement towards greater militancy. However, the solution Moszczeńska came out for at the end of her book testifies to the specific character of the Polish emancipationist movement: this energetic proponent of women's rights did not resort to throwing down the gauntlet to men–instead she asked for empathy and understanding on their part. Her rule of thumb was that reckless egoism on the part of women was more likely to harm than advance the cause. The correct strategy was for women to seek men's solidarity, so that the task of renewing gender divisions could be approached from a common front. That Moszczeńska should have entertained such conciliatory optimism is all the more surprising in view of her own agonistic reconstruction of how gender role divisions historically evolved in the first place.[45]

We find a similar note being struck at Polish women congresses. For instance, the prominent advocate of women's rights,

Maria Turzyma, certainly did not hesitate to interpret the convening of the 1907 Warsaw Women's Congress as an expression of rebelliousness and protest by women–but she saw the true enemy as being the existing state order of the occupying powers, and not entrenched patriarchal power structures at large in Polish society too. According to Turzyma, the demands voiced in Warsaw were not in the least bit feminist, but were simply part of the Polish national struggle for freedom. Freedom and equality for all–including women–was the catchword, a message very much aimed at the address of the occupying powers.[46]

This shows clearly enough that for Turzyma and other likeminded champions of women's rights the ultima ratio to which they devoted all their energies was the securing of national renewal. Thus the Polish women's movement remained subordinate to the wider struggle for Poland's freedom.

Notes to Chapter 1

1. Markowska, D., Rola kobiety polskiej w rodzinie, in: Kobiety polskie. Praca zbiorowa. Warszawa 1986, pp. 184-224, esp. p. 188 f.

2. Moszczeńska, I., Mężczyzna i kobieta, in: Głos kobiet w kwestyj kobiecej. Kraków 1903, pp. 121-142.

3. Markowska, Rola kobiety, p. 190.

4. Cf. inter alia Kutrzeba, S., Ideał i życie kobiety w Polsce wieków średnich. Lwów 1908; Charewiczowa, Ł., Kobieta w dawnej Polsce. Do okresu rozbiorów. Lwów 1938; Lesińki, B., Stanowisko kobiety w polskim prawie ziemskim do połowy XV wieku. Wrocław 1956.

5. Lorence-Kot, B., Child-Rearing and Reform. A Study of the Nobility in Eighteenth-Century Poland. Westport, Conn. and London 1985, p. 47.

6. Lorence-Kot, Child-Rearing, p. 49.

7. Cf. Charewiczowa, Kobieta, p. 16 ff. on the position of women in the various social classes; Lesiński, Stanowisko, p. 102 ff. Czajkowski, A., O prawach kobiet. Diss. in law, in: Kwartalnik Nauk, 1836, No. 3, pp. 224-277, p. 271 ff.

8. Lorence-Kot, Child-Rearing, p. 49 ff.

9. Ibid., cf. p. 51 ff. for some notable instances.

10. Ottmann, R. Beiträge zur Culturgeschichte der polnischen Frauen im

26 WOMEN IN PARTITIONED POLAND

XVI. und XVII. Jahrhunderte. Krakau 1884, p. 6 f.
11. Ibid., pp. 8-20. Cf. also the illustration in Bielski's Sejm Niewieści, in: Wawrzykowska-Wierciochowa, D., Od prządki do astronautki. Z dziejów kobiety polskiej, jej pracy i osiagnięć. Warszawa 1963, p. 47.
12. Kutrzeba, Ideał, p. 21 ff.
13. Cf. Bogucka, M., Bona Sforza. Warszawa 1988.
14. Wawrzykowska-Wierciochowa, Od prządki, p. 45 ff. und p. 62; Charewiczowa, Kobieta, S. 9 ff. Cf. also Shank, M.H., A Female University Student in Late Medieval Krakow, in: Signs, 1987, 12, No. 2, S. 373-380. For examples of these outstanding women personalities, cf. B. Kaczkowski, Z., Kobieta w Polsce–studium historyczno-obyczajowe. 2 vis., St. Petersburg 1895; Ducraine, H., La femme polonaise. Esquisse historique. Paris 1918; Kuchowicz, Z., Wizerunki niepospolitych niewiast staropolskich XVI-XVIII wieku. Łódź 1974(2).
15. For documentation see Lorence-Kot, Child-Rearing, p. 66.
16. Król, p., 101 kobiet polskich. Ślad w historii. Warszawa 1988, p. 75. For details on Jabłonowska's life see Bergerówna, J., Księżna Pani na kocku i siemiatyczach. Działalność gospodarcza i społeczna Anny z Sapiehów Jabłonowskiej. Lwów 1936.
17. Dobra gospodyni, czyli fundamenty ekonomii gospodarskiej osobom młodym do tego zabierającym się potrzebne. Kraków 1784.
18. On traditional upbringing methods as well as on the postpartition repolarization cf. Lorence-Kot, Child-Rearing, p. 22 ff. and 113 ff.
19. Jedlicki, J., Szlachta, in: Przemiany społeczne w Królestwie Polskim 1815-1864. Wrocław etc. 1979, pp. 27-56, esp. p. 48; A. Kahan et alt., Ost- und Südosteuropa 1850-1914. Stuttgart 1980, p. 83; I. Kostrowicka, Z. Landau, J. Tomaszewski, Historia gospodarcza Polski XIX i XX wieku, Warszawa 1975(2), p. 92 ff.
20. Cf. Kieniewicz, The Polish Intelligentsia in the Nineteenth Century, in: K. Hitchins (eds.), Studies in East European Social History, vol. I, Leiden 1977, p. 121-134, here esp. p. 128; N. Koestler, Intelligenzschicht und höhere Bildung im geteilten Polen, in: W. Conze, J. Kocka (Hrsg.), Bildungsbürgertum im 19. Jahrhundert, Stuttgart 1985, pp. 187-206.
21. Kahan, Ost- und Südosteuropa, S. 80.
22. Cf. Herse, S., Frauenarbeit im Königreich Polen. Diss. oecon. publicae Zürich 1912, p. 53 and 56. On wage differentials that were heavily slanted against women cf. p. 73 ff. On the example of Warsaw: Nietyksza, A.,

Przemiany aktywności zawodowej kobiet. Warszawa na przełomie XIX i XX wieku. In: Żarnowska, A., Szwarc, A. (eds.), Kobieta i społeczeństwo na ziemiach polskich w XIX w. Warszawa 1990, pp. 139-160. On problems of migration Mędrzecki, W., Kobieta wiejska w Królestwie Polskim. Przełom XIX i XX wieku, ibid., pp. 130-138.

23. Cf. Walewska, C., Ruch kobiecy w Polsce. 2 cz., Warszawa 1909.

24. On the women's movement cf. Vosberg, F., Die polnische Frauenbewegung. Lissa 1912; D. Wawrzykowska-Wierciochowa, Kobiety wielkopolskie w działalności narodowej, społecznej i wyzwoleńczej 1788-1919. Poznań 1975.

25. Leskiewiczowa, J. (ed.), Społeczeństwo polskie XVIII i XIX wieku. Studia o grupach elitarnych. Vol. VII, Warszawa 1982, p. 474 ff.; J. Komorowska (ed.), Przemiany rodziny polskiej. Warszawa 1975, p. 52 ff. A comparative study of the legal position of women in all three partitioned provinces is an urgent scholarly requirement.

26. Cf. Hulewicz, J., Sprawa wyższego wykształcenia kobiet w Polsce w wieku XIX. Kraków 1939, p. 7 ff.

27. Wawrzykowska-Wierciochowa, D., Od prządki, p. 158 ff.

28. Cf. Król, St., 101 kobiet, p. 82 ff; J. Drackiewicz, Paryż zdradzony czyli Izabela Czartoryska. Lublin 1971.

29. This particular branch of women's engagement is comparatively well researched in the literature. From the numerous extant publications the following may serve as selection: M. Bruchnalska, Ciche bohaterki. Udział kobiet w powstaniu styczniowym. Materiały. Miejsce Piastowe 1933, vol. I-VIII; B. Krzywobłocka, O czarnej sukience i powstańczej dwururce. Warszawa 1964 (3); D. Wawrzykowska-Wierciochowa, Najdziwniejszy z adiutantów. Opowieść o Annie Henryce Pustowojtównie. Warszawa 1986; eadem, Emilia Sczaniecka. Opowieść biograficzna. Warszawa 1970; eadem, Sercem i orężem ojczyźnie służyły. Emilia Plater i inne uczestniczki powstania listopadowego 1830-1831. Warszawa 1982; eadem, Rycerki i samarytanki. Warszawa 1988, S. 153 ff.; M. Złotorzycka, O kobietach żołnierzach w Powstaniu Styczniowym. Warszawa 1972; W. Śliwowska, Polskie drogi do emancypacji. O udziale kobiet w ruchu niepodległościowym w okresie międzypowstaniowym 1833-1856, in: B. Grochulska, J. Skowronek (eds.), Losy Polaków w XIX-XX w. Warszawa 1987, pp. 210-247.

30. Research on women in Poland concentrates on biographies in this historical period as well. Hoffmanowa, Żmichowska and Orzeszkowa use to

be the subject of the history of literature and culture, but not yet of women's studies.

31. Tańska Hoffmanowa, K., Pamiątka po dobrej matce czyli ostatnie jej rady dla córki. Warszawa 1883(10).

32. Cf. Chmielowski, P., Klementyna z Tańskich Hoffmanowa. Zarys biograficzno-pedagogiczny. Życiorysy sławnych Polaków i Polek, No. 9, St. Petersburg, 1898; B. Lorence-Kot, Klementyna Tańska Hoffmanowa, Cultural Nationalism and a New Formula for Polish Womanhood, in: History of European Ideas, 1987, No. 4/5, pp. 435-450. On the subject of "spiritual motherhood" cf. Ch. Sachße, Mütterlichkeit als Beruf. Sozialarbeit, Sozialreform und Frauenbewegung 1871-1929. Frankfurt/Main 1986 and A. Taylor Allen, Spiritual Motherhood: German Feminists and the Kindergarten Movement, in: History of Education Quarterly, 1982, 22, pp. 319-340.

33. Cf. Chmielowski, P., Autorki polskie wieku XIX. Warszawa 1885, p. 226 ff; M. Stępień, Narcyza Żmichowska. Warszawa 1968.

34. Cf. her critical analysis of the emancipation idea in: Kilka słów o kobietach, in: E. Orzeszkowa, Wybór pism, Warszawa 1952, p. 732 ff.

35. Cf. Wawrzykowska-Wierciochowa, Od prządki, p. 182 ff. and 203 ff.

36. Cf. Blejwas, St. A., Realism in Polish Politics: Warsaw Positivism and National Survival in Nineteenth-Century Poland. New Haven 1984.

37. Orzeszkowa, E., Marta. (Transl. from Polish into German.) Berlin/GDR 1984, p. 192.

38. On Eliza Orzeszkowa there exists a comprehensive scholarly literature among which the following titles may be mentioned: Przewóska, M., Eliza Orzeszkowa w literaturze i w ruchu kobiecym. Zarys syntetyczny. Kraków 1909 (2); Żmigrodska, M., Eliza Orzeszkowa. Warszawa 1951; Żmigrodska, M., Orzeszkowa. Młodość pozytywizmu. Warszawa 1965; Jankowski, E., Eliza Orzeszkowa. Warszawa 1964.

39. Cf. Wawrzykowska-Wierciochowa, Udział kobiet w tajnym i jawnym ruchu społeczno-kulturalnym w Warszawie w latach 1880-1914. In: Z dziejów książki i bibliotek w Warszawie. Warszawa 1961, pp. 283-319; Wawrzykowksa-Wierciochowa, D., Z dziejów tajnych pensij żeńskich w Królestwie Polskim, in: Rozprawy z dziejów oświaty, Wrocław etc. 1967, vol. 10, pp. 108-160.

40. On the educational debate and the struggle to secure admission for women to universities see Hulewicz, J., Walka kobiet polskich o dostęp na

uniwersytety. Warszawa 1936; K. Mrozowska, Sto lat działalności kobiet polskich w oświacie i nauce. Kraków 1971.

41. Cf. Warwrzykowska-Wierciochowa, D., Kobiece Koło Oświaty Ludowej, 1883-1894, in: Przegląd Historyczno-Oświatowy, 1959, vol. 2, pp. 49-66.
42. Lubińska, T., O Jubilatce do Jubilatki. In: Z dni Jubileuszowych Pauliny Kuczalskiej-Reinschmit. Warszawa 1911, p. 1-3, here esp. p. 3.
43. On women's journals cf. Zaleska, Z., Czasopisma kobiece w Polsce. Materiały do historii czasopism. Rok 1818-1937. Warszawa 1938.
44. Cf. Walewska, Ruch, p. 21 ff.; Kuczalska-Reinschmit, P., Z historyi ruchu kobiecego, in: Głos kobiet w kwestyi kobiecej, pp. 232-339, esp. p. 311 ff.
45. Moszczeńska, Mężczyzna, pp. 140-142.
46. Turzyma, M., in: Nowe Słowo, 1907, No. 14/15, p. 417, quoted from Wawrzykowska-Wierciochowa, Od prządki, p. 279. Cf. on this point also E. Weickart, Zur Entwicklung der polnischen Frauenbewegung in der ersten Halfte des 19. Jahrhunderts, in: J. Dalhoff et alt. (eds.), Frauenmacht in der Geschichte. Düsseldorf 1986, pp. 338-346, p. 345 f.

2

KONSPIRACJA:
Probing the topography of women's underground activities. The Kingdom of Poland in the second half of the nineteenth century

In 1863 when Mrs. Denisow arrived in Bielsk Podlaski wearing a pale green dress the authorities fined her two hundred rubles because the color green, they said, suggested hope.[2] Why did the choice of apparel, a private matter, constitute a public crime?

Apparently the Tsarist authorities controlling this portion of Poland had the power to define crime at will and did so in trying to stamp out a movement by women called "National Mourning." The green dress episode may be the most absurd of the confrontations which began in 1861 as a commemoration of the thirtieth anniversary of the failed November Uprising against Russia. Warsaw women had helped inaugurate a series of political events by commissioning public mourning masses out of which evolved the fashion for wearing black.[3] Quickly the style spread to parts of Poland partitioned by Prussians and Austrians and even to Russia and Europe where the "Polonaise" style of black apparel became something of a fad.[4] One report describes, with surprise, that even Russian Orthodox believers were adopting the mode! But at a wedding ceremony? It turns out that a wedding party in Podole consisted of men dressed in "czamareks" (a traditional Polish overcoat presumably used in this instance as a symbol of Polish nationalism) and women in black.[5] The tone of surprise and satisfaction which appears in this and other sources whenever a non-ethnic Pole or non-Roman Catholic supports the Polish cause reminds us that ideology had only recently begun competing with family and estate as the primary source of allegiance and identification.

Russian authorities sought to ridicule "National Mourning." They claimed that Polish women had been longing to wear bright colors but that "Russian authorities will not permit such extravagance."[6] This posture strikes the contemporary reader as infantile and raises questions about the level of sophistication on the part of the Tsarist authorities and perhaps Polish society as well.

That not all Poles supported the "Mourning" is evident from an anonymous poem "White and Black" which accused Polish women of doing nothing for their fatherland except wearing black. The author derided the effort as useless and compared its value to an incident in which Russian women had dressed a dog in mourning.[7] Is it possible that a "women's war" of words and actions was waged between Russian and Polish women? (Could we dub it "Putting on the Dog?")

Bruchnalska, the compiler of this information chides the anonymous author for not imitating the numerous sacrifices women made. She remarks that had he imitated the women he would have found that the black dress was an outward manifestation of an inner spirit unifying and sororitizing the women. Two questions occur: one is about the degree of sisterhood among the women and the other is about criticism: its nature, volume and source. Was there conflict between men and women about women's activism? Was the fear of change in women greater than the desire for independence? There is evidence that the men resented the women for various reasons. Possibly a whole topic exists consisting of the varieties of disapproval by Polish men! For now a few examples must suffice. The first is from Walery Wielkopolski's book *Woman:*

> Their (women's) crime consists not only of cutting their hair, smoking cigars, reading learned writing, travelling boldly alone in the world but mainly in breaking away from male authority and striving to be self-

sufficient and even–to build social relations upon this new format. You will recognize them by their bold looks, determined views, free gestures, readiness to undertake hardships which are difficult and unsuitable for their sex. They are brave and bold and the strength of their will develops at the cost of sensitivity and humility. You can easily incline them to heroic virtues but they view domestic virtues as a superfluous commodity; they see weakness and slavery in it. In their behavior they are tough and they humiliate men by their learning and their courage. All of them suffer terribly from the fault of not wanting to be half but total in themselves–they end up being zero.[8]

The author may have been a satirist but there is at least one other instance which fuels the theme of male resentment. Edward Wolinowicz who was born in 1850 described the women of eastern Poland as: sensitive, self-sacrificing, passionate patriots who always led in all the demonstrations and pulled youth after them...they smuggled literature, hid weapons, and then they hid the partisans. One had the impression that most of the men were so politically inept or hypnotized that they reacted too little to the female lead, and women among themselves, with youth in tow, decided everything. They (the women) gave medals for patriotism to agitators and demonstrators and they pilloried, via public opinion, people who were much more sober minded and had greater vision than the emissaries of the National Government. In this manner they (women) created opinions to which the sober thinking people succumbed despite their better judgement. They (the sober minded people) sacrificed their lives and their fortunes by entering the ranks of the partisans.[9]

Is it possible that the 1863 uprising was pushed through by women? What role did women play in instigating and sustaining the rebellion? and what is the significance of events like "Mourning" which preceded the uprising? Bruchnalska cites yet another man, Przyborowski, who claimed that the "religious movement" which is how he refers to political demonstrations, was begun and sustained by people of uncertain future who were willing to risk everything to give their miserable lives some meaning. He called such people murderers of their fatherland adding that "these murderers found eager support among women and parts of the uneducated populace."[10] Is it possible that some identified women's activism with assertion by the lower classes and that, indeed, social change was more frightening to them than the absence of independence?

Bruchnalska traces the beginning of "National Mourning" to the funeral of five people who had died in Warsaw during the anti-Tsarist demonstrations on February 25, 1861. Apparently memoirs from the period allude to the funeral and to the demonstrations. Concurrently Prince Karol Jezierski printed an appeal in the *Gazeta Warszawska* on February 27, 1861 urging women to forego costly apparel.[11]

The authorities are said to have at first tolerated the "Mourning" despite their anger about it. Even the Austrians, commonly considered the mildest of the occupiers, were bothered but the Russian authorities eventually became infuriated particularly since women in the Kingdom removed their mourning on the occasion of national holidays as was the case on August 12, 1862, which was the four hundredth anniversary of the union between Lithuania and Poland. Early that day Warsaw women of lower and higher classes went to church dressed in colorful dresses decorated with multi-colored ribbons. There were many women among those arrested that day.[12] Count Berg, the Tsarist military governor, described the sombre atmosphere in Warsaw in a letter he wrote to the *Petersburg News*. He said that the populace of Warsaw had withdrawn from social life. The theatres were bereft of ordinary people while the few women he saw at one theatre wore black but they turned out to be Russians who had succumbed to the fashion.[13] Further descriptions reveal the various ways in which Poles ostracized Russians. Again from Berg "no sooner a Russian comes in, Poles disappear, children stop playing and run off with their governesses who wear black bands. What a plague we are!"[14]

The prohibition against wearing mourning began on April 1861 after the authorities had fired on unarmed crowds. Not only was the wearing forbidden but merchants were warned not to display black materials in their windows. By 1863 the authorities had mounted the most severe repressions. By mid-July 1863 women who wore black were attacked on the streets of Warsaw by men who tore at their crinolines with hooks. The authorities claimed this was the work of hooligans, some of whom they said they had arrested. But Polish sources claimed that this was the work of government agents![15] By October 1863 the Ober-policmajster of Warsaw passed an ukase demanding that all signs of mourning be abandoned and warning that women of all estates, civil status and age (suggesting that ordinarily these distinctions were significant!) who appeared after October 29 in mourning would be detained and taken to the police station where they would pay a fine. Women on foot were to pay ten rubles while those in hired or public carriages paid fifteen rubles. The owners of conveyances were to pay a ten ruble fine for every woman aboard wearing mourning. Government employees whose wives or children wore mourning were to lose one month's salary.[16]

After Tsarist authorities began fining women in black who could not prove authentic mourning Polish women responded by wearing grey which also became illegal. Brown suffered the same fate as did many ingenious variations upon the same theme. The authorities in Bielsk Podlaski seem particularly aggressive because they even fined those who wore black ribbons! All this created great hardship for the poor women who having nothing else to wear, reports one source, paid the two hundred ruble fine (notice the increase!) or went to the lock up. Mrs. Denisow had tried to avoid a fine and chose light green as a safe color for her visit to Bielsk Podlaski but found to her dismay that hope, as well as mourning, was a punishable offence.[17]

"National Mourning" which dwindled by 1863 turns out to have launched a growing and complex opposition movement by women in the Kingdom of Poland, an entity created by the Congress of Vienna in 1815. From 1815 to 1831 Poles had been ruled under a liberal constitution but following the failed uprising of 1830-31 the constitution was abrogated and replaced by an organic statute which deprived Poles of political rights and much administrative autonomy. While oppositional activities by men had flourished as far back as the initial loss of independence, women launched their drive in the 1860s.[18] In the early nineteenth century Polish girls and women had participated in some illegal activities whose calibre was different from what began in the 1860s. For example, girls had met in covert study groups aimed at self-improvement while women had organized to help the wounded fighters and needy civilians during the November 1830 uprising. Both of these examples illustrate that no conspiratorial model existed which was either fashioned by or for women because the girls who had met for the purpose of illegal study had responded to the initiative of boys while the women of November 1830 acted traditionally in the managerial style of prepartitioned Poland where noble women supervised the health and welfare of their rural communities.

This essay initiates a description of the various underground activities which Polish women undertook in the second half of the nineteenth century. It aims to provoke an interest in the full rendition of this story and all the other stories which reveal the part played by Polish women in national history. So far historians have not been drawn to do this and the events remain as scattered narratives waiting for assembly and description. Consequently when national history is told the women remain obscure. For example, Jerzy Borejsza a contemporary historian, sketches a portrait of the nineteenth century Polish revolutionary and never once mentions women.[20] His silence become puzzling in light of Count Berg's assessment of Polish women written in the wake of the 1863 uprising. Berg was a high-ranking Tsarist functionary who singled out the women because of their zeal, courage and self-sacrifice. He said that the actions of Polish women were unmatched in other countries and of great consequence for the Polish nation. Going further he compared the nationalist behavior of men and women and judged the women as more fervent.

Among Polish men there are differences and the men backslide because they tire of fighting and fall into paralysis but the female population never changes and always maintains the same features. The Polish woman is eternal, unyielding, and an undemonstrative conspirator....A Pole may be

White, Red, or Black and Yellow–in other words of many shades and colors–but a Polish woman can only be Red.[21]

One might question the accuracy of Berg's analysis particularly in the light of his further descriptions which suggest, at least to the contemporary reader, infatuation either with Polish women or his own hyperbole. Whatever he meant and however accurate he may have been, particularly when he said that the character of Polish women had something knightly and masculine in it, he did place Polish women in the midst of conspiratorial activity; in fact he defined them as more constant than the men. All this means that as far back as the nineteenth century Polish women were identified by their contemporaries as active participators in national events. It is time, therefore, to extricate them from a current national history which has falsely buried them by omission–to tell their story accurately–and return them to the national arena according to their authentic role.

Their story will have to be classified according to its own rhythm. In this topic that means distinguishing novel actions by women from traditional ones. Why? Because the crux of change in this instance hinges upon the difference between late nineteenth century Poland and Poland of a hundred years earlier. That independent Commonwealth had consisted of powerful families which came together as a body to constitute public authority. By contrast, partitioned Poland of the late nineteenth century was governed by foreign bureaucrats. We have to assume (and hopefully someone will undertake the task of charting this topic) that Polish women had to pass through several stages before they adjusted their behavior to the new structure. It must have taken time and generations (I speculate) to accept the loss of independence, to relinquish the hope of returning to the old structure in which women served the family's interests, to accept, begin to understand, and eventually learn to effectively use the existing circumstances in asserting their will. In other words, to develop an oppositional style which suited women of that era and their newly minted loyalty to the nation. A transition occurred from family loyalty which had traditionally expanded to include the nation to national loyalty which might include or exclude the family but which made it subsidiary to national interest.

Clearer boundaries existed in the late nineteenth century between private worth and public power than had in old Poland where boundaries had been porous and where public authority was unimaginable without private importance. But in the nineteenth century the private importance of Poles gave them no public authority whereas the public power of Russian bureaucrats was no reflection of their private esteem within the community. Yet despite this division Tsarist authorities presumed to make private behavior a public matter as the "National Mourning" episode demonstrates. The determination of these authorities to control opinion and behavior signals the future in which, as we know, increasingly powerful states would presume to insinuate themselves into all facets of private life. The intrusion of public into private reverses the independent Commonwealth's structure in which private emerged as public.

Women's activities covered a wide range. A handful fought in the 1863 uprising but most appear to have acted in ancillary capacity to the men by serving as couriers, nurses, and liaison, thereby supporting the military actions and their consequences. They helped the "losers" of the uprising by bringing them aid at the Warsaw Citadel prison, by assisting exiles to Siberia and by providing help to families of captured men. They produced and disseminated forbidden literature and they taught children in secret schools. They took part in public political demonstrations such as the "National Mourning" movement and public masses. By the 1870's the socialist movement added another dimension to their agenda.

In the late nineteenth century demands by women covered several different areas which deeper analysis might reveal as syncretic. At this stage it is clear only that three major goals drove women's activities: national independence, social justice, and equity for women. There is no way to assess the number of women activists or how they were allocated with respect to agenda or whether the same women actively pursued all three goals because the statistical work has not been done, so description, for the time being, remains impressionistic as does all else pertaining to Polish women's public input. The same lack of precision exists with respect to the social, economic, ethnic and religious background of the activists. Older sources suggest that the majority were of szlachta background which would mean that opposition continued to be the affair of nobles just as the independent Commonwealth had been a nation for and by nobles. But other types of women, working-class and non-ethnically Polish, also participated according to more recent monographs completed in socialist Poland. The eagerness of the older sources to cite national loyalty in those who had not had status in free Poland, has already been mentioned. In an earlier work dealing with reforms in the eighteenth century I concluded by commenting on the problems accompanying the transition from family governed Poland to a Poland which would include all of her people as members of one family.

The problem which remained was how to sweep up emotionally those who had never belonged to the family–the non-szlachta masses who had always been dispossessed in the Szlachta Commonwealth. The modern concept of nation suggested, and indeed dictated, the participation of all citizens. The Szlachta as well as their fellow travellers, the intelligentsia, made a relatively effortless transition when they transferred their loyalties from their old nation under the Commonwealth to their new nation under occupation. The difficulty lay in persuading those who had never had a nation that they now had one, particularly in the light of the fact, that demands upon their emotional commitment were not accompanied by offers of political, economic, and social equality. The value of these non-relatives, as a national resource, like that of the children in the past, was yet to be recognized.[22]

Not surprisingly Polish women pledged their loyalty to the unfree nation without first acquiring or receiving promise of equal rights. One writer has attributed the late and meager Polish emancipation movement to the preoccupation of Polish women with the national cause.[23] By the 1870's socialism was providing a platform for women who did not identify with Polish nationalism and, given socialist dicta, that must have meant that emancipation became redundant for many. At this stage of inquiry it appears that more Polish women were pledged to nationalism and socialism than to emancipation. It is highly probable that both nationalists as well as socialists assumed that the enactment of their primary platform would–automatically–signify rights for women. But what kind of rights?

How did the holders of power, the authorities, view the women's actions? The attitude of the authorities changed between the early and late nineteenth century. The green dress episode reveals that by the 1860s the authorities were alarmed enough to launch a campaign of prohibitions and penalties against the women while earlier in the century they had mostly ignored them.[24] So asserts Anna Minkowska in her work on conspiracies in 1848. She allows that there are no materials to illustrate this but other authors support her view. Wawrzykowska-Wierciochowa in her latest book on women in the 1863 uprising remarks that it was rare for the Tsarist authorities to send a woman into Siberian exile before 1880. The most severe penalty consisted of internment in Polish convents because there were no political prisons for women.[25] The one exception was Ewa Felińska exiled to Siberia in 1838 for participating in the Konarski conspiracy.[26] There were also some women exiled following the 1863 uprising, one of whom, Helena Majewska Kirkorowa, organized and served as liaison for the leaders of the uprising.[27] In a recent article entitled "Polskie drogi do emancypacji (O udziale kobiet w ruchu niepodległościowym - 1833-1856), Wiktoria Śliwowska demolishes this contention by showing that between the uprising of 1830 and that of 1863 Polish women did much more than participate in study groups. Those categories of activity which appear in the second half of the nineteenth century were already shaping much earlier according to her evidence.[28] It seems probable that when women acted like men or with men they were punished like the men and that the distinction between women's and men's activities lapsed, as far as the authorities were concerned, during the 1880s when the socialist movement was gaining momentum. Careful gathering of data and its analysis should determine whether all distinctions between punishment meted out to men as opposed to women disappeared by the 1880s. Certainly imprisonment in Warsaw and exile to Siberia for women gained momentum in that decade.[28]

At what point did the Russian authorities begin to view women as political creatures akin to men? And was it the nature of the activity which so characterized them or did the authorities begin to view all unconventional behavior by women as political? Did the authorities fashion a model for female conspiracy which mirrored male conspiracy and, in addition, include varieties which were characteristically female? If so, such a model would include actions devised by women and carried out exclusively or primarily by women. Narcyza Żmichowska (1819-1876), leader of a group of literary women, commented on the unusual nature of her group:

> Among our women there exists not a single organization, nor masonry. They have promulgated not a single resolution, have taken no banners, have organized no circles or committees. They are joined by common likes and dislikes but above all by similarity of upbringing and background in that they more or less committed the same errors, got the same ideas and used similar means to gain their ends. People could not believe all of this occurred without oaths.[29]

These women were seeking inner independence but it is known that the authorities kept at least six of them under secret surveillance and that more than one, Żmichowska among them, were incarcerated in convents. Clearly the organizational structure of women's groups was different and was perceived as different.

Between 1861-1864 another organization called "Piątki" (Fives) accepted trustworthy women without regard to social background, nationality, age or faith. This is how Wawrzykowska-Wierciochowa begins their description in *Nie po kwiatach los je prowadził*. She gives the names of three Russian women but no other names to prove her point. Nonetheless, she claims the organization had Catholics, Lutherans, Russian Orthodox and Jewish women. Among them were petty nobles, city women, working intelligentsia, teachers, actresses and wives of merchants and petty tradesmen. The aim of the group was to support the men's military activity. The women collected arms and uniforms, supplied food, transported weapons and information as well as providing medical assistance. The organization forged connections with a group of Russian women in St. Petersburg and Moscow in order to assist men exiled from Poland. "Piątki" functioned in all parts of partitioned Poland and had committees among Poles in Prague, Paris and even America.[30]

The structure consisted of groups of fives. In an administration of five women each formed another group of five with further groups of fives. Then each of these twenty-five women formed further groups. (Sounds like a chain-letter!).[31]

These complexities need exposition as does the posture of the other authorities in Polish women's lives–the Polish men! What in general, was men's opinion about the women's public activities? (Actions extending beyond care of the family constitute public activity). What did public opinion (generally the opinion of men) make of women's activism? What scale of support can be charted with respect to the various activities? It is probably safe to speculate that the greatest approval went to patriotic acts and among those to ones which came closest to women's traditional duties. Teaching Polish culture in illegal primary schools would fit that definition. Within the patriotic camp fighting alongside men in the 1863 uprising would, most likely, garner the greatest disapproval or perhaps discomfort. As for the remaining two groups of activities, it will be interesting to find out, once the work is done, whether socialism repelled Polish men more than emancipation? Once the substantive data is gathered and processed it will be possible to see whether women's activism changed society's ideas about the nature and abilities of women or whether activism, even when approved, was seen as a temporary expedient arising out of dire national circumstances.

At least one of the difficulties which women faced ought to have elicited male sympathy stemming as it did from the absence of men who were imprisoned, exiled or abroad. The women they left behind were forced to fend for themselves, their children and assorted relatives.[32] Adam Próchnik in *Kobieta w polskim ruchu socjalistycznym* (1948) points out that Tsarist repression hit almost every Polish household and "made not only of women but children also–political activists. When men died in battle, women had to assume control not only of their household but also control of public matters."[33] Many women had to find paid employment. Of course, they were ill-prepared to do this and faced great competition for the few types of work which were acceptable for women. Eliza Orzeszkowa (1841-1910) who warrants exclusive and thorough treatment by a historian of women portrayed the plight of the impoverished gentlewomen in her novel *Marta* (1873).[34]

After 1864 the emancipation of peasants added to women's economic ills and intensified their practical need for education. Kamila Mrozowska in *Sto lat działalności kobiet polskich w oswiacie i nauce* refers to waves of impoverished gentry flooding into towns and notes that among them were many women who had hitherto lived on country estates waiting for rich husbands or working as housekeepers and residents.[35] They all found themselves without means of support and their plight became a pressing social problem. Despite the fact that such prominent figures as Aleksander Świętochowski sharply criticized traditional female education claiming that in that sphere women had equal rights with men, nothing changed.[36]

When change came in 1882 it was on the initiative of a woman, Jadwiga Szczawińska who fashioned a system of illegal higher education for women because Russian and Polish universities did not accept women and only a few could afford to travel to Switzerland or France. But that enterprise, whose task was to arm "manless" women to fend for themselves in society, was integrally linked to women's activities in the entire field of education. Wawrszykowska-Wierciochowa says that Polish women played an inordinately important role in education when compared to the role of women in other countries. They shouldered the responsibility of maintaining the national spirit at a time when so many men were absent. They took charge of female education and developed education for the lower classes. This, despite the fact that there were no teachers' colleges for women while men had five. In the 1870's women were just beginning to gain entry to teaching in the legal schools but, according to Wawrzykowska-Wierciochowa, the entire network of illegal schools was in their hands. The growing size and complexity of illegal education is attributable to the fact that by 1885 all legal schooling in Poland was conducted exclusively in the Russian language. Not only did the illegal schools provide training in nationalism but they also took up the slack created by the shortage of legal schools.[37]

"The Flying University" combined with the existing complex of illegal secondary schools to provide advanced classes for women. Marie Skłodowska known to the world as Madame Curie was one of the students. By 1890 it was educating one hundred students and three years later their number had tripled. In 1905 when it became the Society for Higher Learning several hundred students were receiving a university education.[38]

Socialism appears to account for a large segment of women's underground activities particularly in the ebbing years of the nineteenth century. Considering that for the past forty years history in Poland has been written from a socialist perspective we should expect that Polish historians have documented women's roles. But on the other hand perhaps they have not! A cursory glance at this field reveals unexpected ironies. Namely, Maria Bonuszewiczówna, the nineteen-year-old grand-daughter of Tadeusz Kościuszko, the Polish and American freedom fighter, ran the first Polish revolutionary worker's party in 1884 after massive arrests had left the group without leaders. She herself was arrested the following year and after spending eighteen months in the Warsaw Citadel died on her way to Siberian exile. Her diary from that journey was discovered in 1953.[39] She is probably one of many Polish women, from good homes, who committed themselves to socialism.

The part which Polish women played in advancing the cause of socialism appears varied and complex. Just one instance has to suffice for the sake of providing at least a flavor. It is culled from a publication in 1929 intended to honor the work of Maria Paszkowska and her legion of "Dromedaries." That was the name of a group of women who distributed illegal socialist literature in Warsaw.[40] They hid it on their bodies. Paszkowska and her women were also responsible for finding meeting places, delivering conspiratorial correspondence, delivering money to the families of arrested workers, informing comrades of meetings and keeping the agenda.[41] Their youngest recruit was eight years old and she was the step-daughter of the writer Stefan Żeromski. The little girl did not distribute, for her task was to remove hidden documents if the adults were arrested.[42] Clearly, this was still a world in which everyone worked.

When the new century dawned it was apparent that the situation and the behavior of Polish women had undergone many changes since the beginning of the nineteenth century. Underground work serves as a rubric for some major features of the adjustment women had to make to new political, social, and economic conditions in their world. This probe confirms the important and extensive participation by Polish women in public life even though it is merely a prospectus for the work to be done. It declares that the sources exist and that they are rich and complex but untapped except by dedicated and unacknowledged amateurs who exist alongside the historical profession. There is every indication that professional historians, among whom there are many women, are reluctant to delve into women's history out of fear of losing their academic reputation. This "self-censorship" demonstrates that Poland is still a man's world as it was under the Noble Commonwealth, the Partitions, and Socialism and that it may turn out that the occupiers took the women's actions more seriously than their fellow countrymen ever have. Perhaps the new Republic now developing will make it respectable or at least fashionable for historians to document the role of women in the history of the Polish nation.

Notes to Chapter 2

1. Dioniza Wawrzykowska-Wierciochowa "Stan badań nad dziejami kobiety polskiej," Kultura i Społeczeństwo, year VII #1, 1963.
2. Maria Bruchnalska, Ciche bohaterki. Udział kobiet w Powstaniu Styczniowym. (Miejasce Piastowe: Wydawnictwo Towarzystwa Św. Michała Archanioła, 1939) p. 62. The quote is from a Polish newspaper printed in New York in March 1864 and its presence suggests that emigre newspapers might be a valuable source for the history of women. The title refers to the silent heroines of the 1863 uprising while the content represents the most diversified compilation of women's activities that I have encountered. It ranges geographically and topically and in addition reinforces my growing impression that the scattered efforts to document the role of Polish women in national life occurred mainly before World War II. This compilation looks remarkably like an arrangement of primary documents although this author, along with most of the others, footnotes so infrequently as to make the reader wonder why she footnotes at all. What does the unwillingness to footnote represent? That the writer was not trained as a historian? That the writer assumes the materials to be part of the common weal making citations unnecessary? For the historian not steeped in the culture and its materials, tracking down original sources becomes formidable.

The publisher of this rich compendium of women's activism is an obscure Catholic Association indicating that such works did not attract prominent publishers. Clearly, the record of women in public life has been and continues to be the work of dedicated amateurs. Since World War II Polish socialist historians have shown as little interest in the topic as did the bourgeois ones preceeding them. Such is the opinion of Dioniza Wawrzykowska-Wierciochowa the doyenne of writers about women. Her list of publications is impressive and she is to be lauded for keeping the national role of women in the public consciousness but she writes for the general audience in the tradition of the historian by avocation. This genre, open to all, remains apart from mainstream historical writing; consequently it may be helping to retain women outside the realm of national history.

Wawrzykowska-Wierciechowa's most recent book is devoted to women in the 1863 uprising. She faults bouregois historians for their first spinning and socialist historians for continuing to spin the fable that the women in the uprising were mainly noble and that they participated for the love of a fighting man. Not so claims Wawrzykowska-Wierciochowa but she does not provide data to support her contention that the women came from various backgrounds and that they used independent judgement in supporting the uprising. Nie po kwiatach los je prowadził (Warszawa: 1987) p. 20.

3.   Wawrzykowska-Wierciochowa, Nie po kwiatach los je prowadził. (Warszawa: 1987). The author refers to a large collection of "Mourning" jewelry from this era but she does not tell where it is located. Similarly her description of a photograph showing Karl Marx's daughter wearing a Polish "partisan cross" is without reference. p. 22 Wawrzykowska-Wierciochowa does not footnote!

At least one source attributes the beginning of National Mourning to Maria Ilnicka's (1825-1897) poem "To my sisters." A brief account of Ilnicka's family history provides a flavor of the lives of many of her contemporaries: her father died in the uprising of 1831 and she served as archivist for the National Government during the 1863 uprising. She was imprisoned briefly after the uprising's failure. Between 1865-1896 she was the editor of the women's magazine "Bluszcz" (ivy). She was known in Warsaw for her "Literary Tuesdays." Kazimierz Budzyk (ed)., Nowy Korbut (Warszawa: 1968), vol. 7, p. 465-466.

An encyclopedia of Polish women is badly needed to facilitate the history of Polish women and to reveal the extensive participation of women in public life.

4.   Bruchnalska, Ciche bohaterki, p. 63. The quote is from "Moscow News."

5.   Ibid., p. 63.

6.   Ibid., p. 63.

7.   Ibid., p. 53.

8.   Walery Wielkopolski, Kobieta, Kraków: 1860, no page number.

9.   Cited by Dioniza Wawrzykowska-Wierciochowa in Pani Maria Jankowska-Mendelson. Warsaw: 1968, p. 33. She does not identify her source except by name.

10.   Bruchnalska, Ciche bohaterki, p. 12.

11.   Ibid., p. 14.

12.   I am juxtaposing the two dates not Bruchnalska who gives the date for the killing of the five on page 14 and the information about Jezierski's appeal on page 50. The information she gives flows in a stream of consciousness; it cries out for order along a continuous thread.

13.   Berg, N., Zapiski o powstaniu polskim. Kraków 1898, vol. II, p. 401.
14.   Nikolai Berg, *Zapiski o Powstaniu Polskim,* (Cracow: Społka Wydawnicza Polska, 1898) Vol. II, p. 401.
15.   Ibid.
16.   Bruchnalska, Ciche bohaterki, p. 58.
17.   Ibid., p. 59. The amount of the fine appears to have risen about 200% since their initiation when they were ten rubles high.
18.   Wiktoria Śliwowska's "Polskie drogi do emancypacji. (O udziale kobiet w ruchy niepodległościowym 1833-1856), Losy Polaków w XIX-XX w. Warszawa 1987 provides evidence which disputes this contention.
19.   Aleksander Kamiński, Analiza teoretyczna polskich związków młodzieży do połowy XIX w. Warszawa 1971, p. 52. Kamiński points out that women's activism does not pick up until the end of the nineteenth century (he is writing about Polish youth organizations) and then it is most evident in socialist organizations. He gives three reasons why there were no girls in conspiracy before mid-19th century: the lack of secondary and higher education for girls made it difficult to recruit them. There were no models for women since this was a male activity and the emancipation of women among the Polish inteligentsia was late., p. 53.
20.   Jerzy Borejsza, Rewolucjonista polski–szkic do portretu, Polska XIX wieku. Warszaw 1986.
21.   Berg, Zapiski o powstaniu polskim, vol. I., p. 173.
22.   Bogna Lorence-Kot, Child-Rearing and Reform: A Study of the Nobility in Eighteenth-Century Poland, Westport, Connecticut and London 1985, p. 124.
23.   Wawrzykowska-Wierciochowa, Nie po kwiatach los je prowadził, p. 37.
24.   As mentioned earlier the "Mourning" occurred all over Poland but it was the Russians who responded most repressively. Since this is a major episode in the history of women's opposition it needs thorough treatment by someone.
25.   Anna Minkowska, Organizacja spiskowa 1848 roku w Królestwie Polskim, Warszawa 1923 , p. 21 and Wawrzykowska-Wierciochowa, Nie po kwiatach los je prowadził, p. 16.
26.   Wspomnienia podróży do Siberji. Wilno 1852, comes in three volumes. I have seen the first and it describes the conditions of her journey but does not explain the conspiracy. Interestingly enough the account has been

translated into English under the title: Revelations of Siberia by a Banished Lady, published in London in 1852. There is also a Danish translation. (Nowy Korbut, vol. 7 p. 322); Śliwowska in "Polskie drogi do emancypacji." refers to the Konarski conspiracy. Konarski emphasized the role of women in the Association of Polish. People (Stowarzyszenie Ludu Polskiego/SLP). As early as 1835 Konarski was talking of the need to address an appeal to women. Ewa Felińska was Konarski's enthusiastic assistant in the women's section of the SLP. She became the secretary for foreign correspondence as well as many other functions in the association. Felińska, among her other actions, was instrumental in preparing the statute for the women's section, p. 220. The question is, of course, why was there a separate women's section.

27.   Wawrzykowska-Wierciochowa, Nie po kwiatach los je prowadził, p. 102.

28.   Losy Polaków w XIX-XX w. Warszawa 1987.

29.   Minkowska, Organizacja spiskowa 1848 roku w Królestwie Polskim, p. 20. The structure of women's groups was different and was so perceived by at least one women.
Aleksander Kamiński in Polskie związki młodzieży. Warsaw 1968, p. 21, describes conspiratorial activities between 1801 and 1848. He includes the work of women and dwells on the "Enthusiasts" a group of literary women.

30.   Wawrzykowska-Wierciochowa quotes extensively from her source but does not footnote. She provides no information beyond listing the author and title in her bibliography., p. 21.

31.   Ibid.

32.   The shortage of men was partially due to their emigration. Between 1803-1865 ten thousand had left Poland. Stefan Kieniewicz Polska XIX wieku. Warszawa 1986, p. 8.

33.   Wawrzykowska-Wierciochowa quotes Adam Próchnik and lists his article in her bibliography but she gives no page number.

34.   Orzeszkowa has extensive credentials in "public life" but they are too numerous to be listed here. Her novel "Marta" published in 1873 reflects her insistence that women needed to develop their intellectual, emotional and physical abilities. She wanted them to gain constructive knowledge, be educated so as to enter professions and know how to exist autonomously. The heroine of her novel is a widowed woman with a child. Her inadequate education prevents her from working as a teacher, translator, illustrator or dressmaker. Convention prohibits her working in occupations considered

male. Her only solution is to become a seamstress but when she loses that job she is forced to beg and eventually steal. She dies under the wheels of a horse-tram leaving her child to fate. Taken from the entry in Literature Polska: Przewodnik Encyklopedyczny. Warszawa 1985, vol. I, p. 642. This novel is considered to have played a significant role in the history of emancipation and has been translated into fifteen languages. Unfortunately Orzeszkowa left no memoirs. In fact, according to Romana Pachucka in: Pamiętniki z lat 1886-1914 (Memoirs from that period). Wrocław 1958, p. VI, there are no memoirs by representatives of the feminist movement in Poland either in its first phase when it involved women like Tańska, Ziemięcka, Żmichowska nor during the positivist era when neither prominent women like Orzeszkowa and Konopnicka nor lesser ones left their records. There are also no accounts from the first Polish women studying at foreign universities.

35.   Kamila Mrozowska, Sto lat działalności polskich w oświacie i nauce Kraków 1971. An intriguing practice called "White Marriage" was used by some women to gain autonomy in a society where existence without a familiar connection was unthinkable for a woman. These were platonic marriages. In another context, "White Marriages" were also used by Siberian exiles to take advantage of Tsarist family laws. Dioniza Wawrzykowska-Wierciochowa, Pani Maria Jankowska-Mendelson. Warszawa 1968, p. 102. Here is another topic in search of an author.

36.   This article appeared in "Przegląd Tygodniowy" but Kamila Mrozow-ska who cites it in: Sto lat działalności kobiet polskich w oświacie i nauce, p. 9, gives no other information such as a date for the magazine.

37.   Dioniza Wawrzykowska-Wierciochowa, Udział kobiet w tajnym i jawnym ruchu społeczno-kulturalnym w Warszawie w latach 1880-1914, in: Z dziejów książki i bibliotek w Warszawie. Warszawa 1961, p. 286-289.

38.   It is not often that women appear in standard history texts but this item does figure in Norman Davies's: God's Playground. New York 1982, vol. 2, p. 235, probably because in the 1970's a private Society for Academic Courses (TKN) revived the tradition and the name by holding secret classes in major cities. Davies's source for the first Flying University comes from Helena Ceysingerówna, Tajne nauczanie w Warszawie, 1894-1906/7, Niepodległość, 1930 ii., 95-103.

39.   Dioniza Wawrzykowska-Wierciochowa, Udział kobiet, pp. 287-88. The ubiquitous Wawrzykowska-Wierciochowa edited the diary which was printed in 1984 by Książka i Wiedza as Pamiętnik by Maria Bohuszewiczówna.

40.   Życie i praca Marji Paszkowskiej, odbito z druku "Robotnik," Warecka 7, 1929. Nakładem Komitetu Uczczenia Pamięci Marji p. redaktor Leon Wasilewski.

41.   Ibid., p. 75.

42.   Ibid., p. 76.

Rudolf Jaworski

3

Polish Women and the Nationality Conflict in the Province of Posen at the Turn of the Century

This topic, Polish women and the nationality conflict, represents the intersection of social, political, and day-to-day historical questions. On the one hand, it concerns the social situation and the position of Polish women in Posen (Poznań) at the end of the nineteenth century. On the other, it considers their national-political commitment and their connection with the German-Polish altercations during these years, and not least, the place of these two aspects in daily life, for example, in education, family and associational life, and shopping. This overview is only possible and significant because the *Wielkopolanki* (the women of Great Poland) really played a leading role in all of these areas and not last because precisely through their participation, the nationality conflict in Posen had a social breadth and a daily relevance.

It is worth mentioning that little research has been done on the female aspect of Polish self-affirmation in Prussian Poland.[1] Up to now, the necessary social-historical background has been lacking. We know, for example, very little about the occupational structure of Polish working women or their role in nongender specific national Polish organizations, including electoral committees, guilds and trade unions, and the Sokół. Thus this overview can be scarcely more than the beginning of a discussion, one which clearly demands exhaustive and careful examination. The national antagonism in Posen has been chosen as a framework because the woman question and the women's movement in Great Poland at the present research level can be best comprehensively described and characterized from this side. The limiting of the discussion to the province of Posen can be further justified by the leading role which this old Polish historical landscape played in the question for all Poles under Prussian domination. For example, the Polish women's movement in Upper Silesia was initiated primarily due to the personal engagement of the pioneering women from Posen.[2]

When examining the role of women in the nationality conflict in Posen at the turn of the century, one must first take into account that historically there were certain premises for the relatively independent position of women in Polish society, which in the case of the noblewomen even antedated the partition period.[3] After the division of the old Polish federation, the *Polka-Bohaterka* (Polish heroine) was celebrated in romantic literature; thus this prototype of women who conspired side by side with their husbands against foreign domination, actively participating in the uprisings, caring for the wounded insurgents; following their husbands into exile or prison, and, who, having no man at home, held their own. The memory of these glowing female figures remained alive throughout the period of the uprisings and they became guiding figures in the far more peaceful and undramatic activities of the *Polka-Obywatelka* (Polish women citizens) in the following decades.

The example of Emilia Sczaniecka (1804-1896)[4] illustrates that these historical connections were not just idealized constructions, but also represented authentic traditions. This educated Great Polish noblewoman participated in the Polish Revolutions of 1830, 1848, and 1863, and was later involved in the promotion of education in her native region, without the change in her field of activity signifying a break with or a deviation from her fundamental attitude.

The preconditions for the independence of Polish women looked completely different from the lower classes.[5] They were not determined by spiritual freedom and heroic actions, but resulted from the bitter necessity of the struggle for existence.

Since the men either earned too little, or as itinerant workers were simply not there, the women of the urban and rural proletariat were forced to contribute to the support of the family.

During the course of the nineteenth century, the deep division separating noblewomen from the women of other classes was lessened in several ways. Until the turn of this century, Prussian domination produced a clear compression of the middle class of Great Polish society, with the result that women from all social classes were more and more forced to work outside the home.[6] Thus the number of Polish women employed in agriculture increased from 80,896 to 170,379, or by 110.61 percent, between 1882 and 1907. The increase in their numbers in business and industry is ever more clear; during the same period of time the number of Polish women increased from 8,090 to 16,402, or by 131.34 percent. Different classes of women were further brought together by the aspect of Prussian domination that attempted to control as much as possible all areas of life and all groups of Poles, including women. This pressure contributed to an acceleration of the democratization of the Prussian Polish class-based society and brought with it a positive effect on the position of Polish women in society. From the last two decades of the nineteenth century, German-Polish antagonism in the Prussian East was clearly no longer merely a matter of the Prussian government and its executive organs on the one hand and the Polish élites on the other. At least on the Polish side, it was part of the daily life of every man and "every women."

In this situation, the Polish family took on an increased significance, because it represented a sphere that was still more exclusive and screened off than Polish organizations and even than the Polish Catholic Church. It was out of the hands of the Prussian control apparatus and thus represented a last impregnable bastion of "Polishness."[7] In family circles, the Polish language, the use of which was forbidden, even persecuted, in the outside world, was used exclusively. Here, Polish prayers were peacefully prayed, Polish songs were sung, Polish customs were cultivated, and Polish history and tales were related. In this way, the members of the next generation received a thoroughgoing and consistent initiation into the Polish national culture from earliest childhood and were brought up with a corresponding self-confidence. Again, Polish mothers and grandmothers were mainly responsible for fulfilling this important task, surely more as a matter of course in rural families than in urban ones.

Finally, whether a household has the attributes of a *dom polski* (Polish home) or not rested on the shoulders of the women. In the end, for example, how perfectly the children knew Polish, what literature the family read, or whether the daily shopping took place in German or Polish shops depended on them. This sphere of activity of the *Matka-Polka* (Polish mother), who as chaplain of the national fire guarded the home hearth, was consciously understood as a shielded interior space and opposed to an outside world which was in principle hostile.

The internal-external model, which derived from traditional gender roles, was interpreted such, that on the basis of their special tasks at home and in the family, Polish women were thus far less exposed to damaging, denationalizing influences than their husbands, who worked outside. Therefore, Polish women could maintain their pure Polishness and as a result were particularly qualified and called upon to defend and transmit the special character of Polishness.[8] In the same way, feminine goodwill and charity on the one hand were contrasted with the brutal violence of the men's world on the other. Considering that the occupants of this men's world were above all German, especially Prussian, this reproach concerned the Polish men only in part. Thus this sexual contrast was also projected onto the national-Polish level, so that in the end, the entire Polish national movement commended the "soft violence" of feminine inertia and feminine resistance.

Although the framework of the family was transcended and permeated by the increasing entry of Polish women into the work force, the family still remained a privileged female field of activity and was maintained as a Polish refuge. One can in any case assume that the first involuntary beginnings of Polish women's participation in the defense against Prussian attempts at assimilation and denationalization developed in the private family sphere: still lacking a formulated program, guided alone by traditional religious convictions, by the self-evident use of the mother tongue, and characterized by traditional patterns of daily life and the daily requirements of child rearing. If, in addition, the Church and national Polish journalism set up rules of conduct and thus provided ideological support, this intercession for the preservation of Polish nationality must still be designated "prepolitical."

To a certain degree, this was also the case in choosing a marriage partner, although here one already finds a moment of conscious ethnic delimitation in the preference of a co-national husband or wife. Popular traditional provisos against such "unnatural" connections as a Polish woman and a German man–in mixed marriages, this was the dominant form–were expressed in for example the "Wanda legend." Little girls were taught the following verse: *"Wanda leży w polskiej ziemi /bo nie chciała Niemca/ trzeba tylko wziąć rodaka/ a nie cudzoziemca!"* (Wanda lies in Polish earth, because she didn't want a German man. A girl should always choose only a compatriat and never a foreigner for a husband!)[9] In addition, there were the continual warnings of the Polish priests against Protestantism, which was unconditionally equated with Germandom. The ever-decreasing number of mixed marriages up to the turn of the century–in 1910, they represented 1.34 percent of all marriages in the province–clearly demonstrates that the general alienation among the Germans and the Poles had penetrated to this area.[10]

All of the feminine fields of life and experience mentioned until now: family, children, and marriage, had religious connections and again demonstrate the strong influence of the Catholic Church and the Polish clergy on the Great Polish women, which was expressed in women's religious organizations such as the Mary and Mother clubs, but was in no way limited to them. Thus I come to the organized and public efforts of the Great Polish women on behalf of their national identity, which already collectively aimed not only at the maintenance but also at the further growth and development of the Polish nationality.

The organization of women's activities for the protection of Polish interests followed closely upon the general development patterns of Polish club activities in Posen in the field of the so-called "organized work," meaning women appeared first in unpolitical areas. Initially, there was the charity work of upper-class women's groups, under church tutelage. The oldest women's group of this type was the *Towarzystwo Świętego Wincentego a Paulo* (Society of St. Vincent de Paul) founded in 1853 by Polish noblewomen, and which spread rapidly from the city of Posen throughout the entire archdiocese of Posen-Gnesen. It was led by its patron, the Bishop.[11] The support of needy families, hospitals, and day nurseries was the most important activity of this organization, which in the following generations was taken up and expanded by other women's groups. The *Towarzystwo Naukowej Pomocy dla Dziewcząt* (Organization to Support the Education of Young Women) was founded in 1871, based on the Marcinkowski Organization, which limited its concerns to young men. Between 1871 and 1910, this Posen-based organization distributed 2,450 stipends with a value of 310,000 marks to needy and talented young women, chiefly for the training of dressmakers, teachers, accountants, and kindergarten teachers.[12]

The heightened pace of the Prussian Polish policy following the "Era of Reconciliation" of Minister Caprivi brought more and decisive impulses for the social and national-political work of the Great Polish women. A reading hall for women (*Czytelnia dla Kobiet*) was formed in 1895 in the city of Posen; reading halls appeared later in other cities of the province, including Bromberg, Gostyn, Ostrowo, Pleschen, and Samter.[13] In 1909, nine women's reading groups formed a federation, *Zjednoczenie Kobiecych Towarzystw Oświatowych* (Union of Women's Educational Associations). Four years later, 32 women's reading groups were already members of the federation, which had 3,173 members in 1913. A notable characteristic of this federation was the elimination of the Church from the board of directors and the expansion of the organization throughout the entire imperial territory.

There, the *Czytelnia dla Kobiet* began as small discussion groups which were occupied with such activities as recitations from the work of the Polish national poet Adam Mickiewicz. Books by Polish authors and Polish-language magazines from all three parts of partitioned Poland were collected. Thus, the Poznań Women's Reading Hall had 2,363 titles in its collection prior to the First World War. Some women's reading groups presented public lectures on social problems, for instance, "On the Destructiveness of Alcohol," or even on national-political themes such as "Love of the Fatherland and National Education."

Still clearer in its national-Polish orientation was the women's organization *Warta* founded in Posen in 1894.[14] Up to 1913, this semi-legal group had 363 members, who came primarily from the Polish intelligentsia and took a deliberately firm position against the tutelage of many women's groups by the Polish clergy. One of this organization's central tasks was to counteract the anti-Polish tendencies of the Prussian school policy through private initiatives and thus secure for Polish children the possibility of a Polish education. Between 1879 and 1914, under the most difficult, conspiratorial circumstances–private Polish instruction was forbidden–about 24 to 110 predominantly honorary Polish teachers yearly taught Polish twice weekly to some 175 to 750 children in small groups in private homes. Children from poor families had top priority. In this way, about five to ten percent of the Polish children in the provincial capital were taught to read and write Polish. Here, one can speak only of a moral victory. In addition to these efforts, a savings bank for children, the *złota skarbonka* (Golden Passbook) was founded, kindergartenlike installations were maintained, special children's libraries were created, and Christmas parties, amateur theatricals, day trips, and holiday colonies were organized.

The general public work of *Warta* was no less important: its fetes on Polish national holidays, like the yearly celebration of the November 1830 national uprising or honoring such historical personalities as Kościuszko and Staszic, but also famous contemporary Polish women like the writers Maria Konopicka and

Eliza Orzeszkowa. In addition, *Warta* organized large-scale women's demonstrations (*wiece kobiet*). The first took place in Posen in 1899 and had 600 participants; one year later, there were 2,000 participants. Not only the increasing attendance at these meetings, but also the tenor and content of the speeches was impressive. In addition to lectures on educational and household matters, there were regularly speeches concerning Germanization and the national rights of the Poles.

The Polish school strikes of 1901 to 1908 undoubtedly represented a high point in the cultural-political opposition of the Great Polish women.[15] The school strikes deserve particular mention, because in the battle over the prohibition of the Polish language in religious instruction, two levels of cultural self-affirmation of the Great Polish women, which until then had had a parallel existence, came into long-term connection with one another for the first time. The self-confident and active element of noblewomen and the intelligentsia, who had been organized for example in *Warta*, and the until then passive, conservative, and religiously constrained mass of Polish women workers and farmers.[16] We can accordingly observe in the cultural sector alone a gradual widening of the radius of activity in the female sector from the still elite milieu of the small gatherings of noblewomen to the mobilization of the broadest segments of the population.

A similar development also took place in the second main direction of the Great Polish women's movement, which was concerned with preserving material interests. Certain elements of economic and social-political commitment were already of course contained in the previously mentioned women's charity and educational associations. One should not forget the local women's committees, which in connection with a project or cause, collected money for diverse goals, and after achieving a particular goal were again dissolved. Similarly, exhibitions by craftswomen took place in various provincial cities.[17] In addition, there were clearly spontaneous initiatives like a women's meeting at the Posen home of Countess Leonarda Kwilecka on 22 September 1886. It closed with a call for Polish women to limit their expenditures and to buy shares at the Polish Provincial Bank in order to work against the Prussian colonization policy. Later, mass demonstrations for national-economic goals were held, for example, in Urbanów near Posen on 24 November 1912 in connection with the initial execution of the expropriation law. Several thousand participants from nearby villages attended (see appendix).

The organization of the trades of the Polish women workers took place parallel to this. First were the Posen factory workers in 1889, followed by the clothing-manufacture employees, the shop assistants, the domestics, and the farmers.[18] In 1906, most of these provincial organizations amalgamated into the *Związek towarzystw kobiet pracujących z siedzibą w Poznaniu* (Federation of the Associations of Working Women Headquartered in Posen). This federation had 26 associations and 5,782 members in 1911. It organized a dowry, health insurance, and burial fund, and maintained a legal defense office and a labor exchange in Posen as well as in other provincial cities. In addition to their social-political tasks, these associations were always able to do national-Polish educational work, for example through the lectures at their monthly meetings and not through their own publications. The magazine *Pracownica* (Woman Worker), particularly aimed at young, single factory workers, was founded in 1906. *Gazeta dla Kobiet* (Woman's Newspaper), aimed at all working women, both rural and urban, began appearing twice weekly in 1909.[19] In addition to practical advice on health insurance and old-age pension schemes, the upkeep of home and family, and hygiene, it contained articles on Polish history, the defense of the Polish language, and the danger of mixed German-Polish marriages.

The public protest against certain elements of the Prussian cultural and economic policies, the idyll of charity fetes, the discreet work of the reading groups and the finding of positions for servants or clothing-manufacturing workers were widely divergent expressions of female participation in the struggle for Polish national self-affirmation in the province of Posen. Taken together, however, they resulted in a variety of societal undertakings. The most important branches of the Great Polish women's movement, the *Kobiece stowarzyszenia oświatowe* (women's educational associations) and the *kobiece stowarzyszenia ekonomiczne* (female economic associations), were grouped together into two umbrella organizations at the beginning of the twentieth century. Despite different activities and diverging ideological viewpoints–the educational associations were in general more modern and radical than the women's trade organizations which were connected with the Church–there was no basic conflict which alone could prevent the already generally recognized precept of national solidarity.

The driving force for active unification of the Polish women and their organizations was National Democracy, which had been able to incorporate its ideas into so important an association as *Warta,* but also into *Głos Wielkopolanek. Tygodnik społecznonarodowy dla kobiet wszystkich stanów* (Voice of the Women of Great Poland. Economic-National Weekly for Women of all Classes), which dated from 1908.[20] That these efforts toward integration did not stop at the provincial or national border can likewise be attributed to National Democratic influence.

If heroines and Samaritans from Great Poland at the time of the uprisings had as a matter of course played their part in all of Poland, the radius of action and the horizon of ideas of the Great Polish *działaczki* (women activists) in the course of "organizational work" was visibly limited to the province of Posen. This limitation ended only at the end of the nineteenth century, not least due to National Democratic impetus.[21] From that time, interest in women's questions and women's initiatives grew in other areas of partitioned Poland. This interest was expressed in accounts in women's magazines and through direct contact. Representatives from Great Poland took part in an illegal all-Polish women's conference in Warsaw in 1891 and in 1894 and twenty of them attended the centenary celebration of the Kościuszko uprising in Lwów. Great Polish women also participated in a women's meeting at Zakopane in 1899 and again in the first official Polish women's conference in Cracow in 1913. On such occasions, Great Polish participants pushed for solidarity for their national defense struggle in Prussia and were also able to gather ideas for their own work at home. This convergence did not take place without problems. The situation of women in Congress Poland and Galicia was not the same as that of the women of Great Poland and as a result, goals differed. Nevertheless, joint initiatives were possible, namely in the area of national politics. Thus an *Appel des Femmes Polonaises aux Femmes du Monde* (Appeal of the Polish Women to the Women of the World) was published in connection with the school strike of 1901 and the writer Maria Konopicka was able to collect 110,00 signatures for its support in Italy alone.[22]

Conclusions as to the broad effect of the Great Polish women's movement cannot be based on the relatively small groups of their leading speakers, whose number was probably not much more than 100. However, more than 1,000 women attended the large-scale women's assemblies. If not all of the Great Polish women were included, they were, however, still represented by the available initiatives and organizations which represented all social levels. In this remarkable social and organizational range of activities, Great Polish women found no parallel among their East German female neighbors.

A class specific character was distinguishable in the division of work in the female contribution to the struggle for Polish self-affirmation in the province of Posen. Women from the upper classes were chiefly concerned with all questions connected with the preservation and care of Polish culture and education. The women of the business and trade middle class were certainly the protagonists of the attempts at national-economic independence and delimitation, while the representatives of the agrarian and proletarian milieu were prominent on the elementary discussion of speech and religion, as demonstrated by the Polish school strikes.

An indication of the overwhelming significance of the women and their presence in the Polish national movement is the recognition they received from the German opposition. No less a figure than Bismarck said "As long there is still a Polish woman, there will also be a Polish question."[23] Not only the journalists of the *Ostmark* associations pilloried Polish women with national-political convictions. The local and regional representatives of the Prussian state in the province of Posen always kept a watchful and mistrustful eye on the Great Polish women. Thus the Prussian police officials registered attentively the considerable support that female participants provided for Polish assemblies, which were actually not permitted, according to the law on association and assembly, valid until 1908. This was also the case with their own meetings, where the women were reproached by the competent authorities for "encouraging their fellow females into a conscious opposition to Germandom."[24] Occasionally this led to prison sentences, even for such a respected woman as the teacher Aniela Tułodziecka for example who had to serve a fourteen-day prison sentence in 1913, because she had given a Polish-language lecture in Posen on the raising of children. Boarding schools for Polish girls were closed. It is evident from the official reaction that the Great Polish women at the turn of the century were already seen as an increasingly important factor in the nationality differences in the province.

It is not easy to explain the previously mentioned collective activities and organizational associations of the Great Polish women as an expression of a modern emancipation and women's movement in the sense of a struggle for equal opportunities in education and general legal and social equality for women in public life. Certainly there were some elements of this and the very real increasingly public articulation and organizational ability of the Great Polish women speaks for a growth in their independence and self-confidence. But these were side effects rather than aspired to goals.

The programmatic structure of the Prussian Polish women's movement, if one can speak about such a thing, was less aimed at the freeing of women from male domination or at least at the equality of women, than much more a striving for national-Polish self-affirmation under Prussian domination. Also when there was explicit opposition to male domination of the home, of occupational life, and in general of the public front, it was stressed that such protests were not concerned with feminist ambition, but with the demand for a suitable place for women within Polish society, for a place which would make it possible for them to fulfill their social and national tasks and obligations.[25]

Great Polish women's championing of better opportunities in education and occupation took place under such slogans as *Jakie kobiety, takie przyszłości społeczeństwa* (As goes the future of women, so goes the future of society) and its successor, *Wychowanie kobiet to kwestia wychowania całego społeczeństwa* (The education of women is a question of the education of the entire society).[26] That means, however, that the interests of women were not at the center of the endeavors, but had only indirect significance; women were respected as a basic element in Prussian Polish society, without whose help the national defense against Prussian repression would have remained of only limited effectiveness.

It was then only consistent that the Great Polish women's organizations and newspapers adopted the general principles of the "organizational work" extending them unchanged to feminine requirements and field of activities.[27] There was no variation or modification in the sense of broad concepts. One can see how closely bound up with the Polish national movement of Great Poland the woman question remained in that there was little appreciable difference between the expectations the overwhelmingly male "opinion makers" of the Great Polish public placed on the Polish women and the self-imposed ideals and goals of the Great Polish women speakers. The impulses and the fundamental ideas of the Great Polish women's movement consequently did not develop as specifically female problem areas, but were diverted by higher national-political necessities.

The external political stimuli affected charitable activities, educational demands, and representation of occupational interests. The point of departure was necessarily a conservative one: Polish women saw their task first of all as the preservation of the national-Polish heritage in private and semi-private spheres. Since the Catholic Church had had a substantial influence on this heritage, until the turn of this century, the Polish clergy was able to exercise a decisive influence on Prussian Polish women's organizations. This gradually changed in the course of new social and political challenges only at the beginning of the twentieth century. Thus the appearance of Polish women in the Posen nationality conflict took a more lasting, permanent, and agressive shape up to the turn of the century without giving up the prepolitical defense strategies of family and religion.

Notes to Chapter 3

1. See Witold Jakóbczyk, "Ruch kobiecy i rola prasy w Wielkopolsce na poczcątku XX wieku, in: Studia i Materiały do dziejów Wielkopolski i Pomorza 3, 1957, No. 1, pp. 251-54; Idem., Kobiecy ruch kulturalno-oświatowy, in: Studia nad dziejami Wielkopolski 3 (1890-1914), Poznań, 1967, pp. 121-34; Jaworski, R., Kilka refleksji nad dziejami Wielkopolanek w XIX i na początku XX wieku, in: A. Żarnowska and A. Szwarc (eds.) Kobieta i społeczeństwo na ziemiach polskich w XIX w., Warszawa 1990, pp. 25-35; Skopowski, C., Towarzystwo "Warta" w Poznaniu w latach 1894-1939, in: Studia i Materiały do dziejów Wielkopolski i Pomorza 6, 1960, No. 2, pp. 170-208. In addition, one of the contemporary German-National agitational publications of the general secretary of the Deutscher Ostmarkenverein, Fritz Vosberg, Die polnische Frauenbewegung (Lissa, 1912). Biographical descriptions of outstanding female figures in Polish history contain somewhat more information. Compare Dionizja Wawrzykowska-Wierciochowa, Kobiety wielkopolskie w działalności narodowej, społecznej i wyzwoleńczej (1788-1919). Poznań 1977, which has an extensive bibliography. Little attention has been paid to women in Antoni Gsiorowski and Jerzy Topolski, (eds.), Wielkopolski słownik biograficzny. Warszawa 1989.

2. Stefania Mazurek, Z dziejów polskiego ruchu kobiecego na Górnym Śląsku. Opole 1969, pp. 50-65; Wawrzykowska-Wierciochowa, Kobiety wielkopolskie, p. 4.

3. Wawrzykowska-Wierciochowa, Od prządki do astronautki. Z dziejów kobiety polskiej. Warszawa 1963, p. 42ff.

4. Marek Rezler, Emilia Sczaniecka 1804-1896. Poznań 1984.

5. Modern social-historical analysis is still lacking here. See, however, Witold Szulc, Położenie klasy robotniczej w Wielkopolsce v latach 1871-1914. Poznań 1970.

6. See Waldemar Mitscherlich, Die Ausbreitung der Polen in Preussen. Leipzig 1913, p. 12ff, 50, 64-66, 101ff, 129; concerning social and economic developments in general, see the articles of S. Borowski, Teresa Dohnalowa, Czestaw Łuczak, and Witold Szulc in Witold Jakóbczyk (ed.), Dzieje Wielkopolski 2. Poznan 1973, p. 361ff; Stefan Kowal, Społeczeństwo Wielkopolski i Pomorza Nadwiślańskiego w latach 1871-1914. Poznań, 1982.

7. See for example two anonymous contemporary accounts: Spectator, Die polnische Metamorphose. Kraków 1912, p. 51; Wielkopolanin, Walka ekonomiczno-rasowa w Poznańskiem. Kraków 1898, p. 116ff. In addition see Joachim Benyskiewicz's outline of the problem in "Rola rodziny w zachowaniu narodowości w warunkach zaboru" in: Stanisław Kubiak and Lech Trzeciakowski (eds.), Rola Wielkopolski w dziejach narodu polskiego Poznań 1979, pp. 473-483.

8. See also Gazeta dla Kobiet 1 (2 January 1909): 85; Głos Wielkopolanek 13, 28 March 1909, p. 2; 29, 18 July 1909, pp. 1ff; 45, 8 November 1913, pp. 2ff.

9. Quoted by Gazeta dla Kobiet 19c, 21 September 1903, p. 146.

10. Compare Broesike, Deutsche und Polen der Provinz Posen im Lichte der Statistik, in: Zeitschrift des Königlich Preussischen Statistischen Landesamts, 1912, vol. 52, p. 385; Leo Wegener, Der wirtschaftliche Kampf der Deutschen mit den Polen um die Provinz Posen. Posen 1903, p. 36.

11. See Vosberg, Die polnische Frauenbewegung, p. 8ff.

12. According to Wegener, Die wirtschaftliche Kampf, pp. 171ff.

13. See Jakóbczyk, Studia nad dziejami Wielkopolski 3, pp. 126-32.

14. Compare with ibid., pp. 121-26; Skopowski, Towarzystwo 'Warta' pp. 173-202.

15. See John J. Kulczycki, School Strikes in Prussian Poland 1901-1907: The Struggle over Bilingual Education. New York 1981, especially pp. 160ff.

16. This emerges clearly from the personal data in the legal judgements handed down in connection with the Polish school strikes. See Rudolf Korth, Die preussische Schulpolitik und die polnischen Schulstreiks. Würzburg 1963, pp. 165-70.

17. See for example Gazeta dla Kobiet 23, 7 November 1909, pp. 180-83; Głos Wielkopolanek 52, 26 December 1909, pp. 3ff. See also St. Karwowski, Historya Wielkiego Księstwa Poznańskiego 2, Poznań 1920, p. 445;

68 WOMEN IN PARTITIONED POLAND

Wawzryzkowska-Wierciochowa, Od prządki, pp. 294ff.

18. See Vosberg, Die polnische Frauenbewegung, pp. 13-17; in addition the regular reports in the mouth piece of Związek Towarzystw Kobiet Pracujących, particularly the yearly reports of activities, for example Gazeta dla Kobiet 3, 12 February 1911, pp. 1-20; 2, 28 January 1912, pp. 9-13; 3, 11 February 1912, pp. 17-20.

19. Gazeta dla Kobiet 19, 12 October 1909, pp. 145ff; in addition, the index of vols. 1-5 (1909-1913) of this magazine.

20. Compare Jakóbczyk, Studia nad dziejami Wielkopolski 3, pp. 124ff. Until now, Głos Wielkopolanek has not been researched, but its programmatic articles clearly show a National Democratic influence. See for example Głos Wielkopolanek 9, 28 February 1909, p. 1; 26, 27 June 1909, p. 1.

21. See Wawrzykowska-Wierciochowa, Kobiety wielkopolskie, p. 3ff; Idem., Od prządki, pp. 232ff; in addition the regular comments on the women's questions and organizations in Galicia and Russian Poland in "Gazeta dla Kobiet" and "Głos Wielkopolanek."

22. Compare Kulczycki, School Strikes, p. 66.

23. Discussed in Georg C. von Widdern, Das "schlafende Heer" der Polen. Berlin 1912, p. 52; Wawrzykowska-Wierciochowa, Od prządki, p. 292.

24. Compare Jakóbczyk, Studia nad dziejami Wielkopolski 3, No. 49, p. 129; Głos Wielkopolanek 21, 23 May 1909, pp. 1ff; Gazeta dla Kobiet 12, 15 June 1913, pp. 92ff.

25. See for example Głos Wielkopolanek 13, 28 March 1909, pp. 2ff; Gazeta dla Kobiet 21, 22 October 1911, pp. 163ff; 6, 21 March 1912, p. 44.

26. Gazeta dla Kobiet 19, 12 September 1909, p. 23, 7 November 1910, p. 177.

27. This agreement can be very clearly seen in the propagation of the idea of an Einkaufspatriotismus ("Patriotism in Purchase"). See for example Orędownik 282, 7 December 1888; Praca 46, 13 November 1904; Głos Wielkopolanek 17, 25 April 1909; 8, 22 February 1913; 15, 12 April 1913.

Attachment for Chapter 3

Resolution on the occasion of the women's assembly of 24 November 1912 at Urbanów near Posen:

In the sight of God, we the Polish women of all regions and classes assembled at a meeting in Urbanów on 24 November 1912 occasioned by the expropriation of the inheritance of our fathers: the land, the Church and our abodes, resolve from our deepest souls, that we will consciously fulfill our obligation to the Fatherland in belief in its immortality. We solemnly conclude and in consciousness of the significance of the moment:

1.   that we will consider the land, which we have inherited from our fathers or acquired through our own efforts the property of the entire nation, as a holy relic, that we will not sully it through haggling;

2.   that we will strive to repurchase land from foreign hands;

3.   that we will not voluntarily surrender our land to foreign hands, that we will guard our churches, and not voluntarily retreat from the thresholds of our houses;

4.   that we, although violently dispossessed, will not leave our homeland, but will anew place ourselves on guard and that we will influence our fathers, husbands, brothers, and sons in the same sense;

5.   that we will raise our children in a real national spirit, in which we will bestow upon them a pure national education and not send them outside the borders of the Polish lands until they have finished secondary school (*gymnasium*, upper girls' school);

6.   that we will help unenlightened parents or those overburdened by work with instruction of their children in the mother tongue;

7.   that we will always speak Polish and pay attention to the purity of our language;

8.   that we will conscientiously and steadfastly work on all national positions and will join forces to enhance our work for unification;

9.   that we will always and everywhere stand guard over the preservation of the national dignity;

10.   that we will beware of luxury and living above our means and instead of this will propagate for self-sacrifice for national goals;

11.   that we will place our money in Polish cash registers, banks, and

firms, and increase the wealth of society through the creation of indigenous business;

12.   that we will rigorously observe the slogan "Each to his own" with respect to trade, to merchants, and in any professional activity with regard to economic well-being and national dignity;

13.   that we will collect for a national fund...;

14.   that we will deem the propagation of harmonious trade and sincere fraternity of all classes and professions as our most sacred obligation and the mission of Polish women.

SOURCE: *Wojewódzkie Archiwum Państwowe w Poznaniu.* Polizeipräsidium Nr. 2776. Akten betr. die polnische Bewegung in Schrimm 1911-1913, p. 341ff.

4

Galicia: Initiatives for Emancipation of Polish Women

In the middle of the nineteenth century the situation of women in Galicia in legal, social and family terms did not differ from that of women from the remaining areas of the partitioned country. While in other European countries the so-called "women question" was being raised, in Austrian Poland women could still live only by relying on their families. Their role was defined by the Austrian marital law, which was far from according equal rights to men and women, while the social position of women in Galicia depended on their affiliation to a given social class. However, a family model based on patriarchal principles remained among the landed gentry, townspeople, peasants and the working class alike. The choice of a husband belonged to parents; it was they who decided upon the fate of their daughters, who only in exceptional circumstances could follow the choice of their heart. Marriages grounded on financial speculations prevailed among the landed gentry and well-to-do industrialists. It was more common in townspeople's families as well as those of intelligentsia that parents took their children's preferences into consideration and feelings were not ignored, although even here there were cases where blind obedience and submission to paternal will were required. A record by a diarist whose parents did not allow her to marry the chosen man, but who resignedly submitted to their will despite the fact that the decision ruined her happiness and left her with a complex for the rest of her days, was not a solitary case.[1] Literature and prayer-books from the 19th century

71

created the image of a woman in the role of a submissive wife, mother and educator of her children, while the issue of education, its level and independence were not taken into account at all. In the Austrian civil code, in force in Galicia, there were numerous limitations in respect to women, as far as personal law was concerned. They could not act as guardians, curators or witnesses at drafting the last will and testament.[2]

The social activity of individual women in the 1850s was limited to charity and looking after the sick, the poor and children. In order to run such an organized activity, women united in secular, or even more often, religious societies. These organizations established orphanages, poor-houses, educational houses and even schools. Charitable campaigns and philanthropy were the only fields of intense activity for women in Galicia for many years.[3] The outbreak of the January Insurrection in 1863, its course and its further consequences, initiated changes in the traditional situation of women. Although Galicia had not been the theatre of insurgent flights, due to the proximity of its borders it played a very important role in expanding and strengthening the liberation movement. At that time Galician women in particular distinguished themselves, by the sporadic taking up of arms in the uprising but primarily by supporting the national movement with enormous courage and sacrifice. They kept the insurgents in hiding, nursed, looked after and protected the wounded–especially after the tragic battle of Miechów[4]–they served as dispatch-riders carrying weapon, ammunition and messages and proved excellent scouts and activists.[5] They carried out the campaign on behalf of the uprising in secret, yet they managed to create a chain of committees called "Women's Committees" or "Ladies' Committees", with seats not only in Cracow and Lvov, but also in smaller towns of Galicia such as Przemyśl, Rzeszów, Jasło and Tarnów. They played a considerable, however underestimated role in supporting the fight for independence. Many of them were accused of treason and hence persecuted and imprisoned. Women were also the ones who ostentatiously initiated and consequently observed the national mourning in clothing wearing black dresses, black jewelry and black crosses–symbols of suffering. The first stages of women's independent activity at the time of the Insurrection and after its downfall were characterized by very strong patriotic feelings which, in turn, became the motivation for all activities of the Galician women fighting for independence, the Polish language and national status. These were the first signs of the emancipation movement, the first attempts of women to leave their homes and to resist external events.

After the fall of the January Insurrection, the specific political situation, the implementation of martial law in Galicia, the imprisonment or emigration of their fathers and husbands, obliged women to change their traditional way of life. Many men had died in the uprising, others were exiled to Siberia or they worked their way to Western Europe. Then women including those from the manor houses of landed gentry and those from the ranks of townspeople and intelligentsia had to take up the struggle for their own living, as well as that of their children.[6] At that time Galician press and publications increased the amount of information on the development of the feminist movement in Europe. First of all, polemics on the education of women flourished and two different viewpoints were disclosed: a conservative–religious trend averse to any changes, and a liberal one in favour of reforms. The latter was, to a large extent, the reflection of similar changes in the system of economic and social relations. The economic decline of the Galician landed gentry and the fact that many women of that class remained without means was accompanied by the deterioration of trade and the crafts and the influx of women, mainly from Warsaw, who were coming to Galicia in search of education. In this way the Galician women became informed about the attempts of emancipation being undertaken in Russian Poland, and the existing image of a mother, wife and educator, congealed in the moral and religious framework, began to break–slowly but surely.

The act of granting autonomy to Galicia in 1867 by the Austrian government had an enormous impact upon further fate of Galicia. The opportunities for the development of Polish education, learning and culture increased. The polonization of the administrative apparatus opened up opportunities of employment for the Polish people in the national sector which promoted the growth of intelligentsia. Then, voices could be heard demanding some amendment of the situation of women by at least partially abolishing restrictions in the sphere of family life. The idea was to equalize husband and wife in respect to martial faithfulness, to grant women wider civil rights and to admit them to family councils. As regards care of children, there were demands to acknowledge mother's rights to bring up a child, particularly in the case of children under age, and especially the right to appeal against the abuses of paternal powers. In spite of a number of articles on the subject in the press, the achievements were meagre and the discrimination of women was only slightly alleviated.[7]

The disadvantageous situation of women in Galicia was highly influenced by the fact that after Poland had been partitioned, Galicia was long deprived of participation in the economic changes which took place in the more industrial Congress Kingdom of Poland. There, as in Prussian Poland, rapid industrial growth was taking place, obliging women to go to work in factories. In Galicia, the conditions for the development of industry on a larger scale had not yet been created and only in the vicinity of Krosno, Wadowice, Andrychów and Biała did women work in factories; in fact the majority of working women were recruited from urban servants. However, even this sort of work meant some kind of emancipation, especially for peasant women, who were thus able to earn their living and have their own wages.[8] As regards craft, the 1859 Act enabled a widow, after her husband's death, to run a workshop; however not independently but only with help of a qualified journeyman. In the 1860s and 1870s the number of hat and tailor's workshops grew up considerably; hosiery and embroidery workshops appeared, thus increasing the participation of women working independently in crafts. Also, the number of eating-houses and cafe run by women grew up. Women began to appear among the shop staff. They increased in number in the ranks of nursemaids and governesses, not only in the houses of gentry but also in those of well-to-do townsmen and higher orders of intelligentsia. There were few opportunities of employment in the capacity of white-collar workers; perhaps the chances were slightly better in Lvov, as there were more credit-banks and more branches and sections of commercial institutions creating opportunities of employment for women. In Cracow, which was very backward in this respect, women were mainly employed as post-mistresses, accountants, clerks and cashiers in small businesses. In addition, a relatively large group of women made their living by giving private lessons and many of them worked as teachers, especially from the 1870s on.

The number of women teachers increased quickly, leading in time to feminization, especially in primary schools. In the 1875/76 school year, 2750 women teachers worked in Galicia in primary schools; in 1897/98, there were 3292 of them, and by the turn of the century–over 6000.[9] Educational work in elementary and convent schools, as well as in private houses, had been a long established way of making a living, especially for single women. However the rise in number did not mean the improvement of their working conditions , or promotion. Men were promoted into so-called permanent employment (from temporary) much faster than women, even if the latter fulfilled the requirements and had passed the qualification examinations with better marks, or had better education than was required.[10] The employment of women in secondary school education looked somewhat different. There were few women in school at the secondary level, and characteristically, the higher the level of education, the fewer women teachers were to be found.

The new social situation allowed for the expression of new tendencies towards the liberation of women not only in the traditional and economic spheres, but also in regard to education. The necessity of securing financial independence brought to light an educational problem: that of the preparation of women for independent work. The state of girls' schools in Galicia was worse from those in the Congress Kingdom, and the level of education offered was low. According to official reports of the educational authorities, girls' schools for juniors were very primitive; the best situation was reported in convent schools, as for example in the school run by the Benedictine nuns at Staniątki, near Cracow.[11] Though in the 19th century private boarding-schools began to spring up in Galicia, but they were often run by people without proper qualifications who treated their establishment as the source of making money. Boarding-schools did not teach much and the education of women was limited to needlework and music, and sometimes also included a little French. A young diarist admitted that she "has not received much learning" and it was only after her return home from the boarding-school that she tried to supplement her education.[12] The only thing offered by boarding-schools was musical education, and as a result, in almost all houses of the gentry and townsmen wives and daughters played the piano and sang.[13] Galicia completely lacked girls' trade schools. The situaiton was changed in 1867, when the National School Council came into being. Then, the management of elementary and secondary schools, and later also trade schools, was entrusted to the Council, which duly carried out the reorganization of education within the limits of the official acts and regulations in force. It was then that voices were occasionally raised demanding reforms within girls' education, which differed in level from that of the boys and which was, in the estimation of contemporaries, "arranged according to the needs of the sexes."[14] At the same time the intensification of the feminist movement in Warsaw and its influence in Galicia, pushed a small, but vigorous group of social activities of Cracow and Lvov to fight for the cause of women's education. Through the press, they managed to arouse the interest of members of Parliament in this issue, and in the 1880s they provoked an animated discussion in the Galician Parliament. Finally, after long endeavours, at the beginning of our century (in 1904), a reform of girls' education was brought about. The expansion of the activity of convents contributed to the changes in this respect: in 1874 the Ursulines exiled from the Poznań province by the Prussian authorities opened up their boarding-schools for girls in Cracow and Tarnów, while the nuns from the Order of the Immaculate Conception opened a boarding-school and an economic seminary, mainly for girls of landed gentry, at Jazłowiec, Eastern Galicia. Further schools were opened at Niżniowiec in 1883, and at Nowy Sącz in 1897. In Galicia, as in the whole territory of Austria, an interest in trade education, which played an important role in women's emancipation, began to grow. So far, only industrial schools in Lvov and Cracow organized three-year courses of embroidery and ornamental lace-making, as well as four-year courses of drawing and modelling. From the 1870s, schools began preparing women to work as nurses (so far this domain had been monopolized by nuns). Housewives, weavers, dressmakers and milliners began to spring up. In addition, courses teaching cutting, sewing, embroidery, lace-making, corset-making and the like, were started. Also, two-year commercial courses were introduced. The school of embroidery at Maków, the private school of country housewives at Zakopane, the school of lace-making at Kańczugaand Stary Sącz, as well as the school of midwives in Cracow and Lvov, soon became popular. In Eastern Galicia they opened up Ukrainian craft schools and Ukrainian courses of embroidery, lace-making and haberdashery. In this way, from 1882 till 1914, craft education for women was created in Galicia; however it was strictly limited to traditional women's occupations.

Atypical among all this activity tended to create new possibilities of craft education for Galician women were the "Higher Courses for Women", following the English example, which were organized in Cracow in 1868. The organizer, Adrian Baraniecki, was a medical doctor, a collector and a social activist. The courses offered such subjects as natural history, literature with history, fine arts, economy and commerce.[15] The latter did not last for long, because of the lack of interest. At first, the courses lasted for one year, but after the death of the initiator, they were extended into two years. The lectures, held on the university level, were of a scientific nature but designed for the general public, and they were delivered by professors of the Jagiellonian University. Baraniecki's courses were popular. From 1868 till 1891, they were attended by over 3000 women, drawn from all three parts of the partitioned Poland, but characteristically, mostly from the Congress Kingdom, where women had no access to Polish schools. Baraniecki's courses, being a novelty on a nationwide scale, were a substitute for a university, for they allowed women access to an education approximate to academic education, and served as a preparation for further studies. Hence Dr. Baraniecki was considered a forerunner of higher education for women.

In the second half of the 19th century, secondary education for women in Galicia was practically non-existent. That is why the opening of the first three government teacher-training seminaries for women, in 1871(Cracow, Lvov, Przemyśl), was tremendously significant in the development of education. On finishing the seminary, the teachers took an examination entitling them to work in primary schools; and then, if they wished, the second examination entitling to teach in secondary schools. These women's seminaries were immensely popular in Galicia. It may be as well to quote a project which was put forward by the School Council in 1874, to extend the duration of training in the seminary up to four years. The proposal was justified not only by the desire to raise the level of education of the candidates, but also by the inconvenience caused by their great number. The addition of the extra year was to discourage the candidates from enrolling.[16] The seminaries were mainly attended by the daughters of the Galician intelligentsia; some of them no longer young, but they enrolled with the hope of gaining qualifications necessary to perform intellectual work. The first women students who later went to the Galician and foreign universities were recruited from among the students of these seminaries. Thus the teacher-training seminaries provided a substitute for a real secondary school for girls, and they gave them opportunities to learn and to obtain a profession. They opened up the way towards emancipation for those women who were seeking independence.

With no secondary schools available in Galicia, women had the possibility of taking secondary school finals in two appointed grammar schools for boys: at St. Ann's in Cracow, and at Franz Joseph's in Lvov. It was not an easy thing, however. The finals required a long and thorough preparation. That is why, starting from the 1880s, an idea emerged to open a grammar school for girls in Galicia; from the 1890s on the project was strongly supported by the press and, above all, it was partonized by "Przedświt" (Harbinger), a publication for women issued in Lvov. In 1893, women-activitists grouped around "News-Room for Women" in Lvov, collected about four thousand signatures on the petition to the Galician Parliament within a few days to support the initiative; while in Cracow, beside N. Cybulski, professor of physiology, and Adolf Gross, Kazimiera Bujwidowa, who was the wife of a professor of medicine of the Jagiellonian University, an activist from the Congress Kingdom, was the chief initiator of the new grammar school for girls. They won the battle for the first Polish private girls' grammar school which was opened in Cracow in 1896.[17] The completion of the school prepared girls for a job requiring higher qualifications or provided the qualifications needed to enter a university. However, the school did not obtain the right to carry out finals, and the graduates continued to take the examination at St. Ann's. It was not until 1907, after years of repeated efforts, that the school obtained the necessary consent. It was only in our century during the process of establishing classical and real grammar schools for girls that the conditions in secondary school education for girls improved.

"Przedświt," the already mentioned daring women's periodical, excelled in influencing–quietly but consistently–public opinion in favour of the new project of creating a grammar school for girls. From 1895 it was backed up by "Ster" (Helm), a feminist fortnightly review dedicated to the education of women. In 1897 a petition to Parliament was printed in the paper asking for another grammar school for girls, this time in Lvov. It was argued that in the face of the worsening economic situation women were more and more in need of extending their range and means of making money. It is clear that economic needs became the main source of women's desire to obtain education, and the press reflected very accurately the growth of their aspirations and the range of their fight. Besides the demands for a grammar school, the issue of admission of women to universities was always present in both periodicals. According to the regulation of 1876, women could attend university lectures in the capacity of guest auditors only, with the permission of the appropriate dean, but they had not any rights resulting from the fact. Those women's progressive periodicals that created a favourable atmosphere as regards higher education for women were attacked by the conservative press and publications; even the Minister of Education in the Austrian government, P. Gautsch, stressed the preparation for the role of future wives and mothers in his speech on the education of girls. The dispute on higher education for women continued and became increasingly heated while the Galician government adopted a wait and see policy. At the same time the case was being discussed in Vienna. Then a group of feminists from Cracow, with Maria Siedlecka, Maria Turzyma and invaluable Kazimiera Bujwidowa, began a written and oral campaign on behalf of admitting women to universities. Naturally, they collaborated with the activists from Lvov, Maria Wysłouchowa among others. They persuaded Jan Karłowicz, the famous etnographer and linguist, to make a speech at the Conference of Naturalists and Physicians in 1891 and to put forward a demand to create the possibility for Polish women to study at the Galician universities. The great battle took place three years later, in 1894 at the Congress of Polish teachers in Lvov. There, Bujwidowa delivered an excellent speech in which she addressed the Congress, demanding the admission of women to universities as accredited students. The atmosphere of the conference rooms was not favourable to the issue, and the animated discussion revealed the split of the teachers into two groups–for and against the project. In spite of the situation, the speaker managed to break the ice and she succeeded in having the resolution adopted. It was an important step forward in the fight for equal rights. Bujwidows took advantage of the victory in her further work. She began to encourage women to apply for admission to the Jagiellonian University. In 1894/95 there were 64 applications of this kind, and although they were not answered positively, the issue had been broached and it obliged the Galician universities to make definite decisions.[18] The attitude of the professors of both universities was divided; however only a

minority sympathized with the demands of the women's movement. This became evident both in Cracow and in Lvov when
further applications for admission arrived. When three students
applied for admission to the Faculty of Pharmacy of the Jagiellonian University–all three from the Congress Kingdom and
with certificates of the so-called "pharmaceutic help" which had
been recognized in Warsaw as equivalent to grammar school
finals–they were supported by a group of progressive professors
(O. Bujwid, B. Ulanowski, W. Zakrzewski). Through the media-
tion of the Jagiellonian University Senate, they applied again to
the Ministry of Education in Vienna. The answer was that they
would be accepted as guest auditors, that is, without being
entitled to the university degree.[19] Besides, they had to obtain
permission to attend lectures from each lecturer separately. "We
were kindly received everywhere and we obtained the required
permissions without problems," wrote Jadwiga Klemensiewiczowa,[20] one of the students. In 1895 another three students
from the Congress Kingdom enrolled in Pharmacy and in 1896,
eight women were admitted to the Faculty of Philosophy in
Cracow. The following applications came in a wave that could
not be stopped.

    In the meantime, the first woman who applied to the Medical
Faculty in Lvov, in 1895 was rejected by the Ministry; she was
offered a place at the Faculty of Philosophy, instead. However,
in the Faculty office the applications were handled ambivalently;
the prospective students were instructed to apply individually to
the Ministry but at the same time the Faculty organized academic
courses for women, modelled on the English pattern, and on the
Higher Courses of A. Baraniecki. Although the influx of women
was sizeable, and the professors were excellent, the participants
did not come up to the expectations of the women's movement.
However, when in 1897 the Minister of Education consulted the
universities of Cracow and Lvov as to their opinion on admission
of women, the Faculty of Philosophy in Lvov totally supported
the women's demands, thus showing more progressiveness than
in Cracow. In Cracow, on the other hand, it was concluded, that
women could actually be admitted as ordinary auditors, on the

same principles as men, however, the admission to lectures would depend on the permission of the individual lecturer, and lectures for women were to take place separately from men. Finally, on March 23, 1897, the Ministry of Faith and Education granted women permission to study at the Faculty of Philosophy of both Galician universities on condition that they were Austrian citizens over 18, with their finals completed in a classical Austrian grammar school for men. In 1898 the decision was extended and foreigners who had passed their finals abroad could also seek admission, however, the decision lay in the hands of the Ministry. Two years later, in 1900 women were admitted to medical studies. The fight for equal rights for women in regard to admission to universities ended up in partial victory. They obtained the possibility to study at the Philosophical and Medical Faculties, but they were not admitted to the Law Faculty, the Academy of Fine Arts or technical studies. However, soon they proved themselves no less capable than men, both in Humanities and Sciences. In the first academic years, after having obtained the right to study, there were no ordinary women students at the Faculty of Philosophy in Cracow, as none of the candidates had completed their finals; so there were only extraordinary students admitted. In Lvov, there were two ordinary women students but the majority belonged to the extraordinary group. In the following years the percentage of women studying at the Faculty of Philosophy grew up considerably; e.g. in Cracow in 1900, there were 11 percent; 15 percent in 1905, and in 1915 as high as 52 percent.[21] The systematic rise in the percentage of women indicated that this faculty enjoyed a special popularity; for a while it was also the only accessible way to higher education. "These were my happiest years," wrote a student of the Philosophical Faculty of the University of Lvov in her diary, when after long efforts she finally got enrolled and managed to finish her studies in due course.[22] The first woman student of the Medical Faculty of the Jagiellonian University in Cracow was Helena Sikorska (the sister-in-law of Władysław Sikorski, the Prime Minister and the Commander-in-Chief of the Polish Army during the Second World War), who having completed her finals at St. Ann's grammar school, obtained the permission from the Ministry and started her studies in 1900; in 1906 she received a grade of the doctor of medicine–the first woman's grade from the Galician University. Although the Galician feminists started their campaign to get to the universities of Cracow and Lvov almost a quarter of a century later than the women from the Congress Kingdom attending foreign universities (and the cause of this situation lay in the differences between the two economies), the fight was spirited. They managed to overcome prejudice on the part of the professors and male colleagues who feared the competition of women at work, and to prove their capabilities. Another battle was fought to admit the Galician women to the posts of professor's assistants and to examinations qualifying for assistant-professorship.

Having higher qualifications should have meant for women better paid jobs. Unfortunately, the majority of women graduates of the Faculty of Philosophy from Galicia gave private lessons; only few of them were employed in the teacher-training seminaries. The situation of women working in elementary schools was even worse; especially of those employed as temporary teachers. Their earnings were very low and the responsibility was high. The same applied to the salaries of a large number of women clerks, but the worst financial treatment fell to the share of those employed in small craft workshops producing clothes. Their earnings left them on the verge of starvation. Women employed as workers in factories were very exploited and their earnings were lower in comparison to men's. Thus, the Galician women had no possibilities to make use of their education or specific qualifications. In all aspects of employment they were less privileged than men, more exposed to risks of umemployment and not admitted to responsible positions. However, this state of affairs made women ready to take up the difficult fight for their rights and they tended to unite for this purpose. It was the Galician teachers who realized the significance of joint efforts first, and they created the "Association of Women Teachers" in Cracow, as early as 1873. At first, the activity of the association was confined to granting allowances and loans, but later a library, a reading-room and the employment agency for private teachers were added.[23] They also actively joined in organizing mass meetings and gatherings, and soon a similar association came into being in Lvov, aiding women in obtaining qualifications necessary for a given job, e.g. by organizing courses preparing for entrance examinations to the so-called faculty schools. In Przemyśl, the mutual aid society of teachers was created.[24] The women's movement, which began to take a more definite shape in Galicia, was more prominent in Lvov than in Cracow. The "Society of Women's Labour", which came into being there in the 1870s, established a school of cutting and sewing, together with the compulsory education, according to the existing programme.[25] From 1886 on, the "News-Room for Women" of Lvov assembled a few hundred members who wanted to establish "a center of intellectual life". They took part in campaigning for the admission of women to higher education, for executive posts in education, for the equal legal status of women teachers and for places in the Schools Councils. The "News-Room for Women" created in Cracow in 1889 organized, apart from solemn celebrations of national anniversaries, courses on floriculture, hairdressing, embroiders, etc.[26] In Lvov, a school for servants named after Żulinski was established, where instruction was given on Sundays; in Cracow "St. Zyta's Society of Servants" came into being in 1899. In 1901, in Lvov, a society was created acting as an employment agency with its own newspaper. At the end of the 19th century, also in Lvov, "St. Joseph's Society of Women Producing Clothes" came into being, followed by St. Anthony's society that ran its own sewing workshop and cutting and sewing courses. Women-workers of the state-owned cigar factory in Cracow (opened in 1875) though large in number, created their own society relatively late; it was not until 1900 that "St. Joseph's Society" was created to bring financial and moral support. The movement of the women's intelligentsia, apart from the "News-Room", was assembled in Galicia in "Ladies' Circles" of the Society of People's School. Its members, beside demanding access to higher education and to a wider range of jobs, opened up reading-rooms, schools and they organized national celebrations and excursions. Beside Cracow and Lvov, the Przemyśl circle was very active; it established four people's schools as well as the Stanisławów one in Eastern Galicia which also opened up a few schools.[27] A positive role was also played–especially in fight for higher education–by the "Józef I. Kraszewski Society", which organized lectures and raised scholarship funds.[28]

According to the 1867 Act on societies in Austrian law, women were excluded from political parties, so they could fight for equal rights only indirectly, through the members of these groups. A resolution on the women issue might help women to get onto legislative bodies. Thanks to the abovementioned campaign by the "Association of Women Teachers", a woman was elected to a School Council for the first time in Lvov, and then the Galician Parliament carried a motion that henceforth, a woman would be a delegate in the Cracow and Lvov School council. This was, of course, significant for education; however, the issues of social and political equality were more difficult to achieve. The Galician women did not have, with few exceptions, the rights to vote for Commune Councils, or Parliament. The Commune Council Act of 1866, as well as the statutes of Cracow and Lvov from the late 1860's, decided that only men were entitled to vote and be elected, and those women who paid national direct taxes on property, enterprise or income. However, the right to be elected was restricted to men, and if a women fulfilled the requirements to be elected, her husband or plenipotentiary with a written authorization voted in her name. Thus, in towns, it was mainly owners of tenement houses and industrial or commercial enterprises, as well as women living on interest who voted.; clerks, teachers, actresses or women employed in crafts or the health service were deprived of this right. In the 1880's, in Cracow, where they created three electoral groups, about 740 women voted; this includes 320 owners of real property, 400 owners of industrial and commercial enterprises and only 20 women living on interest.[29] The issue of elections to the Galician Parliament in Lvov and to the State Council in Vienna was far more important. According to the electoral law of 1867, only women paying high taxes, that is owners of large land estates, real property and workshops of considerable size, had the right to vote for the State Council and for the Parliament. According to the electoral law, both referring to the community councils and to Parliament, in cases of married women it was the husband who performed the voting; in other cases it was a plenipotentiary.[30] Women's activities at first focused on the problems of job training, secondary school education and admission to universities, put off the fight for electoral rights for later. As part of the campaign for the electoral reform in Galicia in 1890, the social-democratic party spoke up for political equality for women. Soon the significance of demands for electoral rights for women of the emancipation movement was understood. At the women's mass meeting in Lvov in 1892, which assembled about 200 participants, a resolution was carried demanding the general election include electoral rights for women. In the following years the battle grew more heated, in mass meetings in Cracow in 1893, and in Lvov from 1894 till 1895 the necessity to ensure political rights for women was strongly stressed. The campaign was extended into working classes from the Bielsko-Biała constituency. In 1893, at a joint meeting of men and woman workers of that area, the postulates of full electoral rights, regardless of sex were put forward. In the meantime, a new reformed electoral law brought into being in 1896, established the fifth electoral group; however women were not included in it.[31] Until the outbreak of the Great War, women in Austrian Poland had not received full electoral rights, although they solicited actively for them in the press as well as through the resolutions to Parliament at mass meetings. It was a very dynamic and animated fight and, although not crowned with success, it proved the political maturity of the Galician women.

The Galician women's movement of the second half of the 19th century was very complex. It expressed tendencies towards liberation in the spheres of the economy, morality, education as well as legal, social and political fields. A writer recorded in the 1870's "Sad is the fate of those poor women, who are orphaned or early widowed; they must work very hard indeed, for a humble living and their work is unpopular for the sake of competition".[32] The economic situation of the Galician women did not change much within fifty years, which was important in the process of formation of unions and associations for the sake of equality. The outlook on the women issue was changing slowly but permanently; the issue began not only to be perceived and fought, but also supported. The feminist movement in Galicia had reached, in comparison to the original stagnation, considerable success through these years, especially in the sphere of education. Because of the political situation in Austrian Poland and considerable political liberties, it was also characterized by a strong patriotic current. It had an impact upon close cooperation with associations from other partitioned territories and, with time, the women's fight for equality of rights merged with political and patriotic activity and liberation tendencies.

Notes to Chapter 4

1. H. Kunachowiczowa, née Kadłubowska, Dziennik z lat 1856-1860, in: Kapitan i dwie panny. Krakowskie pamiętniki z XIX wieku. Prepared by: Irena Homola and Bolesław Łopuszański, Kraków 1980, pp. 200-317.

2. K. Grzybowski, Historia państwa i prawa polskiego, vol. 4: Warszawa 1982, p. 438.

3. T. Męczkowska, Ruch kobiecy, Warszawa 1907, pp. 9-10: M. Estreicherówna, Życie towarzyskie i obyczajowe Krakowa w latach 1848-1863. Kraków 1968, pp. 35-37.

4. W. Tokarz, Kraków w początkach powstania styczniowego i wyprawa na Miechów. Kraków 1924; M. Kietlińska, née Moher, Wspomnienia. Compiled by Irena Homola-Skąpska, Kraków, 1986, pp. 208-215.

5. M. Bruchnalska, Ciche bohaterki. Udział kobiet w powstaniu styczniowym. Miejsce Piastowe 1933, pp. 93-144; L. Zembrzuski, Rola kobiety w dziejach obcej i polskiej wojskowej służby zdrowia. Warszawa 1927.

6. D. Wawrzykowska Wierciochowa, Od prządki do astronautki. Z dziejów kobiety polskiej, jej pracy i osiągnięć. Warszawa 1963, pp. 203-231, eadem., Z dziejów kobiety wiejskiej. Warszawa 1961, pp. 121-123, eadem., Nie po kwiatach los je prowadził. Warszawa 1987, pp. 10-15.

7. A. Pawłowska, Kwestie etyczno-obyczajowe w prasie kobiecej przełomu XIX i XX wieku, in: Studia Historyczne 30: 1987, pp. 571-588.

8. I. Ihnatowicz, A. Mączak, B. Ziętara, Społeczeństwo polskie od X do XX wieku. Warszawa 1979, pp. 480-485.

9. B. Czajecka, Z domu w szeroki świat (a typescript of monography in the course of issue).

10. I. Homola, Kwiat społeczeństwa...Struktura społeczna i zarys położenia inteligencji krakowskiej w latach 1860-1914. Kraków etc. 1984.

11. J. Hulewicz, Sprawa wyższego wykształcenia kobiet w Polsce w wieku XIX. Kraków 1939, pp. 103-104; Romana Pachucka, on her arrival at Lvov from Warsaw, was taken aback by the difference in the level of learning between the Galician and Warsaw schools. She also noticed, what the girls from Lvov thought of: R. Pachucka, Pamiętniki z lat 1886-1914. Wrocław 1958, p. 68.

12. M. Kietlińska, née Moher, Wspomnienia, p. 323.

13. T. Strumiłło, Szkice z polskiego życia muzycznego. Kraków 1954, p. 110.

14. Projekty reform szkolnictwa ludowego w Galicji u progu autonomii 1860-1873. Compiled by C. Majorek, Wrocław etc. 1980.

15. J. Kras, Wyższe Kursy dla kobiet im. A. Baranieckiego w Krakowie 1868-1924. Kraków 1972.

16. C. Majorek, System kształcenia nauczycieli szkół ludowych w Galicji doby autonomicznej (1871-1914). Wrocław etc. 1971.

17. Petycja kobiet do sejmu. Przedświt, Lwów 1893, No. 10.

18. Zachara J. Historia pierwszego na ziemiach polskich gimnazjum żeńskiego im. Emilii Plater w Krakowie, in: Sprawozdanie gimnazjum im. E. Plater w Krakowie za rok 1936/1937.

19. Ster 1897, No. 7.

20. J. Hulewicz, Walka kobiet polskich o dostęp na uniwersytety. Warszawa 1936, pp. 32-33.

21. J. Klemensiewiczowa, née Sikorska, Przebojem ku wiedzy, Wrocław. Warszawa etc. 1961, pp. 229-230.

22. J. Klemensiewiczowa, née Sikorska, Przebojem, p. 232.

23. Z. Tabaka, Analiza zbiorowości studenckiej Uniwersytetu Jagiellońskiego w latach 1850-1918. Kraków 1970.

24. R. Pachucka, Pamiętniki, p. 79.

25. Głos kobiet w kwestii kobiecej. Warszawa 1903, p. 326.
26. Pamiętniki Zjazdu Kobiet Polskich odbytego 11 i 12 maja 1913. Kraków 1913, pp. 132-160.
27. J. Hulewicz, Sprawa, p. 247.
28. W. Reutt, O szkolnictwie galicyjskim. In: Kobieta współczesna. Księga zbiorowa. Warszawa 1904, pp. 239-242.
29. Pamiętnik Zjazdu, pp. 132-160.
30. P. Kuczalska-Reinschmit, Z historii ruchu kobiecego, in: Głos kobiet w kwestii kobiecej, pp. 271-329.
31. I. Homola, Kuria inteligencji w krakowskiej Radzie Miejskiej/1866-1914/, in: Inteligencja polska pod zaborami. Warszawa 1978, pp. 107-157.
32. S. Warmski, Prawo kobiet w państwie austriackim. Lwów 1910.

5

Girls' Education in the Kingdom of Poland (1815-1915)

A wider interest in the question of bringing up and educating girls is apparent in Poland in the middle of the 18 century. It was reflected in the views of leading representatives of Polish pedagogical thought of that period. For example, sharp criticism of the eduction of girls at that time was given by Hugo Kołłątaj, who called for a reform of their education, demanding patriotism and further knowledge be included in the process.[1]

The Commission of National Education, under the influence of Polish and West-European pedagogical thought, turned its attention to the matter of educating girls. However it did not undertake the reform of female education nor organize its own secondary schools, but it made efforts to attain a permanent supervision of private girls' boarding-schools. As a result, the "Przepisy od Komisji Edukacji Narodowej Pensjonarzom i Mistrzyniom dane" ("Regulations given to Headmasters and Headmistresses from the Commission of National Education") were published in 1775.[2] It must be said, however, that the Commission did not recognize equal educational right for women and did not fully appreciate the social importance of their education. It seems that the attitude of the Commission towards that problem must have been influenced by contemporary prejudices of society, mostly nobility, against wider concern with girls' education.

The work on improving the state of education of Polish women initiated by the Commission was stopped by the third partition of Poland in 1795. Given the lack of state independence, the matter of upbringing and educating girls gained real importance. Faced with the real danger of losing their national identity, Polish society began to understand that properly educated and brought-up women or mothers could play a leading role in keeping up the national consciousness of the younger generation. This conviction called for a search for the way best suited to local conditions to solve the problem of girls' education at the beginning of the 19th century.[3]

The most favourable conditions for creating a Polish national system of education at the time existed in the Warsaw Duchy formed by Napoleon I in 1807. The educational authorities of the Duchy, i.e. the House of Public Education and later the Board of National Education, took over and creatively expanded the achievements of the Commission of National Education in the field of educating girls. The development taking place in educating women in Europe at the turn of the 19th century stimulated further interest in dealing with the issue.[4] The interest of the House of Public Education in the education of girls was already shown in the "Raport o stanie edukacji publicznej i jej funduszach" ("Report on the State of Public Education and Its Funds") from December 1, 1807. The House wanted, among other things, to raise the level of girls' education by founding a school for governesses.[5] But, because of the lack of funds to realize that project, the House focused its attention on the education of girls at the elementary level first. That was also a result of the generally understood necessity to extend education to all classes of society. The efforts of Stanisław Kostka Potocki, the head of the House, resulted in the increase in the number of girls in elementary schools. At the same time, the work on improving didactic and organizational levels of schools and private girls' boarding-schools was continued. Those schools were directly subordinated to specially created Departmental Controlling Bodies for Female Schools and Boarding–Schools. These collective social bodies consisted of the most eminent women in a given Department (administrational unit) who, combining "a perfect upbringing with attributes of mothers and citizens", supervised the education of girls.[6] After creating the

Bodies, the House of Public Education issued the "Regulament pensji i szkół płci żeńskiej" ("Regulations for Female Schools and Boarding-Schools") on March 9, 1810.[7] That act was an effort to set in order all the matters connected with educating girls. Accordingly, a clear division into schools and boarding-schools was made. A uniform programme of education and moral guidance was set up in the both types of educational institutes. It must be said that, unlike at the time of the Commission of National Education, now much greater attention was paid to sanitary conditions in girls' schools and private boarding-schools as well as to personal hygiene and the physical training of girls. According to the "Regulament...," the curriculum included: Polish, French and German languages, arithmetic, book-keeping, the history of Poland and general history, geography, knowledge of hygiene and of the physical and moral bringing up children, the rudiments of astronomy, knowledge of useful and harmful plants, drawing, women's works and information about food (kinds, prices and the ways of serving it), about prices of: furniture, of various kinds of services, payment for domestic servants, etc. Moreover, each girl, if talented enough, could learn music or dancing.[8] It was a rather extensive programme, covering a large variety of subjects, and also characterized by utility. Evident care was taken to prepare girls for their roles as wives and mothers looking after both the intellectual as well as the physical development of their children.

The educational authorities of the Kingdom of Poland (established in 1815) continued the girls' educational policy as determined by the House of Public Education.[9] The Governmental Commission for Religious Beliefs and Public Enlightenment (in Polish: Komisja Rządowa Wyznań Religijnych i Oświecenia Publicznego; thus the abbreviation KRWRiOP later in the text) confirmed the regulations of the "Regulament..." from 1810 as mandatory and insisted on the need for a qualifying examination by persons who wanted to open a school or boarding-school. In 1817 in the Kingdom of Poland there were 79 girls' schools and boarding-schools in which 1115 girls of noble descent were educated. But already in the following year the number of those schools decreased by 56 and the number of girls in them by 972.[10] Thus the percentage of girls being educated, compared with the total number of female youth in the country, was low. But quite soon the emergence of capitalism which changed the traditional feudal economies and forced the declassed noble families to move to the towns, made them understand the importance of education for their sons and daughters; education became a chance for a better future. All those changes brought a natural increase of interest in the question of education of girls. That problem was recognized to be of such social importance that it was discussed at two succeeding sessions of parliament in 1818 and 1820.[11] As a result, the educational authorities undertook the task of improving the state of girls' education. First of all, the KRWRiOP prepared a bill "Urządzenia pensji i szkół dla młodzieży płci żeńskiej"("Arrangements for schools and boarding-schools for the youth of female sex"). The bill based on the "Regulament..." from 1810, was ratified at the session of the KRWRiOP on March 28, 1821.[12] According to the new act, private schools and boarding-schools for girls were divided into two groups: a) lower-with two classes, b) higher-with four classes. Both types of schools were subordinate to Voivodeship School Controlling Bodies which consisted of representatives of the Roman-Catholic clergy, commissioners of voivodeship commissions for education and rectors of voivodeships.

There were also women "of known enlightenment" invited to work in the Controll Bodies and their task was to look after the moral education of girls. The programme of education for girls, as determined by the 35th article of the "Urządzenia...", included: a knowledge of religion together with history of the Old and New Testament, Polish, French, and German languages, arithmetic, instruction in "natural sciences used for elementary everyday skills and house economy," geography, the history of Poland and general history, calligraphy and drawing, needle-work and, following a special agreement with parents, dancing and music, that is, the so-called "talents."[13] The knowledge acquired by girls in the process was to be enlarged by additional reading which however was obligatory. Influenced by the minister of religious beliefs and enlightenment, Stanisław Grabowski, a list of books which should be available in the libraries of girls' schools and boarding-schools was added to the "Urządzenia...". The list contained 49 titles of books by both Polish and foreign authors. Among Polish authors, works by Ignacy Krasicki, Krzysztof Kluk and Franciszek Karpiński dominated; among foreign authors, Marie Beaumont, Stephanie Genlis and Philantropist Joachim Heinrich Campe appeared most often. The list also included works by Polish female writers, namely Izabela Czartoryska and Klementyna Tańska.

In order to provide girls' schools and boarding-schools with qualified pedagogical staff, the KRWRiOP issued in 1825 the "Instrukcja obejmująca kwalifikacje mistrzyni, guwernerek, nauczycieli i nauczycielek" ("Instruction including qualifications of headmistresses, governesses, male and female teachers") and a year later the "Szczegółowa instrukcja względem sposobu dawania nauk po pensjach i szkołach płci żeńskiej" ("Detailed instruction concerning the way of teaching the female sex in schools and boarding-schools").[14] In the "Instrukcja..." the educational authorities instructed the examination commissions to thoroughly examine the pedagogical abilities of candidates for headmistresses and governesses. During the examination the candidates had to show that they had "at least general knowledge of subjects planned to be taught in girls' boarding-schools, so that they could, with nobody's help, form their own opinions". In turn, the "Szczegółowa instrukcja..." was a kind of didactic guide for teachers in girls' schools and boarding-schools.

Although the norms for qualifications were fixed, there was a lack of properly prepared teaching staff in female school and institutes. In this situation the educational authorities decided to open the "Governesses" School in Warsaw on May 1, 1825; the school followed the model of Berlin's Luisenstiftung.[15] At first, its role was limited to completing the education of governesses working in Warsaw, but in 1826 it was transformed into the Governmental Institute for Educating the Female Sex with a three year course of teaching. To give the schoolgirls a chance of applying theory to practice, a model boarding-school was formed at the Institute, with Zuzanna Wilczyńska as headmistress.[16] In this way, the idea born at the time of the Commission of National Education and the Warsaw Duchy was realized. However, the 20th article of the "Urządzenia..." clearly assumed that the education given in the school must be superficial and must beconnected with the role of women as wives and mothers. Thus the conservative view on the education of girls was not completely overcome. Nevertheless, considerable progress in the field of the education of girls was made in the Kingdom of Poland. This issue had also become more important within the society as was reflected in contemporary publications.[17] The greatest influence on the course of the education of girls was exerted by Klementyna Tańska-Hoffmanowa who paid much attention to that problem in her pedagogical and practical activities.[18] In 1830, that is, at the end of autonomy of the Kingdom of Poland, there were 74 private schools and boarding-schools where 1910 girls were educated.[19] That meant that only a small percentage of girls from noble families were involved in school education and the girls of urban middle class and peasant descent were a minority in schools.

The failure of the November Uprising in 1831 resulted in the change in the political situation in the Kingdom of Poland. The Russian authorities especially persecuted education. In 1832 they formed the Government Commission for Inner and Religious Affairs and Public Enlightenment, where the matter of education was clearly subordinated to the main purpose of the tsarist policy towards the Polish nation, which was to make Poles obedient to the Russian tsar. At the same time a special committee appointed by tsar Nicolas I in Petersbourgh prepared a project to reform education in the Kingdom of Poland which was accepted by the tsar in 1833. The act did not abolish the previous organizational regulations concerning female schools. It opened, however, legal possibilities of gradual undermining of Polish national spirit in the education of girls. The tsarist authorities entrusted the task of realizing that anti-Polish policy to Matylda Abramowicz who was brought from Typhlis and appointed the general inspector of female schools in the Kingdom of Poland.

She immediately began to introduce changes in female schools. First of all, she removed patriotic and political subject matter from the curriculum. In 1833, following her suggestions, the tsarist authorities introduced the teaching of the Russian language in the Governmental Institute of Educating the Female Sex and the teaching of the history and geography of Russia in that language in private schools and boarding-schools.[20]

The subordination of the educational system of the Kingdom of Poland to the Ministry of Education of the Russian Empire in the school year of 1839-1840, was a signal of new, strict course in the educational policy. Special attention was paid to the Governmental Institute of Educating the Female Sex which was already (since 1839) under direct supervision of the empress. The purpose of the supervision was to eliminate Polish influences in the school where the curriculum was gradually limited and the Russian language and culture where expanded. In 1840 Nicolas I confirmed a new law for the Institute and changed its name to the Institute for the Education of Maidens. Three years later the Institute was moved to the town of Puławy which was given the new official name of New Alexandria after the tsar Alexander I; therefore the Institute was called the Alexandrian Institute for the Education of Maidens.[21] According to the new law the school, at governmental cost, was supposed to educate the daughters of Russian indigent clerks and military men staying in the Kingdom of Poland and prepare some of the girls for the job of governess. The full course of schooling lasted 6 years and included the following subjects: religion, Polish, Russian, French and German languages and literatures, arithmetic, the history and geography of Russia, selected knowledge of natural history and physics, pedagogy, calligraphy, drawing, music and singing, and needle-work. With the consent of the headmistress, schoolgirls could also take private lessions in a subject not included in the curriculum.[22] It must be said that the subject matter of all the subjects taught was deliberately adapted to serve the main purpose of an education inculcating respect and obedience as well as love of the Russian monarchy.

While the Governmental Institute for the Education of the Female Sex was reorganized, the work on new regulations for private female schools was continued. In the school year 1838-1840 in the Kingdom of Poland there were 57 female schools and boarding-schools, almost half of them[23] in Warsaw. In all those schools 2261 girls were educated.[24] As a result of legislation in St. Petersberg, the "Ustawa dla instytutów naukowych prywatnych, guwernerów i nauczycieli domowych" ("Act for Private Educational Institutes, tutors and house-teachers") was issued on January 18, 1841.[25] The act, based on one from 1828, stated that the curriculum in private female schools could not be superior to the programme in district male schools. Consequently, the teaching of natural sciences in female schools was eliminated.

Further changes in the female school system of the Kingdom of Poland were introduced after Aleksander II was enthroned as tsar of Russia. He stated that the education of girls did not meet the requirements of the time and ordered that the education of women should be broadened and that more social classes should be included in school education. In October 1856 the law "O najwyższej woli co do urządzenia zakładów naukowych rządowych żeńskich w Królestwie Polskim" ("About the Highest Will Concerning Arrangement of Governmental Female Educational Institutes in the Kingdom of Poland") was issued. Its intention was seemingly to open possibilities of education to girls from the lower social classes.[26] In fact, its purpose was to weaken the national spirit in Polish families and private educational institutes. For, at that time Polish women of the upper social classes quite freely demonstrated their patriotism, which often made those Poles who were ready to co-operate with the Russians complain they were being prevented from conducting their rational politics. Realizing their intentions, in 1858 the tsarist authorities opened the Governmental Female Boarding-School in Warsaw with a 5 year course of education and a year later the Governmental Female High School with a course lasting six years.[27]

In September of 1860 five otherfemale schools with 6 year courses were opened: in Lublin, Radom, Płock, Kalisz and Suwałki, and also one class with 4 year course at the Governmental Female High School in Warsaw.[28] After opening these schools, all the female schools were removed from the competence of the Inspector of Warsaw Educational District and Ministry of Education and directly subordinated to the Empress Mary. In the Kingdom, the governor, on behalf of the empress, was in charge of female schools.

The curriculum in government female schools was somewhat more extensive than the one in private schools. Besides religion and languages (Russian, Polish, French and German), girls learned arithmetic, natural history, housekeeping, geography, the history of Russia and general history, pedagogy, hygiene, calligraphy, drawing, needle-work and church singing. Those alumnae of the Governmental Female High School in Warsaw who had good grades received the degree of "higher governess" and those who had worse grades the degree of "lower governess".[29]

The beginning of the 1860s brought a more liberal attitude on the part of the tsarist authorities, which was the result of military failures. In the Kingdom of Poland this was clearly visible in the field of education. By 1861 the Governmental Commission for Religious Beliefs and Public Enlightenment had been restored and, under the direction of margrave Aleksander Wielopolski, started working on the project of a school reform. The liberalization of social and political life gave Polish society a chance to express their opinions concerning the education and upbringing of the younger generation. It must be said that conservative voices dominated in the matter of the education of girls. In May 1862, tsar Aleksander II confirmed the "Ustawa o wychowaniu publicznym w Królestwie Polskim" ("Act on Public Upbringing in the Kingdom of Poland") prepared by the KRWRiOP.[30] The act introduced considerable changes in the network of governmental female schools. Of the 8 governmental schools formerly existing, only 2 were left. One of them was the Aleksandrian-Marian Institute for the Education of Maidens in Warsaw which was formed by joining the Aleksandrian Institute in Puławy with the Governmental Female Boarding-School in Warsaw; the other one was the Governmental Female High School in Warsaw with the statute confirmed on November 18, 1862.[31] The Institute consisted of 6 classes and an additional pedagogical class whose purpose was to educate governesses. The subjects most emphasized in the curriculum were religious and moral upbringing and French and German languages. The Russian language was limited to two hours a week in the three highest classes, and the teaching of natural sciences, physics and chemistry was selected so as to be of practical use in housekeeping. Thus the utilitarian purpose of girls' education was clearly exposed. That programme was to be completed by selected information on psychology, logic, hygiene and pedagogy. However, little time was spent acquainting school girls with those subjects, namely one hour a week in the two highest classes. For a separate fee, schools girls could learn singing, music, dancing and English and Italian in the time free from obligatory classes.[32]

The educational programme of the Aleksandrian-Marian Institute became a model for the Governmental Female High School. In the educational programme of the School, consisting of six classes and without the additional pedagogical class, the amount of hours for learning geography, general history and calligraphy was reducted, while the amount of hours for learning arithmetic was increased. The alumnae who wanted to get teaching qualifications had to go through two years practice as coaches or tutors and pass the appropriate examination before the Pedagogical Council of the Aleksandrian-Marian Institute.[33]

In the 1863-1864 school year, the KRWRiOP ordered that the curriculum of the Governmental Female High School be introduced in all private high schools and boarding-schools.[34] The curriculum in lower and elementary private female schools was not changed. There was also virtually no increase in the number of those schools. In 1863 there were 55 female high schools, 19 lower and 89 elementary ones.[35] That was much too little in relation to the needs. The outburst of the January Uprising (January 22, 1863) ended the policy of co-operation with the tsarist authorities conducted by a part of the Polish upper classes. The main representative, Margrave A. Wielopolski, who was increasingly criticized by Russian military and civil circles, was granted a leave of absence and went abroad. The school reform which he had started was stopped and withered away. After suppressing the uprising, the tsarist authorities increased their oppression of the Polish nation. But there was also another factor which considerably influenced the situation of schools in the Kingdom of Poland: the social and economical changes taking place at that time. The emancipation of the peasants in 1864 resulted in diminishing the leading social role of the nobility. Hundreds of declassed noble families moved to the towns, searching for better conditions of life. The general change of social relations was accompanied by violent ideological fights which took on various forms. The sharpening antagonism between capitalism developing in the Kingdom and an increasingly powerful proletariat became fertile soil for the development of a socialist movement whose programme was in basic contradiction with the ideals of the non-political "organic work". Both the idea of "organic work" as well as Warsaw positivism with its motto of "rudimental work", which were the result of criticism of the backward social and economic relations, served the interests of the privileged social classes and were to ensure the successful development of the Polish bourgeoise.[36]

The change of social and economic relations in the Kingdom of Poland took place at the time when the emancipation movement aiming at the legal, social and economic liberation of women began to develop in Western Europe and in the United States of America. The movement met with broad support in the Kingdom of Poland where, after the failure of the January Uprising and resulting deportations of Polish men to Siberia, a considerable number of lonely women had been left behind who had to take care of their families, and this entailed the necessity of earning their living. Under these circumstances, in addition to the women question, the question of the education of girls became particularly important: it was necessary to prepare them to live in the new social and economic conditions. The problem, however, was perceived differently by Polish society than by the Russian authorities. Nicolas Milutin sent to the Kingdom of Poland by Aleksander II, officially proposed to extend the network of public female schools but the real purpose behind this was to take the education of girls out of private hands and put it under full control of the authorities.[37] The purposes of education should be modified in such a way that girls would become loyal subjects of the Russian monarchy. Following this assumption, Milutin prepared plans for new educational laws for schools in the Kingdom of Poland, and Aleksander II confirmed them on September 11, 1864 in Jugenheim.[38] One of the five laws concerned the creation of female 6-class grammar-schools and 4-or-3-class grammar sub-schools. The justification of the need to create such schools for girls said that " necessity requires us to create a general system of educating women, according to the needs of various social classes, since mental and moral shaping of the female population will be the best guarantee of proper education of future generations."[39] Thus the Russian authorities understood that the proper education of Polish women was a guarantee of political and social peace.

The act about grammar schools and grammar sub-schools confirmed by Alexsander II was modelled on Russian legislation and provided a general outline. Therefore further work on it began immediately. In January 1865 a Russian grammar sub-school together with an elementary school were opened in Warsaw. In the first days of March 1866, female grammar schools were opened in Warsaw, Lublin, Radom, Płock, Suwałki and Kalisz, while 4-classes grammar sub-schools were opened in Piotrków Trybunalski and Warsaw. Besides, a female 3-classes grammar sub-school was opened in Warsaw.[40] The curriculum of a female grammar school included: religion, Polish language and literature, Russian and French or German languages, mathematics, geography of the Russian Empire and the Kingdom of Poland, physics and the general knowledge of cosmography, natural history, the history of Russia and general history, calligraphy, drawing and needle-work. There were also lessons in singing and gymnastics, treated as non-mandatory subjects and, for a separate fee, lessions in dancing. The language of the lessons was Polish at first, but history and geography were taught in Russian. The diploma received after completing the course of education of a grammar school permitted a schoolgirl to be a private tutor. The curriculum in 3 or 4-classes grammar sub-schools corresponded in principle to the programme of particular classes in grammar schools. The final certificate of a grammar sub-school gave girls the right to enter the fourth or fifth class of a grammar school, unless the period of time between completing the school and entering the class was longer than 6 months.[41]

The new organization of the female school system was accompanied by greater pressure from the tsarist authorities to "russianize" Polish youth and the society in general. To hasten the process, the Russian authorities divided the society of the Kingdom of Poland into various national and religious groups. To justify the act, the authorities claimed it was necessary to protect national minorities from, as they put it, Polish propaganda and the danger of "polonization." Under the guise of caring about girls of protestant beliefs a female 6-classes grammar school was opened at the Main German-Evangelical School in Warsaw in 1866.[42] The following year female grammar schools and sub-schools were opened in Chełm, Łomża, Siedlce and Suwałki for girls of Lithuanian and Ukrainian (Greek-Catholic belief) nationalities.[43] In those schools the language used for lectures was Russian, which clearly revealed the Russifying intentions of the authorities. The curriculum was almost identical with the one in schools for Polish girls. That project to found schools resulted in 10 female grammar schools existing in the Kingdom of Poland in 1868: 4 Polish, 2 Russian, 1 Lithuanian, 1 German and 2 bilingual ones. Besides the grammar schools, there were also 5 grammar sub-schools: 1 Russian, 2 Polish and 2 bilingual ones.[44]

After the failure of the January Uprising, the educational policy of the tsarist authorities in the Kingdom of Poland aimed at fully subordinating of schools to the authorities and depriving Polish society of the possibility of influencing the direction of its development. Following the tsarist act of May 27, 1867, the KRWRiOP was liquidated and replaced by the restored Warsaw Educational District which was subordinated to the minister of education of the Empire. The District was governed by inspectors who faithfully carried out orders coming from St. Petersburg. Some of them, like Teodor Witte and Aleksander Apuchtin, were well-known as persecutors of the Polish language and any Polish influences in schools.[45] It was T. Witte who introduced, in the school-year of 1868-1869, the teaching of all subjects in female schools in the Russian language. The only exception were teaching Polish and religion. In consequence, all books in the Polish language were removed from Polish schools and the same curriculum and textbooks as those used in schools in Russia were introduced. The final step unifying the Polish school system with the Russian one was the extension of the Russian act on grammar schools and grammar sub-schools in female schools in the Kingdom of Poland in 1872.

While developing the governmental female school system, the tsarist authorities began to close down convent schools and boarding-schools and to limit the number of private schools. The authorities were convinced that all those schools educated girls in a spirit of enmity towards Russia. Therefore, following the act of Alexsander II on Roman-Catholic monasteries (1864), female schools and boarding-schools run by convents (Nuns of the Visitation, Nuns of the Order of the Holy Sacrament, Benedictines and Norbertines) were changed into governmental public institutes.[46] At the same time, all the female private schools became the object of intensive Russification. The first step was taken in 1869 when Alexsander II confirmed the act "O wprowadzeniu w prywatnych zakładach naukowych Warszawskiego Okręgu Naukowego nauczania niektórych przedmiotów w języku rosyjskim" ("About introducing the teaching of some subjects in the Russian language into private educational institutes of Warsaw Educational District").[47] The official justification of that law was that Russian was the language in governmental female schools and therefore should also be in private ones. Although private schools did not give their alumnae any degrees, they still were very popular in Polish society.[48] It was mostly as a result of the atmosphere of the education provided by Polish teachers who were often outstanding scientific workers. The programme of teaching carried out in those schools was usually of a double character: 1) the official one, confirmed by tsarist educational authorities, 2) the unofficial one including forbidden subjects like Polish literature, the history and geography of Poland.[49] Therefore private schools did not present a uniform educational system. It was rather a conglomerate of more-or-less well organized schools of different didactic levels. Their number, in spite of numerous obstacles from the Russian authorities, was increasing considerably. They were mostly small institutes but, because of that, they were much more difficult for the tsarist police to control. At the end of the 19th century and the beginning of the 20th century there were two-, three-, four-, and six-class female boarding-schools. The level of teaching and ideological attitude of a school or a boarding-school depended, to a great extent, on the owner or the headmistress. Thus, according to the political views and inclinations of headmistresses, boarding-schools conducted their educational and didactic work in a clerical-conservative, national-patriotic, progressive-democratic, aristocratic or middle-class spirit.[50]

The Russian authorities were very reluctant to give permissions to open private female schools and boarding-schools of any level higher than two classes; especially those with a 6 class programme had difficulty getting permission. That is why lower-level boarding-schools arranged illegal higher courses where schoolgirls were taught Polish history, literature and geography. Apart from this, at the end of the 19th century Polish society began to arrange an "underground" network of elementary schools with the purpose of protecting their children from Russification. Those secret schools worked in very difficult housing and financial conditions. They could not provide any school certificates or official qualifications. The teachers working in them were in constant danger of being arrested and sent to Siberia, while parents of schoolgirls were fined. Attending a secret school however, gave a sense of freedom and independence of thought and also guaranteed an education in the national spirit. Nevertheless, only courageous parents decided to choose such a risky way of educating their daughters.[51]

Female high schools, both governmental and private, aimed at providing girls with a general, classical education and they usually did not prepare the girls well for life. Given that situation initiatives appeared proposing the founding of technical schools for girls. The first school of that type was founded in Warsaw in 1869 by Wilhelmina Schmidt. The subjects taught there were book-keeping, book-binding, retouching, and type-setting.[52] The next technical schools for girls were opened in the 1880s and 1890s influenced by the creed of useful work spread by Warsaw positivists. Besides Warsaw, institutes of this type were also opened in Kalisz, Lublin, Płock, Radom and Włocławek. Apart from getting qualifications in schools, girls also began to get them by the traditional way of apprenticeship. Among others, the alumnae of female grammar schools who wanted to get the qualifications to become pharmacists or dentists made use of that traditional way. They practised as apprentices for 3-5 years with experienced pharmacists or dentists and then tried to get permission to take the State theoretical and practical examinations in order to obtain professional qualifications. However, it was an obstacle-ridden and difficult way to get the desired qualification. The difficulty in qualifying as dentists was changed only in 1891 when a governmental Dental School for women was opened in Warsaw. The course lasted for 2.5 years and only pupils from female grammar schools might apply to enter the school.[53] With no access to universities both in the Kingdom of Poland and the Empire and realizing the necessity of going beyond the level of higher education provided by grammar schools, more enlightened women began to develop a self-education movement at a university level at the beginning of 1880s. Various self-education circles appeared at that time. In 1885 Jadwiga Szczawińska-Dawidowa joined them together into a system of permanent courses aimed at educating youth (both female and male) at a university level. The most eminent academic men in Warsaw e.g. Ludwik Krzywicki, Jan Władysław Dawid, Adam Mahrburg,

Piotr Chmielowski, Tadeusz Korzon, Samuel Dickstein, Wacław Nałkowski and others taught the courses. To avoid the control of the tsarist police, the classes took place in different private houses and therefore were called the Flying University. In the year 1905-1906 it was legalized (with some restrictions in its curriculum) as the Society of University Education Courses. It was a kind of Polish university which conducted classes in 4 departments: mathematical-scientific, the Arts, technological and agricultural.[54]

The struggle of Polish society for democratic school entered a new stage with the outbreak of the revolution in 1905. The school strike, closely connected with the revolution, resulted in a liberalization of the tsarist educational policy. On November 14, 1905 Nicolas II signed the act which gave the Ministers of Education and of Finance the right to give permission to schools and boarding-schools to use Polish as the main language. The teachers and schoolgirls of those schools, however, did not have the rights and privileges granted to the didactic staff and schoolgirls of government or semi-government schools.[55] To make use of the possibilities given by the tsarist act, female schools were set up in almost every town. In spite of some difficulties raised by over-zealous tsarist clerks in the years 1908-1912 the gradual increase in the number of female schools was not restrained.[56] The increased number of female schools was not paralleled, however, by their quality and organizational level. The curriculum was outdated in many schools. Other schools, on the other hand, tried to introduce subjects which up to then had been taught only in male schools. All those factors exerted a negative influence on the level of education of girls.[57] In 1914, on the threshold of World War I, there were 24 governmental and private-with-governmental-rights female grammar sub-schools in the Kingdom of Poland. Besides, there were 118 female private schools without governmental rights. Those were 1 philological school, 6 commercial schools, 4 co-educational ones and 107 others.[58] The invasion of the Kingdom of Poland by German and Austrian-Hungarian troops in 1915 put an end to the Russian occu-

108 WOMEN IN PARTITIONED POLAND

pation and opened a new but not easier period in the history of
female educational system in this part of Poland.

Within a span of a hundred years (1815-1915) a lot of organizational and curricular changes in the education of girls in the
Kingdom of Poland took place. A more complete presentation of
them is not possible within the limits of this article. Nevertheless,
it must be stressed that the system for education of girls in the
Kingdom of Poland, although rooted in the times of the Commission of National Education and possessing many deficiencies,
essentially fulfilled its task. Sufficient evidence for this is the fact
that generations of Polish women, in spite of the ruthless pressure of Russification, were fully able to maintain their language,
culture and national spirit and conquer the difficult trials with
which they had been faced in history.

Note to Chapter 5

1. H. Kołłątaj, Listy Anonima i Prawo polityczne narodu polskiego,
opracowali B. Leśnodorski i H. Wereszycka. Warszawa 1954, vol. 2, p. 93.

2. Przepisy od Komisji Edukacji Narodowej Pensjonarzom i Mistrzyniom
dane, in: J. Lewicki, Ustawodawstwo szkolne za czasów Komisji Edukacji
Narodowej. Kraków 1925, pp. 69-83.

3. J. Hulewicz, Sprawa wyższego wykształcenia kobiet w Polsce w wieku
XIX. Kraków 1939, p. 7 and passim.

4. There was much more attention payed to women's education in the
West (for instance in France) as well as in the East (Russia).

5. Archiwum Główne Akt Dawnych (AGAD), Rada Stanu i Rada
Ministrów Księstwa Warszawskiego, II. 140, p. 24.

6. Gazeta Korespondenta Warszawskiego i Zagranicznego, 1809, No. 23,
p. 340; J. Lipiński, Sprawa z pięcioletniego urzędowania Izby Edukacyjnej.
Warszawa 1812, pp. 72-74.

7. Regulament pensji i szkół płci żeńskiej. Warszawa 1810.

8. Ibidem, p. 6 and passim.

9. AGAD, I Rada Stanu Królestwa Polskiego (I RSKP), 99, p. 109; 122,
p. 459.

10. Ibid., 99, p. 166.

11. Zdanie o Raporcie Rady Stanu u dwuletnich czynności Rządu w

Girls' Education in the Kingdom of Poland 109

imieniu połączenia Komisji Sejmowych Senatu przez ks. Adama Czartoryskiego dnia 24 kwietnia 1818 r. (b.r. i m.w.),p. 19. Cf. AGAD, I RSKP: 138, p. 14.

12. Urządzenie pensji i szkół dla młodzieży płci żeńskiej. Warszawa 1821.

13. Ibid., pp. 20-21.

14. Komisja Rządowa Wyznań Religijnych i Oświecenia Publicznego, (b.m.w.), 1826, pp. 1-6; Szczegółowa instrukcja względem sposobu dawania nauk po pensjach i szkołach wyższych płci żeńskiej. Warszawa 1826.

15. Zbiór Przepisów Administracyjnych Królestwa Polskiego. Wydział Oświecenia. Warzawa 1868, vol. 5, pp. 351-355; Programmat kursu nauk wykładanych w Instytucie Rządowym Wychowania Płci Żeńskiej. Warszawa 1827, p. 3 and passim.

16. Zbiór Przepisów Administracyjnych, pp. 357-409; S. Duchińska, Pamiętniki, in: Eadem., Pisma. Lwów 1893, p. 63.

17. A. Nakwaska, Krótki rzut oka na terażniejsze wychowanie Polek, in: Pamiętnik Warszawski, 1820, pp. 238-252; Myśl o wychowaniu kobiet przez L., in: Pamiętnik Warszawski, pp. 348-373.

18. Cf. Hoffmanowa z Tańskich, K., Pamiątka po dobrej matce, czyli ostatnie jej rady dla córki, przez Polkę. Warszawa 1819. The author was a teacher of moral ethics at the Instytut Rządowy Wychowania Płci Żeńskiej (State-run institute for the education of girls). Since 1878 she worked as an inspector for boarding-schools and private girls' schools in the Kingdom of Poland.

19. Biblioteka XX. Czartoryskich w Krakowie, msp. 5257, p. 89.

20. Cf. Zbiór Przepisów Administracyjnych, vol. 1, 2. 125-143; vol. 3, pp. 127-197 and vol. 5, p. 423.

21. Ibid., vol. 5, pp. 427-571.

22. Ibid., pp. 427 and 435.

23. R. Gerber, Szkolnictwo Królestwa Polskiego w okresie międzypowstaniowym, in: Rozprawy z Dziejów Oświaty, 1960, vol. 2, p. 123.

24. Zbiór Przepisów Administracyjnych, vol. 5, pp. 739-779.

25. Ibid., pp. 471-475.

26. Ibid., pp. 475-535.

27. AGAD, Protokoły Rady Administracyjnej Królestwa Polskiego, 137,pp. 402 and 665. Cf. K. Poznański, Reforma szkolna w Królestwie

Polskim w 1862 Wrocław etc. 1968, p. 41.

28.   Zbiór Przepisów Administracyjnych, vol. 5, pp. 535-538.
29.   Ibid., vol. 1, pp. 397-425; vol. 4, pp. 313-353; T. Manteuffel, Centralne władze oświatowe na terenie byłego Królestwa Kongresowego (1807-1915). Warszawa 1929, p. 37.
30.   Zbiór Przepisów Administracyjnych, vol. 5, pp. 565-603.
31.   AGAD, Protokły Rady Administracyjnej Królestwa Polskiego, 146, pp. 552-555. Cf. K. Poznański, Reforma, p. 251.
32.   AGAD, Protokoły Rady Administracyjnej Królestwa Polskiego, 147, p. 322; Zbiór Przepisów Administracyjnych, vol. 5, pp. 589-603.
33.   Wojewódzkie Archiwum Państwowe w Lublinie, 503. Pismo KRWRiOP z dnia 25.08.1863 r.
34.   K. Poznański, Reforma, p. 252.
35.   Cf. J. Rutkowski, Historia gospodarcza Polski. Poznań 1950, vol. 2, pp. 233-238; A. Juzwenko, Rosja w polskiej myśli politycznej lat 1864-1918, in: Polska myśl polityczna XIX i XX w., vol. 1. Polska i jej sąsiedzi. H. Zieliński (ed.), Wrocław 1975, pp. 27-65.
36.   Issledowanija w Carstwie Polskom po Wysoczajszemu Powielieniju proizwiediennyje pod rukowodstwom senatora Stats-Sekretaria Milutina, 1864, vol. 4. Kopija do wsiepoddanniejszej dokładnoj zapiski, pp. 2-4.
37.   Dziennik Praw Królestwa Polskiego, 1864, vol. 62, vol. 327-333.
38.   Ibid., p. 329.
39.   AGAD, Protokoły Rady Administracyjnej Królestwa Polskiego, 158, pp. 758-759. Cf. K. Poznański, Reforma, p. 310.
40.   Dziennik Praw Królestwa Polskiego, 1864, vol. 62, pp. 201-231.
41.   J. Ender, Szkoła elementarna w Królestwie Polskim w dobie reform Wielopolskiego, in: Przeglad Historyczny, 1928, vol. 27, pp. 9-10.
42.   Cf. A. Winiarz, Zinocza gimnazja u Chołmi dlia ukrainskogo nasjelienia (1866-1915), in: Naszu Kultura, 1985, No. 2, pp. 12-14, No.3, pp. 11-12.
43.   K. Poznański, Reforma, p. 312.
44.   T. Manteuffel, Centralne władze, pp. 46-50 and 68-69.
45.   J. Hulewicz, Sprawa wyższego, p. 69.
46.   E. Staszyński, Główne kierunki rozwoju szkoły prywatnej w Królestwie Polskim, in: Rozprawy z dziejów oświaty, 1963, vol. 6, p. 125.
47   J. Klemensiewiczowa, Przebojem ku wiedzy. Wrocław 1961, p. 141.

48.   T. Wojeński, Walka o szkołę polską w okresie rewolucji 1905 r. Warszawa 1960, pp. 10-12.

49.   J. Szczawińska-Dawidowa, Pensje żeńskie, in: Głos, 1905, No. 35, p. 28; R. Pachucka, Pamiętniki z lat 1886-1914. Wstępem i objaśnieniami opatrzył J. Hulewicz. Wrocław 1958, pp. 19-24; J. Klemensiewiczowa, Przebojem, p. 82.

50.   H. Ceysingerówna, Tajna szkoła w Warszawie w epoce caratu. Warszawa 1949, p. 26 and passim: H. Mortkowicz-Olczakowa, Panna Stefania. Warszawa 1961, p. 56; D. Wawrzykowska-Wierciochowa, Z dziejów tajnych pensji żeńskich w Królestwie Polskim, in: Rozprawy z dziejów oświaty, 1967, vol. 10, p. 114 and passim.

51.   J. Miaso, Szkolnictwo zawodowe w Królestwie Polskim 1815-1915. Wrocław etc. 1966, pp. 179-182.

52.   Kształcenie i warunki dentystek, in: Kalendarz Kobiety Polskiej, 1911, p. 116; J. Klemensiewiczowa, Przebojem, pp. 189-226.

53.   R. Wroczyński, Myśl pedagogiczna i programy oświatowe w Królestwie Polskim na przełomie XIX i XX w. Warszawa 1955, p. 112; K. Wojciechowski, Oświata ludowa 1863-1905 w Królestwie Polskim i Galicji. Warszawa 1954, p. 37; J. Miaso, Uniwersytet dla Wszystkich. Warszawa 1960, pp. 17 and 31.

54.   Cf. Nowa ustawa dla szkolnictwa prywatnego, opracowanie Biura Pracy Społecznej. Warszawa 1914.

55.   Cf. Nasza walka o szkołę polską 1901-1917. Warszawa 1932, vol. 1 and 2, Warszawa 1934.

56.   J. Łowieniecka, Rzut oka na naszą szkołę średnią żeńską, in: Szkoła Polska, 1906, p. 383.

57.   K. Konarski, Dzieje szkolnictwa w byłym Królestwie Kongresowym 1915-1918. Kraków 1923, pp. 247 and 276.

Małgorzata Czyszkowska-Peschler

6

SHE IS - A NOBODY WITHOUT A NAME
The Professional Situation of Polish Women-of-Letters in the Second Half of the Nineteenth Century

On her own she is a nobody, a cipher that only amounts to something when combined with another number. She is–a nobody without a name. Servile spinelessness, pious blindness, silent self-denial, unctuous patriotism, a lack of trust in her own powers–this is the gender ideal propagated by Tańska's pen.

With this attack on Klementyna Tańska-Hoffmanowa, the somewhat retiring spokeswoman in the 1820s of certain rights for women, Aleksander Swiętochowski began an article, published in "*Przegląd Tygodniowy*" in 1873, that argued in favor of granting women access to higher education.[1]

And Narcyza Żmichowska–a thinker, if ever there was one, truly ahead of her own time–saw the time of struggle for women's rights as being essentially a thing of the past, since the basic breakthrough had already been achieved. She wrote, "Society seems to be telling women, 'Study, if you can and must; achieve as much as you have it in you to achieve; but know too that you will have to make your way alone. That means that if you get into trouble, don't expect anyone to come running; there will be nobody you can fall back on.' And what's more, women are getting the message too; they are ceasing to envy men; they take pride in the progress they have made, and are riding it for all it is worth; and, above all, they realize that, from now on, if they are to get anything at all, it will have to be by their own unaided efforts. We refrain from talking of a "struggle" or "using force", for we wish to convince our women readers that the time of taking things by storm is now over; the things we have fought to achieve are no longer forbidden us; thus the struggle is over."[2]

This conclusion turned out to be somewhat premature. Admittedly, there had been considerable changes in the social structure since 1816, the year in which Miss Tańska published *Pamiątka po dobrej matce*–changes that had become especially conspicuous around the time when Żmichowska's penned her preface to Tanska's works in the mid-1870s.

For Żmichowska, Tańska-Hoffmanowa was "actually the first woman in Poland to live by writing".[3] And that proved possible because her first book scored an instant success–the one that was to earn Swiętochowski's derision so much later on.

> One must realize that when Miss Tańska published *Pamiątka po dobrej matce* in 1919, a woman-of-letters was still an interesting curiosity in our country. One still thought in terms of such glossy, meretricious rhymes as *Ze szlacheckiego dworku* by Elżbieta Drużbacka; *Domownik* by Wanda Malecka had been already circulating around Warsaw in manuscript form for a year. More frequently it was ladies from socially privileged circles or such high-born personalities as Princess Czarto-ryska, the wife of General von Podale, and their daughter Princess Marya Wirtemberska who took up the pen. Their works were invariably praised to the hilt–in all likelihood out of a sense of tactful chivalry, perhaps too with a touch of courtly deference, though in all likelihood it was no less the result of the kind of abashed indulgence which was soon to touch off the rapturous reception accorded the seven-year-old Józio Krogulski. Not, to be sure, because his music was so exquisite, but because he was so tiny in stature...[4]

Who does in fact qualify as Poland's first professional woman-of-letters? Żmichowska names Tańska-Hoffmanowa, and the latter certainly looked on writing as her chosen field, writing "I can only adhere to an author's trade; this beloved and in every way laudable occupation will both feed me and preserve my happiness".[5] It should not be forgotten, though, that she also worked as an inspector of girls' schools and as a teacher at the Institute for governesses.

There are other names that occur to one: for example, Aleksandra Borkowska-Chomętowska (1828-1898), who edited the "*Kółko Domowe*" and the"*Wieczory Rodzinne,*" and who has been described as "the first woman in Warsaw to make a career out of doing editorial work".[6] Then too there was Felicja Kaftal, "the first woman to engage in journalistic activity...[who was] on the staff of the "*Kurier Poranny*".[7] These are names and verdicts drawn fairly much at random. Still, there is no doubt that Tańska was the illustrious predecessor of these and all the other women to be reviewed in the following pages.

Writing as a Professional Outlet

In the mid-19th century, the various branches of the writer's trade were not yet clearly differentiated.

Thus we find Wacław Szymanowski writing in 1855, "The idea of a 'man-of-letters' is at best a generality referring to someone who engages in scholarly pursuits and has a literary output to show for it".[8]

Thus a man (or indeed woman)-of-letters was someone who could turn out articles or essays on a wide range of topics or, alternatively, someone who was not averse to trying his or her hand at any or all of the going literary genres. But in none of the available sources for the period between the 1830 and 1863 insurrections is writing actually refered to as a profession. The statisticians' lists of the times make no mention of writers, journalists, or independent scholars, simply because virtually nobody to speak of regarded writing as capable of providing a living–certainly not as a full-time activity and not even as a significant part-time one. On the other hand, there seems to have been a large group of potential writers, publicists, and journalists who found only part-time or temporary employment for their talents. Thus in 1858 Ludwik Jenike experienced no difficulty in assembling a team of journalists for his newly founded weekly *"Tygodnik Ilustrowany"*. The publisher Samuel Orgelbrand also had no trouble in hiring 115 scholars to work on his *"Encyklopedia Powszechna"*.[9] However, it must also be said that there were some who turned to writing not as a source of income, but because they wished to express their political convictions; there were also some who were simply concerned to record their own experiences; and there were some to for whom writing was simply an intellectual exercise or even just an agreeable pastime. Ryszarda Czepulis-Rastenis has calculated on the basis of her research that there were around 150 professional writers between 1832 and 1862 that can be documented as such; but she considers the real number to have been twice as high. Of the members of the *Intelligenzja* writing professionally in the period 1814-1826–estimated incidentally at some 1100 for both Poland and in exile abroad, and irrespectively of whether it was done for a living or not–Janina Kamionkowa puts the proportion of women active in their ranks at only 10%.[10]

Though the political and social position of the *Intelligenzja* certainly differed from one part of Poland to another, the professional life of writers can be globally characterized without too much fear of distortion. In the 1860s, the number of magazines rose; the publishing houses expanded their activities; and the work of journalists, writers and artists gradually took on the character of a remunerated job like any other–i.e. it was no longer invariably engaged in as a side pursuit. But this new profession was marked by irksome features unknown to the other more established independent professions. For one thing, it offered no long-term job security; for another, the flow of commissions was irregular and sometimes impossible to predict. That this was so was principally due to the magazines' practice of operating with few permanent staff members; instead, they preferred to operate a freelance system, whereby commissions were farmed out to a pool of writers and journalists. Needless to say, this kept the latter dependent on them for their living and also for the opportunity to see their work into print.

Adequate social security provisions took a long time in

coming. Not until 1899 were the statutes of a *Kasa Literacka* finally approved by the authorities of the Polish Kingdom, thus clearing the way for the formation of the first professional body representing the interests of writers and journalists. The Society of Polish Journalists (*Towarzystwo Dziennikarzy Polskich*) was founded in Lvov in 1894, recruiting its membership from all those journalistically active "irrespective of sex" ("bez względu na łeć") though admittedly it demanded somewhat stiff membership fees. In return it pledged to represent the material and moral interests of its members, and even set up a retirement fund.

This may explain why so many journalists chose to retain their excruciatingly run-of-the-mill jobs as officials on the payroll of state institutions, e.g. as grammar school teachers or as private tutors. Władysław Ludwik Anczyc, a poet and playwright highly acclaimed in his day and age, was not only proprietor of a printing press and a bookshop, but also numbered a vinegar manufactory among his possessions. Some lived off their assets or off endowments, and among these some indeed were women. Women writers dependent by necessity or by choice on their own efforts to make a living normally found themselves forced to train as teachers or governesses, since no other educational avenues were open to them.

Hipolit Skimborowicz, in an obituary notice published in the *Tygodnik Ilustrowany* in 1878, cited no less than fourteen contemporary Polish writers who had died destitute in proof of his contention that literature still could not provide a living for those laboring on its behalf.[11]

In addition, professional journalism was still struggling for social recognition; and the relation of the journalists themselves to having their literary output thus find its way into print was fraught with ambiguities. For the authors, however, it was enticing to reflect that the periodicals bearing their work "can penetrate to quarters where no book ever reached".[12] Another consideration certainly not without importance was the instant remuneration that could be expected. But Józef Ignacy Kraszewski, who was equally versed in the anguish suffered by writer and editor alike, has given us his reflections on the drawbacks:

The wretched thing about journalism is that, once it has got its claws into you, it puts paid to all further efforts at learning, extending oneself and climbing higher. Even the greatest talent succumbs to the general law. Condemned to a incessant round of work, damned to bolt one's nourishment in ways that are not always good for one's health and which, in any case, one seldom has a chance to digest at leisure, the journalist eventually falls victim to mannerisms and one-dimensionality, latching onto a certain style of writing so that from then on he writes more like a machine than a human being.[13]

Another problem was that the author's prestige could at times suffer in the eyes of his readers if he stooped to engage in journalism. Świętochowski testified tellingly to the harmfulness of "journalistic hackery", i.e. the financial dependence of those engaging in it–and indeed did it in a manner that would certainly have won the approval of the parties involved–by taking the glittering *feuilletons* by Prus that appeared in the *"Kurier Warszawski"* and comparing them with the somewhat less illustrious activity of peeling potatoes. Prus, for his part, saw himself too as being kept far more than he liked from getting on with the real task of writing as a result of his "journeyman's labor" ("parobcza robota") performed for magazines.[14]

The extent to which the editors had a controling say varied from case to case, depending on the kind of magazine, its constituency and its general standing. Naturally, the emoluments paid to the contributors varied in like fashion. That one could expect to earn more in Warsaw than in Cracow had the status of a general truth. There was also a great difference between the going rate per line paid out to publicists and that which authors could command. Rates paid per line fluctuated in Warsaw between 2.5 kopeks (*"Niwa"*) and 20 kopecks (*"Bluszcz"*).

Sewer (Ignacy Maciejowski) has left us with a record of his own personal finances, according to which he earned an average of some 839 zloty per annum during the years 1885-1888–which corresponds more or less to the salary of a local official at the lowest rung of the pay scale.

Drawing top incomes were the bestselling authors Kraszewski, Korzeniowski and Kaczkowski, who could command an average of 2000-3000 rubles for a novel. Orzeszkowa received 1000 rubles for each volume of "*Nad Niemnem*". For her work on the staff at "*Świt*", the publisher Lewental paid Maria Konopnicka 2000 rubles per annum, plus free lodgings in his house, plus extra remuneration for those of her works published in "*Świt*".

It was not just the generally very low emoluments paid that was a sore point. Complaints about material distress were, in any case, rampant in this profession. But what most led to resentment were the scandalous practices consistently resorted to by editors and publishers, who thought nothing of withholding payments due, breaking contracts, and dictating the lowest remunerations possible. Thus, we find Adam Flug reporting to Konopnicka on the 5th of September 1896 that, when Maria Ilnicka–who had been chief-of-staff of "*Bluszcz*" since 1865, developed eye problems–Glücksberg, the editor, cut her salary from 120 to 50 rubles, and later on did not even pay her this.[15]

This "sublime '*Bluszcz*',"[16] whose subtitle was "Pismo Tygodniowe Ilustrowane dla Kobiet", was no doubt held in complete contempt in intellectual circles; but the fact is that there is scarcely a single ranking author of the 19th century whose work did not appear in its pages at some time or other. This journal–whose "subjective and sentimental effusions penned by our hapless women editors have so sorely importuned the reading public,"[17] as one detractor put it–was edited some thirty years long by this same Maria Ilnicka, a childless widow, who had penned the manifesto of the January Rising of 1863. Her literary productions were full of moral exhortations and dripping with sentimentality. In her salon smoking was tabooed–because the cigarettes came from Russia. Ilnicka, who would "break out in tears so easily", certainly had the respect of her intellectual contemporaries–though this was given less for her role in running this "Illustrated Weekly Magazine for Women" than for her personal integrity. Thus we find one admirer writing:

I feel a sense of personal gratitude for the probity of her talent and her social position. An authoress without any affairs–let's face it!–that must be respected and indulged for all its worth.[18]

This was the same Ilnicka whose Catholic background and receptivity to clerical influences so much filled Orzeszkowa with consternation for the fate in Warsaw of the freshly arrived Konopnicka–the same woman who looked on family as the highest good, who only approved of women working when they had no other choice, and who is credited with having made "*Bluszcz*" into a more progressive organ than it had a reputation for being.[19]

Case One

We know how it came about that Maria Konopnicka moved to Warsaw with her six children. We know all about how she cooked, cleaned, sewed, gave tutorials, and still found time on the side to write. And we know too about how she became admired as a poet within a few years.

...Konopnicka finds herself in great vogue there [in Warsaw], not only as a writer but as a woman. Evidently she is universally regarded as both an inspired poet and one of the most beautiful women in society. An extraordinary fate. Until she was in her thirties she resided on the land, unknown, always on the verge of poverty, her hands always occupied by running a household and caring for her children. But by the time she was in her forties she had become acclaimed as an inspired poet, a citizen of the world, and a beautiful woman to boot.[20]

Then she was offered the chance to take charge of the literary supplement of a new magazine–a prospect which had "only one disadvantage, namely that it [was] to be a women's magazine."[21] Despite her misgivings she accepted nonetheless. Orzeszkowa reported to Michał Balucki on the 15th of November 1883: Her "material position, previously quite precarious, would be stabilized as a result...Now that she can be more reassured about her own and her children's future, she will certainly go on to write more and more beautiful things."[22] Konopnicka was able to win the major talents for "*Świt*"; her name and her diplomatic skills–wielded in her correspondence with amazing adroitness–were of such a kind as to inspire confidence.

Nonetheless, her success was only short-lived. The initially high number of "*Świt*" subscribers in the first year (2000-2500) sank rapidly again. The editor protested against what she called "obstructionism touched off by every independent sentence".[23] After two years of editing "*Świt*", she retired from her journalistic post with a great sense of relief, then to spend the last twenty years of her life in perennial wanderings abroad. Always with a weather eye out for the cheapest accommodation; always making the trek to the pawnbroker. Sometimes the pennies in her purse would just be enough for a bread roll and a bunch of grapes; sometimes there was enough for a midday meal, which she would share with Dulebianka. We know all about the "paroxysms of poverty"[24] she went through. That was the price that she paid, the price she was willing to pay, for "the only possession of those oppressed by fate–freedom."[25] For, she said:

> A human being is not like a spider that can go on spinning its threads out of itself forever. A human being needs to be open to all the movements of life; she needs to work up her perceptions and impressions into an artistic form. In other words–if she is to write at all–she must tune her soul the same way an instrument is tuned. To be cut off from what is redolent of spiritual nourishment, from what is not to be found in books but only in real life, necessarily withers up the intellect. It is no different from practicing any other profession: the ground under your feet, the right conditions and environment, this is something you simply must have.[26]

This danger was something many women writers were no stranger to, irrespective of their country of origin or the period they lived in. The limited worlds of experience inhabited by most women writers was singled out by Virginia Woolf as an enormous drawback for their literary development. Thus, we find

Konopnicka writing to Orzeskowa in a letter dating from 1882:

> Because of the very nature of their position in society women tend far too much towards narrow and onesided trains of thought. Banned from the broad terrains and vast struggles of life, constrained within the admittedly exalted but anything but far-reaching realm of family obligations, they are loath to permit their thoughts to roam beyond this limited field of view.[27]

Eliza Orzeszkowa roamed with her thoughts further and more passionately than many others caught up right in the heart of things, despite leading what to superficial inspection seemed a confined life which she herself experienced as a disadvantage. She explained her feelings as follows:

> I can say openly that I am a *"fille de mes oeuvres"*. Nobody ever gave me any advice, nobody aided me intellectually...I spent long years in cramped rooms with my family living on top of me, without a sense of space, deprived of intellectual friendship and good conversation, without the slightest support or help from outside. Only twice did I manage to go abroad. Years went by without me ever laying eyes on a work of art or even listening to music. My other colleagues in the writing profession–those who live in Warsaw or abroad–are no more than names, at best known to me from their works only or sometimes from once or twice catching a glimpse of them.[28]

Case Two

There was another woman writer who suffered particularly under the external circumstances of her life–who back in the third quarter of the 19th century was highly regarded, even looked up to as an authority, but who today is forgotten by the general public, though scholars quickly warm to her as soon as they immerse themselves in her person and work.

> The first impression a perusal of Żmichowska's pedagogical works leaves in the reader is disturbing and oppressive: one is confronted with

an exceptionally talented woman who was capable of giving birth to myriad creative ideas, whose flashes of thought were far ahead of her time...; but who, as a result of being caught up in the socio-political realities prevailing in the Russian-occupied part of Poland, was condemned to virtually complete inactivity and fruitless exertions...The external circumstances of Żmichowska's life–meaning, on the one hand, the stifling narrowness of life in the Polish Kingdom during the time of Paskiewicz and, on the other, the never ending battle against poverty that had to be waged by the author of *Poganka*–condemned her to a life of constant struggle against the strictures of fate.[29]

Narcyza Żmichowska was a lyric poetess, novelist, private tutor, translator and girls' school teacher, as well as a penner of pedagogical tracts, text books and teaching curricula. Moreover, she kept up an unflagging stream of personal correspondence that clearly shows that, had other political and personal circumstances permitted her aspirations and self-image to unfold along different lines, she would have made a first-rate publicist.

It is to be doubted that she was "as cold as a frog, as systematic as the Germans, and more than a little haughty",[30] as Teofil Lenartowicz's caricature of a thumbnail sketch had it (proffered despite the fact that he had a high regard for her talent, dignity and patriotism). The thousands of letters she penned during her lifetime communicate a quite different impression: she emerges as a keen-eyed, highly educated, tolerant, not to mention warm-hearted and spirited woman. The way her friends made a real cult out of her speaks volumes. Born in 1819, her own personal fate–despite her engaged stand on behalf of women's rights (especially the right to work and earn an income, to which she attached very great importance)[31]–was to be that of remaining trapped within the rules and conventions of the traditional social order. She was full of good advice and encouragement for others to go out and explore brave new worlds; as to her own situation, though, she was to find no way out. She would not admit to being a feminist; and the thought of being thirty-three years old and still unmarried filled her with apprehension at the jibes she anticipated:

> I am approaching thirty-three; being still unmarried at this age is a fate
> worse than being an elderly spinster, for at any moment it can give rise
> to ridicule. (Letter to Augusta Grotthusowa written from Lublin Prison
> the 13th of June 1851).

On the other hand, she was troubled by the marriage of her niece, Maria Glogerówna, since she recognized in this girl the signs of a creative woman with the potential to take charge of her life in the new, modern way and to go on to fulfil her talents:

> As far as Marylka's marriage is concerned, I can feel no joy whatsoever,
> not for all Roman's wealth, nor for all the French polish lavished on his
> upbringing, nor for his being the son of an marshall from the nobility.
> Perhaps it's because Marylka–this very same Marylka who was best cut
> out to tread the artist's road of earning one's own living and embracing
> honorable poverty, and hence to set a shining example for our moaning
> and groaning little group–is now about to drift off into a comfortable life
> essentially devoid of merit?(Letter to Anna Skimborowiczowa, the
> 22nd of January 1854).

Żmichowska's thinking outstripped her times. But her *gefühlswelt* was rooted in Romanticism.

Żmichowska announced her own death as a poet quite early on, just as she first reported the onset of old age at the age of twenty-five. Her writing difficulties were partly due to her complicated domestic arrangements. To write at all she needed absolute tranquillity; yet she spent the greater part of her adult years living in the large families of her sisters, with children romping around in every room. Then too, she needed her sleep, meaning that she was incapable of working into the small hours of the morning. That, at any rate, was one of the explanations she offered. On the other hand, her whole life long she was plagued by doubts about the value of her work–doubts that kept her from completing many works, and which elicited from her the following ironic comment:

> Take even these wretched four volumes of the *"Works of Gabryella"*–well, you can just see for yourself how full of beginnings and middles they are, and how nothing is carried through to a conclusion anywhere. (Letter to Bibianna Moraczewska, the 11th of February 1868).

Pressured from all sides–from family members, friends, editors and publishing houses–to get on with her writing, she could invariably be counted on to come up with a good reason for saying no. When in 1866 Maria Ilnicka tried to win her for a collaboration with *"Bluszcz"*, this merely drew forth a declaration from Zmichowska to the effect that what she was able to reveal about herself and her view of things was not fit to print, but that she could not write any other way. Her unprintability she ascribed less to the Russian censor than to the bigotry of Polish society–which, in her view, bore the blame for the low level of the literature of her day.[32] Ilnicka did not contradict her.

Zmichowska was not one to demand masterpieces from others; even mediocre literature and journalistic work had its honorable place in her scheme of things:

> Not even the most absurd story by Miss Szmigielska ever really cut you or me to the quick; nor were we ever offended by the most interminably rambling poem by Pruszakowa–on the contrary, I remember that when it first appeared *"Dwa dwory"* quite found my favor, and I still read the narratives of Zosia Węgierska with pleasure.[33]

Indeed, as the newly published author of 1841 averred to Anna Skimborowicz in a candid statement of her writing credo:

> Talent I have none...To write at all, I must wait for a moment of rapture; I must first become aglow with love in some reflection of an eternal truth before the right images, these powerful authenticating signs, stream into my consciousness. (Letter of the 25/26th of July 1853).

But we have still to hear the most intimate and probing confession of this woman, who was only willing to accept marriage if construed in the sense of a felicitous partnership–indeed one where domestic felicity was firmly placed in the line of duty–and who saw a women's true fulfillment as lying rather in the pursuit of a vocation, or in the shouldering of obligations to her next of kin or to society as a whole:

> Never in my whole life did my love call up an answering response of love–not even for twenty-four hours; no, not even for one single hour! That is why I am incapable of writing any more. Because in certain things with every step I take I feel–an emptiness. (Letter to Izabela Zbiegniewska, the 30th of December 1866).

There is no doubt Żmichowska would have made an outstanding gifted publicist, had she not chosen rather to channel her insights and understandings–steadfastly deepened over a whole lifetime–into the literary outlets that cost her such untold pains; or had she been able to discard the nagging awareness that she was writing for publication. She indeed had the makings of a fearless publicist capable of exerting a significant influence on public opinion. She never held back from championing unpopular opinions–whether in politics, where she came out against armed struggle just prior to the January Rising of 1863; or in matters of social policy, where she was a sharp critic of the society of her day. Admittedly the positions she defended found no printed expression in the gagged-and-bound press; but they did receive a certain airing through her voluminous correspondence which, in her collected opus, is not separable from her literary works.

Zmichowska unleased a storm of indignation in 1844/1845 when she vehemently defended the right of the young Zofia Mielęcka (*née* Kamińska) to leave her husband, whom she had been married to at the age of sixteen, and to set up house with a friend and lover, the journalist Feliks Węgierski.

Case Three

The scandal unleashed by the young women's action threatened to have a direct effect on the life of the rebellious Narcyza Żmichowska when her friend Helena Turno, whose daughter was Żmichowska's pupil, voiced doubts that she might be a bad influence on the children. But Narcyza stuck to her guns and was not so easy to browbeat:

> And, in the event, I am just giving vent to what my conscience tells me, namely that in this case I have acted correctly, unselfishly and honorably.[34]

Zofia, by now married to Węgierski, lived with her second husband in Cracow, where she got her first grounding in journalism during his sickness. After his death in 1849, she moved to Paris where, at the beginning of the 1860s, she was to write six children's books, some of which first appeared as magazine installments.

> Only highly talented women who also have a heart," wrote the critic A. Szabranski in the foreword to the second edition of Zofia Węgierska's *Legendy Historyczne,* "can manage a really useful little book on the upbringing of women. For they know best about all the mysteries of female thoughts and feelings; they are acquainted with every frailty of the fairer half of the Creation, and can dispense help and advice liberally to fit each individual case. Among the no mean number of our lady writers of distinction, Mrs. Kamińska stands out through her compeling vision of reality, her beguiling principles, and the uncommon charm of her candid and unclouded style that is so redolent with mellifluity and tenderness. We would like to urge Mrs. Kamińska in no uncertain terms to once again take up this work of such importance to our native land...[35]

Węgierska, however, had turned her back on "mellifluity and tenderness", and was not to be persuaded. Ten years beforehand she had begun to write reports for *"Biblioteka Warszawska"* from her Paris base, and over the years other Polish magazines were added to the list. Despite the fact that all her children's books were reissued in new editions throughout the 1860s, her royalties naturally did not stretch far enough to cover her living expenses in Paris. Moreover, it is conceivable that the author herself had outgrown a style she found increasingly cloying and precious. In any event, she smuggled into her *"Legendy"*–written for the edification of small girls, be it noted–the tale of an amorous affair which did not end entirely harmlessly and of an unforeseen incestuous relation with the heroine's half-sister, who was a nun into the bargain. This somewhat sullied paragon of virginal purity incurred the critical ire of the reviewers, and set them off on mental wild goose chases that were not borne out by any of the other tales and which certainly had nothing in common with the intentions of the author.

From then on, our author contented herself with writing only reports, "on the scientific, literary and artistic life" of Paris, but without trying her hand at anything of higher artistic pretensions according to the conventional canons. One critic wrote that, although her name was least well known of all, she enjoyed the largest circle of readers in Poland. The unknown author of the *"Parisian Chronicle"* made quite a stir and occasioned much curiosity. Readers puzzled over who it might be, convinced that, since the author wrote of himself in the male gender, "he" must indeed be a man. When the truth came out, there were the inevitable charges of a "betrayal of femininity".[36]

Węgierska wrote regularly for a number of magazines, i.e. the *"Biblioteka Warszawska"* (1853-1869), the *"Gazeta Codzienna"* (1859-1861), the *"Gazeta Polska"* (1861-1869), the *"Kurier Wileński"* (1860-1864), *"Czas"* (1865-1869), and *"Bluszcz"* (1866-1869). On top of this, she wrote several reports for *"Słowa"*, the Polish daily newspaper in Petersburg (1859), as well as three others for *"Hasło"* in Lvov (1865), the magazine that was eventually taken over by J.I. Kraszewski.

Her work found the approval not only of the public but also of her fellow writers. Kraszewski enlarged on the pitfalls of the writing trade:

> The chronicles of Węgierska...are unparalleled among us [writers]: they succeed well enough in combining charm with serious-mindedness, are always artfully varied, yet never seem to lose their appeal and lack of pretension. There is nothing more difficult to manage than a commissioned report–most of them bore the reader with their routine and over-cautious approach.[37]

Her personality commanded the admiration of the friends and acquaintances who flocked to the tiny salon held each Sunday in the rue Laval 25. Especially highly regarded was her independence which she had won and contrived to maintain by virtue of plain hard work.

> Without adequate financial reserves to fall back on, alone except for the pen in her hand, she put in long hours of unremitting and arduous work that gradually brought her the independence she so much desired, as well as allowing her to safeguard and preserve the sense of human dignity that was fundamental to everything she undertook. Back in her Polish motherland she had numerous friends and acquaintances, as well as her family and a far-flung network of relatives–thus the way would have been clear to solicit their support, had she chosen to do so. That would have given her a life that was if not well-off then at least comfortable enough, freed from the burdensome and fatiguing tasks [of her Paris exile].[38]

It should also be mentioned that Polish royalties were much lower than those paid by French magazines, though Węgierska had to foot the same living expenses as her Parisian colleagues:

> Even the most lightweight of French *feuilleton* scribblers would have been surprised in no small degree to learn of the meager size of the emoluments paid by Polish magazines even to an established woman writer whose work was eagerly competed for by rivaling editors.[39]

From the few sources we possess that shed light on Węgierska's life, a picture emerges of a woman who not only was "an heroic worker of the greatest talent"[40] but also was indefatigable in the service of others. Her correspondence with Seweryn Boszczyński testifies to the touching concern, the sense of responsibility, the disinterested desire to help, and the absolute dependability that characterized her relation to the elderly author of "*Zamek Kaniowski*". To this must be added her letters to the journalist Stefan Buszczyński and to her close friend Cyprian Norwid. Moreover, these sources make it clear that the three were by no means the only ones to elicit her solicitude and efforts to help. For Buszczyński and his Cracow-based newspaper "*Kraj*" she combed Paris looking for suitable correspondents;[41] and for her publisher Goszczynski in Warsaw she did the same. She took Norwid's manuscripts into safe-keeping as a service of trust; for many an unknown text she was its first reader, proof-reader and editor. Whenever her friends and circle of acquaintances needed someone to turn to, no effort was too great for her: she was not niggardly of word and deed until the problem was solved. In fact, they rarely had to even ask in the first place. She did what she could to help her circle secure financial support, acting as a go-between, representative or negotiator, as the case might be.

At the beginning of each month, "as regular as a chronometer,"[42] she would take her report to the post-office: for each magazine there might be 20 to 30 printed pages worth of manuscript to be sent. In the PAN Library in Cracow three letters of Węgierska are preserved that were written to the "*Biblioteka Warszawska*" in 1865 and 1868. Characteristically, in the one case, the non-payment of an overdue quarterly emolument is the subject at issue (Węgierska always insisted on being paid at quarterly intervals). In another letter, we find her writing about a report she thought had got lost in the mail, but about whose eventual arrival the editor's office had not bothered to inform her. Likewise her letters to "*Gazeta Polska*" and to Kraszewski consist mainly of resubmissions of bills requesting payment of overdue emoluments and of complaints concerning unanswered letters. Though elaborate assurances of undiminished esteem and full understanding for the position of the overworked editor are not lacking, to be sure, and indeed give the letters a chivalrous tone, the bottom line is plain enough: as a colleague, she requests punctual payment of what is hers by right since, "as one who belongs to the ranks of those who have to live from their work, [she] cannot wait for ever".[43]

A sense of the daily difficulties faced by a press correspondent–of whatever sex–comes across well in the letter to Kraszewski written on the 1st of July 1862:

Dear Sir,
Together with my usual "Chronicle" dispatch sent to Mr. Kronenberg on the 1st of June, I included a request that my quarterly earnings be transfered by the middle of the month. When I received no answer I repeated my request, asking furthermore if you would kindly correct the address given as mine on the cover of the magazine. The result was–complete silence. The address has not been altered and the magazine is still just drifting around–and, worst of all, the "Chronicle" did not appear in the magazine. What can be the explanation for all this? I simply have no idea.

Today I enclose my text for July, which brings us up to the second quarter. I would ask you most urgently to entrust someone with the task of letting me know what is going on and to accede to my frequently repeated requests for remittance of payment.

I know you are heavily burdened by your tasks, which is enough to fill me with guilty qualms about troubling you with this letter–but who else do I have to turn to? Please favor me with an answer on these points, and rest assured that I am fully cognizant of the honor to be your humble and faithful servant.

Yours faithfully,
Zofia Węgierska[44]

Węgierska was particularly distinguished by her conscientiousness and loyalty. When Buszczyński tried to win her for the new liberal and democratic Cracow-based magazine "Kraj", she turned him down because accepting would have meant having to renege on another commitment. She would much rather have cut her ties with the conservative gazette "Czas", whose political line she was as much at loggerheads with as she was personally with the chief editor, Lucjan Siemieński. But the path of duty was clear enough:

> My conscience makes it impossible for me to participate in the murder of "*Czas*". For me to take such a step, "*Czas*" would have to be more than the tedious, sugary, stifling bastion of received opinion that it is–it would have to be an enemy of our land too. But enemy it is not, only incompetent–and, bound to it as I am by many years of collaboration, I would consider it disloyal to go over to the rival camp taking lock, stock and barrel with me and brandishing a weapon.[45]

Norwid diagnosed the cause of Węgierska's death in the poem he dedicated to her memory, "*Na zgon Poezji*": "Umarła ona na ciężką chorobę./ Która sie zowie: pieniądz i bruliony".

Węgierska herself regarded her work as an inescapable part of her life, though she was aware it undermined her health:

> You yourself have tasted Parisian life, so you know how time here races away with the pace of a locomotive. How is one supposed to discharge the business of the day while still functioning at a peak of activity, can you tell me that? When on top of one's daily work one adds keeping up contacts with other people, plus allowing for some ten hours or so of idleness–then no wonder one just can't keep up with the obligatory tasks any more.[46]

And once again:

> I was in bed for two days–yesterday hardly able to speak–today still very weak–but still at my station, with a pen in my hand.[47]

A witness described to Stefan Buszczyński the manner of Węgierska's death:

> Over a long period the habit of overtaxing her strength with her work had undermined her delicate health. Then thirty hours of suffering–initially brought on by a light cold–sufficed to push to the

point of no return a body which had been held together less by its own power than by that of the soul.[48]

Case Four

Volume IV of the "*Compendium of Polish Literature*" devotes an entry of nearly ten full pages to the work of a woman writer "the details of [whose] life", its author confesses, are "unknown to us"[49]–though he goes on to say that she belongs "beyond any doubt to our outstanding novelists and is in fact the only humorist we have."[50] In 1876, some seven years after Węgierska's death, Norwid was filled with enthusiasm for this woman, whose novels had already been acclaimed by Piotr Chmielowski in the same issue of the "*Biblioteka Warszawska*" where the last "*Kronika Paryzka*" by Węgierska also appeared (Volume 4, 1869).

Writing under the pseudonym of Zbigniew, Maria Sadowska had been turning out novels, short stories, humorous sketches (*humoreski*) and literary essays ever since 1859, with most of them appearing in the Warsaw-based magazine "*Przegląd Tygodniowy*". 1879 seems to have been the year of her last publication: the short story "*Sądy Boże*", which appeared in "*Przegląd Tygodniowy*".

Straight-jacketed in an unhappy marriage, this woman writer (who was born in 1835) lived in Paris with her husband and two daughters from 1867 on. She is said to have been carefully brought up, to have been highly educated, and to have worked for some time as a teacher. However, it seems that she increasingly took to drinking and/or succumbed to a psychic ailment–this can be documented back to 1876 when her acquaintance with Norwid began. The last sign of life we have from her is apparently an appeal for help directed to Prince Czartoyski on the 21st of January 1880 begging for the loan of 100 francs for two months. Desperately she confides that she is in a "very distressing, indeed a humiliating position", since she is reduced to living "on credit."[51] She is said to have died around 1890–"in the gutter", as was said by some; or "in the madhouse", as others had it.[52]

Though the "cases" reviewed cannot claim exemplary character, and each one must stand for itself alone, there is, for all that, a sense in which they do reflect the experience of a far more sizeable group of women in the second half of the 19th century than is commonly admitted.[53] This is so despite the worst possible circumstances then prevailing in a patriarchally structured Polish society, whose attention was necessarily monopolized by the imperative of national survival to the point where it had little patience with new social currents, let alone being ready to recognize in women's emancipation a legitimate social development whose time had come. The fate of those women who did not have the spotlight of posthumous fame trained on them remains a chapter that future scholarship has yet to write. Indeed it still remains to be determined whether enough original material survived the ravages of the last war to permit their story to be told. When hunting for the kind of information rarely drawn on by the general histories or the studies of literary history, there is no choice but to go back to the original source materials–in particular to the correspondence of the literary *milieu* under investigation, both published and unpublished, but also to the archives of the magazines and newspapers, as far as these are available.

At this point it is appropriate to mention the names of some of the women who were active as writers or as journalists but whose fate it is to have been less well known or even completely forgotten.

The *Rys dziejów literatury polskiej* put out by Zdanowicz and Sowiński in 1877 and which, according to Sienkiewicz and Prus, "exemplified a certain amount of talent", groups together on several pages the names of most of the women authors known to us from a large number of scattered sources. In the section on the first half of the century, there are fairly extensive sections dealing with Klementyna Tańska and Elżbieta Jaraczewska. Apart from these authors, Anna Krajewska-Nakwaska, Karolina Potocka-Nakwaska, Łucja Rautenstrauchowa, Wanda Malecka, Paulina Krakowowa and Karolina Wojnarowska are praised for their literary achievements. The two last-mentioned authors followed up and further developed Hoffmanowa's ideas, albeit working independently of each other. Moreover, Paulina Krakowowa and Gabriela Puzynina have left us their memoirs as important documents of the times.

After mid-century, we find far more women making their mark who did far more than simply pen occasional pieces. Julia Molińska-Wojkowska, in her literary works, devoted herself to the poor and dispossessed, publishing magazines in Posen together with her husband. Józefa Śmigielska-Dobieszewska turned her back on her well-to-do home background, because she prefered to earn her way by the fruit of her own labors. She made her literary debut with a play and a novel, before going on to edit magazines; in the seventies, she wrote socially critical reports from Galicia for the positivistically inclined "*Niwa*", besides being a leading figure in the debate over the emancipation of women. It was she who made the proposal that women-of-letters should band together and found an organization to promote the struggle for women's rights.

Seweryna Duchińska (Pruszakowa, in a second marriage), writer and publicist, succeeded Węgierska after the latter's death as Paris correspondent for the "*Biblioteka Warszawska*". In 1897 she celebrated her 50th year of literary work.

Not to be forgotten is that *wunderkind* and—in later years—curiosity of Warsaw cultural life: Deotima—Jadwiga Łuszczewska.

Writing in 1877, the authors of the influential "*Compendium of Polish Literary History*" singled out Orzeszkowa, Sadowska and Walerya Marrené-Morzkowska as three "exceptionally vigorous talents" in the literary field addressing social and moral problems and the role women could play beyond their usual gender-imposed fate as wife and mother, i.e. "against the dictates of nature and tradition"—though they did not omit to add that, as a field, it was "not quite appropriate for wives and mothers".

The same *Compendium* also went on to mention a Mrs. Meyerson, a Jewess from Lublin, who published a novel about Polish Jews in 1868. Zofia Meller wrote popular plays for the stage, while Maria Bartusówna in Lvov and Anna Libera (who earned her way through life as a seamstress) were both celebrated lyrical poets.

Though no doubt each time combined slightly differently, we find much the same names repeating themselves in Korbut and Feldman's publications and in the *"Dzieje literatury pięknej w Polsce"* of 1918. Several others active in journalism deserve mention as well: for example, Maria Szeliga, both novelist and feminist, who wrote for both the Polish and the French press; and also Aniela Tripolin, who today is completely forgotten as a writer but who was an acquainted with Konopnicka.

Celina Gładkowska published (under the pseudonym of Julian Marosz) in the *"Gazeta Świąteczna"*, a magazine for farmers. Here she was succeeded, after her death, by Amelia Bortnowska. Antonina Feldówna-Śmiszkowa (using the pseudonym of Antoszka) likewise wrote for the *"Gazeta Świąteczna"* and for *"Zorza"*, the latter being a daily newspaper read by the rural population. Faustyna Mokrzycka also wrote articles of a popular scientific nature for the same publications. Natalie Korwin-Szymanowska wrote 16 novels, 6 collections of short stories as well as reports on Polish literary life for French and English newspapers, not to mention articles for Warsaw-based women's magazines–all under the pseudonym of Anatol Krżyzanowska.

Aleksandra Borkowska-Chomętowska launched the fortnightly magazine *"Kronika Rodzinna"* in 1868 and edited it till 1896. Jadwiga Papi wrote novels whose success evoked comparisons with those of Kraszewski, beside collaborating with children's and family magazines. Felicja Kaftal grew up in Berlin but, after her marriage, moved to Warsaw, where she first had to learn Polish before embarking on a career as a writer; shortly after the launching of the independent newspaper *"Kurier Poranny"* in 1877, she was appointed its social columnist.

Zofia Chłopicka-Klimańska worked as a publicist for a radical democratic newspaper *"Gwiazda"* (Kiev 1846-1849); also for its successor *"Pamiętnik Naukowo-Literacki"* (Vilna 1849-1850), which she financed, and later on for Warsaw magazines as well. She also wrote novels.

Zofia Urbanowska was closely connected with the family of Josef Sikorski, who succeeded Kraszewski as chief editor of *"Gazeta Polska"*. This country girl who wanted to study and have a career became a member of Sikorski's household. Apart from doing correction work for this magazine, she spent several months each year with the family in Zakopane, where she took charge of the household. Later she took a room at the girls' school of Jadwiga Sikorska and wrote bestseller novels for adolescents. She also became a member of the editorial board of *"Przegląd pedagogiczny"*.

In the years after 1867, the universities of Europe gradually opened their doors to women students. However, until the first generation of women was trained and graduated, teaching was the only professional avenue with any intellectual pretensions to speak of that was accessible to women. For women of literary talent the way lay open to publication, indeed increasingly so after the advent of the "new press" of the Positivists. To take this way, however, necessitated a more advanced stage of individual emancipation than the society of the day actually permitted its women.

From the 1870s on, we find the positivistically inclined publicists—men in the main, to be sure—addressing the question of women's rights, especially the issues of access to education and of a career outside the home, and pushing these into the forefront of public awareness. This they did with such tenacity and for such a length of time that they indeed succeeded in inducing a certain alteration in this awareness. Bronisław Trentowski, the founding figure of the "Polish national teaching philosophy", who died in 1869, was the last prominent representative of intellectual life to give vent to such gusts of spleen as in his testy apostrophization of educated women as "erudite cows".

But traditional habits of thought and conduct frequently proved too strong to be overcome. Zmichowa was adamant in her rejection of the accolade of *"emancypantka"* in her own case; and Konopnicka poked fun at the feminist activities of her friend Maria Dulębianka. A full-scale women's movement, in the real sense of the word, never grew up in Poland.

It is appropriate to close by citing this judgement by Eliza Orzeszkowa on the significance of Polish women writers for the society of her day and age:

Arguably greater than in any other country was the influence of women writers on Polish womanhood as a whole...Even as early as in Druzbacka it is possible to recognize the characteristic pattern of the Polish woman-of-letters in an incipient stage. The talented poet in her fell victim to the passionate citizen and indignant moralist that were no less part of her nature. To a degree we were all harmed by this in our later artistic unfolding.[54]

Notes to Chapter 6

1.   Jan Hulewicz, Sprawa wyższego wykształcenia kobiet w Polsce w wieku XIX. Kraków 1939, p. 157.

2.   N. Żmichowska, Słowo przedwstępne do dzieł pani Hoffmanowej, przez Narcyzę Żmichowską, in: Pisma Nacyzy Żmichowskiej (Gabryelli). Warszawa 1886, vol. 5, pp. 573 f.

3.   Polski Słownik Biograficzny: "Dzięki swej pracy literackiej stała się H. pierwszą kobietą w Polsce żyjącą z pióra, choć borykała się nieraz z długami za druk. W r. 1823 otzymała zasiłek Komisji Rządowej Wyznań Religijnych i Oświecenia (3000 zł). Dowodem uznania dla tej pracy było mianowanie jej od r. 1825 "eforką" tj. wizytatorką dwóch szkół i dwóch pensji żeńskich. W r. 1826 objęła bespłatnie wykłady "nauki obyczajowej" w nowo utworzonym Instytucie Guwernantek."

4.   N. Żmichowska, Słowo przedwstępne do dzieł pani Hoffmanowej, p. 491-492.

5.   Die achtundzwanzigjährige Klementyna Tańska in ihren "Pamiętniki" am 31. Dezember 1826, in: Ryszarda Czepulis-Rastenis, "Klasa umysłowa". Inteligencja Królestwa Polskiego 1832-1862 Warszawa 1973, p. 196.

6.   Bartlomiej Szyndler, Tygodnik ilustrowany "Kłosy" Wrocław etc. 1981, pp. 61-62.

7.   Zenon Kmiecik, Prasa warszawska w latach 1886-1904. Wrocław etc. 1986, p. 14.

8.   W. Szymanowska, Aleksander Niewiarowski, Wspomnienia o cyganerii warszawskiej 1964, p. 67.

9. R. Czepulis-Rastenis, Klasa umysłowa, p. 113.
10. Ibid., p. 196.
11. Ludwig Jenike, himself employed as an official with the auditing authorities, listed in his memoirs the names of nine fellow writers who made their living working for this relatively small state-run institution. R. Czepulis-Rastenis, Klasa umysłowa, pp. 267 and 318.
12. B. Bolesławita (J. L. Kraszewski), Z roku 1869. Rachunki. Rok czwarty. Poznań 1970, pp. 537-538.
13. Ibid.
14. Prus, "obiera kartofle". Cf. Ewa Baworska, Problemy życia literackiego drugiej połowy XIX w. w oczach ówczesnej krytyki, in: Problemy życia literackiego w Królestwie Polskim drugiej polowy XIXw. Wrocław etc. 1983.
15. Maria Szypowska, Konopnicka jakiej nie znamy. Warszawa 1965, p. 228.
16. Orzeskowa on the 13th of November 1883, quoted in: Szypowska, Konopnicka, p. 309.
17. Announcement published in "Przegląd Tygodniowy", heralding the appearance of the first number of "Świt". Quoted in: M. Szypowska, Konopnicka, p. 312.
18. Żmichowska 1867, quoted from: T. Żeleński (Boy) (ed.), "Narcyssa i Wanda." Listy Narczy Żmichowskiej do Wandy Grabowskiej (Żeleńskiej). Warszawa 1930, p. 195.
19. J. Hulewicz, Sprawa wyższego wykształcenia, pp. 164-165.
20. Orzeszkowa to Jan Karbwicz, the 6th of May 1884. Quoted from M. Szypowska, Konopnicka, pp. 303-304.
21. Konopnicka to Orzeszkowa, the 24th of January 1882. Quoted in M. Szypowska, op. cit., p. 303f.
22. Tadeusz Czapczyński, "Świt" pod redakcją Marii Konopnickiej. (Materiały do twórczości Konopnickiej jako publicystki i redaktorki) In: Prace polonistyczne. Series X (1952), p. 238.
23. Konopnicka to Teofil Lenartowicz, 1st of May 1886. Quoted from Czapczyński, "Świt," p. 240.
24. Konopnicka to her daughter Zofia in 1896. Quoted in: T. Czapczyński, Tułacze lata Marii Konopnickiej. Przyczynki do biografii. Łódź 1957, p. 23.
25. To Lenartowicz, the 1st of May 1886. Effective from the 1st of April, W. Marrené-Morzkowska had taken over the editorial responsibilities for the

literary supplement of "Świt". Quoted in: Czapczyński, "Świt" pod redakcja Marii Konopnickiej, p. 240.

26.   T. Czapczyński, Tułacze lata, p. 19.

27.   M. Szypowska, Konopnicka, p. 302.

28.   Grodno 1896. Quoted in: Eliza Orzeszkowa, O sobie...Wstęp. J. Krzyżanowski, Warszawa 1974, p. 121.

29.   J. Hulewicz, Sprawa, pp. 83 ff.

30.   Henryk Biegeleisen, Lirnik Mazowiecki, Jego życie i dzieła w świetle nieznanej korespondencyi poety. Warszawa 1913, p. 243.

31.   "Pieniędzmi ugruntuje równość małżeńska i władzę macierzyńską; z pieniędzmi, gdy chce, dziś już może sobie ukształcenie zapewnić." N. Żmichowska, Pogadanki. Quoted in: J. Hulewicz, Sprawa, p. 90.

32.   Cf. letters to Izabella Zbiegniewska, the 30th of December 1866 and the 18th of June 1871. Żmichowska's letters are quoted, unless otherwise indicated, from N. Żmichowska, Listy. Pod redackcja S. Pigonia. Do druku przygotowała i komentarzem opatrzyła M. Romankówna, Wrocław etc. 1957-1967.

33.   Letter to Wanda Grabowska, the 1st of June 1866. Quoted in: "Narcyssa i Wanda", p. 115.

34.   Letter to Helena Turno, the 24th of April 1845.

35.   A. Szabrański, "Legendy Historyczne" przez Bronisławę Kamińską. Wydanie drugie przejrzone. Poznań 1863. Quoted in: Biblioteka Warszawska, vol. III, 1863, Kronika Literacka, pp. 521-526.

36.   Przeniewierzenie się kobiecości, in: W. Korotyński, Zofia Węgierska. Nekrolog, quoted in: Tygodnik Ilustrowany, the 4th of December 1869.

37.   B. Bolesławita, Rachunki. Z roku 1869, p. 659.

38.   L. Kapliński, Rocznik Towarzystwa Historyczno-Literackiego w Paryżu. Rok 1869. Paris 1870, p. 230.

39.   Ibid., p. 230.

40.   Letter from J.I. Kraszewski to T. Lenartowicz, the 19th of November 1869. Quoted in: W. Danek (ed.), J.I. Kraszewski and T. Lenartowicz, KorespondencjaWrocław etc. 1963, p. 143.

41.   This was not all that easy, as Węgierska related to Buszczyński: "Zaraz po odebraniu twojego listu obejrzałam się w koło szukając korespondenta politycznego, któryby choć trochę był podobny do idealnego portretu jaki mi kreślisz. Mówię trochę, gdyż o znalezieniu takiego ideału ani marzyć nie można. Wiedzieć powinieneś ze polacy mający pozycyę, konneksye, a

nawet chociażby tylko obiad–już żadnej obowiązkowej pracy się nie po-dejmują. Piszą korespondencye tylko głodni i nie odziani–a tacy dobrze informowani być nie mogą dla tej prostej przyczyny, ze tam nie wchodzą gdzie można się czego dowiedzieć." Letter of the 28th of February 1869. List XXXIX. Quoted in: J. Mikolajtis (ed.), Listy N. Żmichowskiej i Z. Węgierskiej. Częstochowa 1934.

42. Letter from Węgierska to the Biblioteka Warszawska, the 15th of February 1868. Original preserved at Biblioteka PAN w Krakowie. 719. Mf 81; Zbiór autografów C. Walewskiego. vol. VIII.

43. Letter to J. I. Kraszewski, the 1st of August 1862, original manu-script preserved in the Biblioteka Jagiellońska. Msp. 6483 IV. Korespon-dencja J. I. Kraszewskiega. Listy z lat 1844-1862. vol. 22. Korespondencja od Zofii Węgierska 1862. pp. 226-245.

44. Ibid.

Łaskawy Panie,

Posyłając 1. czerwca zwykłą Kronikę pod adresem pana Kronen-berga, prosiłam o odesłanie w połowie miesiąca mojej kwartalne należności. Nie otrzymawszy odpowiedzi ponowiłam prośbę, prosząc również o po-prawienie na opasce dziennika mylnie wydrukowanego adresu mojego–Milczenie zupełne. Adres nie poprawiony, dziennik się błąka–a co gorsza Kronika nie wydrukowana w Gazecie. Jaki powód tego wszystkiego? Daremnie zgadnąć usiłuję.

Dziś wysyłając sprawozdanie lipcowe, rozpoczynające drugi kwartał, proszę Pana usilnie żebyś polecił komuś wytłomaczenie mi Zagadki, oraz zadośćuczynienie ponowionej prośbie o wysłanie pieniędzy.

Zatrudnienia Pańskie tak liczne, iż czuję wyrzut sumienia trudząc go moim listem–Ale do kogoż mam mówić? wskaż Pan i bądź przekonany o moich chęciach służenia Mu

Zostaję z wysokiem uszanowaniem

Zofia Węgierska

45. Listy N. Żmichowskiej i Z. Węgierska. Częstochowa 1934. List XXXIX, the 28th of February 1869.

46. Letter to Buszczyński, the 1st of June 1868. List XXXIV. Ibid.

47. Letter to Norwid, September/October (?) 1869. Listy Z. Węgierskiej do C. Norwida. Opracowała Izabela Kleszczowa. Quoted in: Pamiętnik Literacki 1976, No. 3. p. 205.

48. Letter by K. Bawroński to Stefan Buszczyński, the 20th of Novem-

ber 1869. Listy Narcyzy Żmichowskiej i Zofii Węgierskiej, p. 68.

49.	Leonard Sowiński (ed.), Rys dziejów literatury polskiej podług notat Aleksandra Zdanowicza oraz innych źródeł opracował i do ostatnich czasów doprowadził Leonard Sowiński, vol. IV. Wilno 1877.

50.	Ibid., p. 373.

51.	In the Biblioteka XX. Czartoryskich in Cracow is preserved the original of a letter not listed in Korbut (Rękopis nieoprawny w archiwum Władyslawa Czartoryskiego) whose contents is as follows:

Rue des Maronites	1 styczeń 1880
Belville

J.O. Xiąże! Chociaż nie mam szczęścia znać J.O. Xięcia, wszelakoż, wiem dostatecznie od wielu polaków o Jego szlachetnej i wspaniałej dobroci–osmielam się przeto prosić, (chociaż to mnie wiele kosztuje) o pożyczenie mi na 2. miesiące 100 fr – Mąż mój postąpił niegodnie ze mną–i w skutek czego zostaję w nader bolesnej pozycjii.–a nawet upokarzającej, bo żyję na kredyt...

Nie wchodzę w detale, by nie nudzić J. O. Księcia, o rzeczy, które wie z ust moich szan. pań Rustejko–i jeśli Xiąże Pan, raczy go zapytać o mnie to będzie poinformowany suwerennie.

Kończąc ten list–mam sobie za zaszczyt pisać się Jaśnie Oś. Xięcia uniżoną sługą.

Maria Sadowska
née C Römer de Brzezina

52.	J. W. Somulicki, Ostatni romans Norwida. Quoted in: Stolica 1967, No. 17, p. 1011.

53.	Such famous names as Orzeszkowa, Zapolska, Eleonora Ziemięcka and Maria Rodziewiczówna need only be mentioned in passing, since the reader will be familiar enough with their life histories.

54.	Quoted in: M. Szypowska, Konopnicka, p. 300.

Maria Nietyksza

7

The Vocational Activities of Women in Warsaw at the Turn of the Nineteenth Century

In the nineteenth century Warsaw was the largest urban center in the Polish territories, a center with a high rate of development. In the mid-1860s it had over 240,000 inhabitants. It did not significantly expand its administrative boundaries until the outbreak of World War I. Urbanized suburbs were developing beyond these boundaries from the end of the nineteenth century. In the first year of the twientieth century the population of Warsaw exceeded 700,000, and in 1914 it amounted to about 885,000. On the eve of the Great War Warsaw, together with its suburbs, had about one million inhabitants.[1]

Sources allow us to ascertain the component parts of the city's demographic growth (without the suburbs), i.e., the proportion of the natural to the migratory increase from the beginning of the 1880s until 1914. Nearly half (some 48%) of the increase was due to the inflow of population.[2] This means that Warsaw was a center of intensive immigration.

It was not only its demographic potential, but also its function that distinguished Warsaw from other Polish towns. This old capital of Poland had retained some traits of a metropolis, despite the partitioner's endeavours to reduce its role to that of a provincial capital. Warsaw was a strong cultural and intellectual center, the administrative center of the Polish Kingdom, and also a center where economic decisions were taken. Many branches of industry were developing in Warsaw and the surrounding area, and handicrafts continued to function and develop. As early as the 1870s Warsaw became an important railway junction. The city had extensive trade links, and the necessity of meeting the needs of several hundred thousand inhabitants fostered retail trade and services.[3]

The Warsaw Labor market was therefore variegated and absorptive. It offered much wider opportunities of employment than did the towns with no well–developed economic and especially productive function. In purely industrial towns, too, the situation was less favorable, for as a rule, their servicing, educational and cultural functions were underdeveloped and the dominant role of one or two branches of industry made employment dependent on fluctuations in the economic situation.

Of great importance for the subject dealt with in this paper was the religious and national composition of Warsaw's population, because of the different demographic and socio-vocational characteristics of the individual groups.[4] The general proportions of the religious denominations are illustrated in Diagram 1. Alongside the basic Catholic group (Polish), there was a numerous Jewish population, the percentage of which was steadily increasing. This was a clearly distinctive community, polonization having embraced only a relatively small part of it. As will be shown further on in this paper, the Jewish population made significant impact on the processes and phenomena concerning the population of Warsaw as a whole.

The main statistical sources for the demographic and vocational structure of the inhabitants of Warsaw are the one-day censuses of 1882 (local Warsaw census) and 1897 (general all-Russian census). The next census was not held until 1921, that is, in independent Poland. Not many conclusions can be drawn from a comparison of the censuses of 1897 and 1921, because different methods were used in conducting them and in the grouping of data in the published material, because of the effect of what is called the great incorporation of the suburbs into Warsaw in 1916, and the consequences of the Great War, which are difficult to ascertain. The data for 1913 and 1914 quoted in this paper and concerning the total number of inhabitants, the proportion of the sexes and the religious composition of the population come from the registers kept by the municipal authorities of Warsaw.[5]

During the period under review women outnumbered men in Europe. It was the same in the Polish Kingdom. The numerical preponderance of women was greater in Warsaw and this was undoubtedly due to intensive immigration, for women predominated among the immigrants, accounting, according to the censuses, for just over half of the inhabitants born outside Warsaw, namely, for 51.9% in 1882 and for 52.4% in 1897. There were 1,112 women per 1,000 men in 1882, 1,109 in 1897 and 1,076 in 1913.[6] It is worth pointing out that this numerical superiority was decreasing.

Vocational activeness is indicated by the proportion of gainfully employed persons to the total number of persons of a given population.

Table 1.
Gainfully employed women in Warsaw in 1882 and 1897
(percentage of the total number of women)

	Women		
Year	Gainfully employed	Without a paid job	Total
1882	25.8	5.0	30.8
1897	24.2	5.2	29.4

Source: M. Nietyksza, Ludność Warszawy na przełomie XIX i XX wieku (The Population of Warsaw at the Turn of the 19th Century), Warszawa 1971, data from Table 35, p. 138.

The figures in Table 1 show a slight drop in the vocational activeness of women between 1882 and 1897. The same period witnessed a greater drop in the index for men (from 64.4% to

61.3%) and consequently, in the index for the entire population of Warsaw (from 46.6% to 44.4%).[7]

This seems to be in contradiction to the intensive immigration into Warsaw, a large part of which consisted of persons of productive age. We must therefore find out if the indices are reliable. If, after a possible correction, they continue to show a drop, we shall have to seek another explantion.

We know that neither census mentions the unemployed. They must have been included in the group of gainfully employed people, probably mainly in the group of casual workers (unskilled workers employed on a daily basis) and the group of people of unknown occupation. Their number must have been small in both cases (1882–the beginning of the crisis, 1897–the peak of the boom) without any signficant influence on the index of vocational activeness.

An important deficiency is, however, the exclusion of relations helping in family businesses, who have been listed as vocationally passive. This was a large group, especially in industry and small-scale trade, and a large part of it consisted of women. Since the 1921 census distinguishes this group, we can approximately define the error resulting from the incomplete data of the earlier censuses.

In 1921, relatives helping in family businesses in Warsaw accounted for 2.3% of all gainfully employed persons, in trade for 5.6%, in industry and handicrafts jointly for 3.2%; the last index should be applied only to handicrafts and consequently should be appropriately raised. Jews played a considerable role both in handicrafts and in trade. In 1921, relatives helping in family businesses accounted for 6.2% of all gainfully employed Jews, the corresponding index for Catholics being only 1.2%.[8]

This means that the absence of this category in the nineteenth century censuses has lowered the Warsaw population's index of vocational activeness. Has it also deformed the trends of changes? It must have done so, for the percentage of Jews, and consequently also that of gainfully employed persons not indicated in the censuses, was growing in the city. It is difficult to achieve a precise correction, but there is no doubt that: first, the indices concerning women were lowered more than those concerning men, and secondly, the decreasing trend was, in fact, weaker.

In evaluating women's vocational activeness we should not confine ourselves to correcting the information contained in the censuses but also take into account the various factors which influenced this activeness. First and foremost there are the factors which, though difficult to measure, undoubtedly led to an increase in vocational activeness, such as the women's emancipation aspirations, characteristic, above all, of the intelligentsia, and economic pressure, which affected women of various social milieus.

Among the factors which can be presented statistically are: changes in the age and sex structure of Warsaw's population; changes in its religious composition, which are important in view of the different demographic characteristics and the vocational structure of the individual religious denominations; the effect of the labor legislation introduced in Russia in 1882, which was particularly conspicuous with regard to the adolescent group (12-17 years).

I will omit detailed statistical investigations and confine myself to stating their results and importance for the question we are dealing with.

What we need in order to make an analysis of vocational activeness is a classification of the population into age groups which would allow us to set the productive age apart. We must bear in mind, however, that the age limits of this group are of a formal character, since it is difficult to unequivocally establish when the productive age starts and when it ends. In research we are often hampered by the classifications employed in the publications of census results.[9] As a rule, the 15-59 year age group is regarded as a productive age.

Table 2.
Total Population (in percentages)

Age groups	1882 men	1882 women	1882 jointly	1897 men	1897 women	1897 jointly
0-14	32.0	29.0	30.4	33.4	30.2	31.7
15-59	63.2	65.2	64.2	61.5	63.2	62.4
60 and more	4.5	5.4	5.0	5.0	6.5	5.8
age unknown	0.3	0.4	0.4	0.1	0.1	0.1
	100.0	100.0	100.0	100.0	100.0	100.0

Source: M. Nietyksza, Ludność Warszawy..., data from Table 37, p. 143.

The figures in Table 2 show that in the years 1882-1897 Warsaw witnessed a drop in the percentage of people of productive age. This concerns both men and women, the drop being slightly higher with regard to women. At the same time, the percentage of children and elderly people grew.

In a city with a large influx of population one would have expected an opposite trend. But there are two reasons for these changes in the age structure. First and foremost, Warsaw witnessed a great growth in its natural increase from the mid-1880s until the mid-1890s; the drop which followed was much slower.[10]

The other factor is the specific character of the migration of Jews, who constituted a large part of the inflowing population. They settled in the city with their entire families, whereas the Catholic (and also Protestant) immigrants were mostly of productive age. These differences in the character of the immigration are reflected in the shape of the age pyramids of the individual religious groups (Diagram 2).[11] The diagrams showing the sex and age structure of the Catholic and Protestant populations are pyramids of progressive populations with a deformation typical of the populations of large cities, that is, a large percentage of the central age groups, resulting from immigration. The age pyramid of the Jewish population is almost the shape of a regular triangle, the only trace of immigration being evident in the group of females between 10-19 years of age in 1897; the most numerous were the youngest age groups.

I have already mentioned that the numerical superiority of women declined in Warsaw between 1882 and 1914. Let us now see what the sex proportions in the three age groups were in the light of the censuses (Table 3).

**Table 3. The Population of Warsaw by Sex
and Age in 1882 and 1897: Proportions of the Sexes**

Age groups	Number of women per 1,000 men	
1882	1897	
0-14	1023	1020
15-59	1166	1156
60 and more	1342	1459

Source: M. Nietyksza, Ludność Warszawy..., p. 144.

In the oldest age group (the least numerous) we do not see a drop but a considerable increase. In the youngest group the numerical superiority of women decreased slightly. A distinct drop is evident in the middle group, between the ages of 15 and 59.

Thus two factors were responsible for the relative drop in the employment of women in Warsaw: the drop in the percentage of women of productive age and the decrease in women's numerical superiority over men in this age group.

The interdependence between vocational activeness and age reveals different characteristics in the case of men and women. (Table 4).

Table 4. Vocational Activeness of Men and Women in Warsaw by Age Groups in 1882 and 1897

Age groups	Gainfully employed (in percentages)[x]			
	women		men	
	1882	1897	1882	1897
0-14	7.2	5.2	9.5	5.3
15-59	40.1	39.2	90.2	89.1
of which:				
15-19	45.6	48.6	66.3	60.4
20-39[xx]	38.4	37.1	94.4	93.7
40-59[xx]	39.2	37.0	99.0	98.7
60 and more	45.1	46.2	93.4	91.7

x   Percentage of the total population of a given age group.
xx   Division into 20-year age groups, as in the 1897 census
Source: M. Nietyksza, Ludność Warszawy..., data from Table 39, p. 147.

The threefold division into age groups shows the greatest vocational activeness in the oldest group, over 60 years of age, that is, formally, in the post-productive age. The division into subgroups shows the highest index for women between the age of 15 and 19 and for men between the age of 40 and 59. In the older age groups of productive age the percentage of gainfully employed women was considerably lower, probably because of marriage and the rearing of children, while the percentage of gainfully employed men increased greatly in these groups. We see a great difference between the male indices for the 15-19 age group and the 20-39 year group, and a relatively small increase in the next group (with indices exceeding 90%).

Men's vocational activeness was, on the whole, more than twice as high as that of women; the difference was small only with regard to children, the index for girls being 7.2% and for boys 9.5% in 1882. In between the censuses, the drop in the employment of boys was much greater than that for girls, as a result of which the vocational activeness of both boys and girls became equal and stood at just over 5% at the end of the 19th century.

This was undoubtedly the influence of factory legislation, which was applied with greater stringency to boys, who worked mostly in industry and handicrafts, than to girls, who were employed mainly in domestic and other personal services, that is, in occupations which had no legal regulations.[12]

If we look at the indices of all the age-groups in Table 4 we see that in 1882-1897 vocational activeness increased in only two groups: the groups of women between the age of 15 and 19, and of women over 60.

Changes in the demographic structure and legal, economic, social and psychological (emancipation aspirations) factors influenced the vocational activeness of women in Warsaw in different ways.

The reservations about the preciseness of the census information (the fact that relatives helping in family businesses were not taken into account) and the objective (demographic) reasons for the drop in the vocational activeness of all the inhabitants of Warsaw (including women) do not yet adequately explain why the vocational activeness of the adult population decreased. There are reasons for thinking that this was due to the increase in the percentage of Jews in Warsaw, for the Jewish community was considerably less active vocationally than the rest of the population. As regards the period under review, only the 1897 census allows us to work out the approximate indices for the various groups distinguished by the language criterion. These indices are confirmed by the information contained in the 1921 census, which is more precise, for it takes into account gainfully employed relatives helping in family businesses.[13]

In 1897, among the gainfully employed people of the largest nationality groups (distinguished by the criterion of language) women accounted for 37.6% in the Polish group and for 29.3%

in the Jewish group. Since the percentage of the Jewish population increased in the years 1882-1897 and the percentage of women among the gainfully employed people remained at an unchanged level (35.1%), there is no doubt that the vocational activeness of Polish women kept increasing.[14]

The need to take up paid work was becoming increasingly urgent for women in the second half of the nineteenth century, but the opportunities were limited.

At the end of the 1860s and the beginning of the 1870s, women accounted for only a few percent of the white-collar workers in Warsaw. The main occupations accessible to women in this field were teaching, the upbringing of children and auxiliary medical service. Women were also represented in the arts (theatre, ballet, singing) and began to take up editorial jobs. The road to these occupations was barred by traditions and social barriers; formal barriers also appeared. By the ukase of 1871 the Russian authorities barred women from access to office work in state institutions.[15] The difficulty of acquiring an education was a great obstacle for women who wanted to pursue a professional career. In addition to just a few secondary government schools for girls, many private schools, frequently on quite a high level, were opened in Warsaw in the 1870s and 1880s, as if in response to the slogans concerning women's emancipation. However, they did not prepare the girls for any trade or profession, nor were they entitled to grant matriculation certificates. Besides, women were not admitted to universities in the Russian Empire. At that time they had access to only a few European schools of higher learning. Women's self-tuition circles, which gave rise to a specific secret school, the so-called Flying University, were a substitute for university studies. The Flying University, organized in the mid-1880s, had four faculties and was on a very high level, particularly as regards the humanities and social sciences. It is estimated that some 5,000 women studied at this university during the 20 years of its existence. In 1906 the Flying University was transformed into the Society of Scientific Courses, a legal institution. Up to 1915, nearly 70% of its students were women.[16]

In petty bourgeois circles it was easier for women to be active in trade than in handicrafts. Artisans' assemblies did not begin to admit women until the mid-1890s. Dress- and underwear-making and the production of artificial flowers were the crafts most frequently taken up by women. Women of the impoverished intelligentsia and landowning families also looked for a living in these branches (less frequently in trade). Widows sometimes managed a workshop or a shop left by the husband. Research into the petty bourgeoisie in nineteenth century Warsaw shows that women from this class were very active, running their own businesses or working in their fathers' or husbands' artisan workshops or shops. This confirms the supposition that quite a large group had not been included in the category of gainfully employed persons. It also shows the distinctive characteristics of the Jewish petty bourgeoisie, which constituted the overwhelming part of the Jewish community in Warsaw.[17]

Hired physical labor provided a livelihood for more than two-thirds of the working women in Warsaw. The great city attracted many young women looking for work, even children without any qualifications. They found employment mostly as servants, less frequently did they take up casual work. Handicrafts, especially the production of clothing and fancy goods, were developing dynamically, offering women many possibilities of earning a living. The importance of industry was growing gradually and its growth accelerated at the beginning of the 20th century. Industrial workwomen were employed in a greater variety of branches than they were in handicrafts.[18]

Since we have two censuses from the last two decades of the nineteenth century for Warsaw, we can not only reconstruct the population's vocational structure, but also point out the changes which took place during that time, and this seems to be particularly interesting. Even though the two censuses list the individual trades in different groups, it has been possible to find comparable categories. It has turned out that an overwhelming majority of the occupations listed in the two censuses can be classified into separate branches of the economy, that is, that the criterion of objective occupation can be applied. There are, however, some important exceptions. Casual laborers, that is, unskilled workers usually employed per day in physical work, have been listed as a separate group. They have been left as a separate group, for there are no data which would allow us to ascertain the proportions working in industry, handicrafts, trade or transport. Similarly, private clerks are listed as a separate group, no mention being made of the institutions which employed them. However, they are listed in Section 5 (see Table 5) which comprises public administration, courts of justice, private administration, the Church, the health service, education, science, literature and the arts, in brief, white-collar workers employed in state, social and private institutions as well as professional people. It is also worth pointing out that Section 8 has been distinguished on the basis of formal criteria and embraces greatly differing categories.

In nineteenth century censuses the gainfully employed people are defined as "independent persons" or "persons having independent occupations", while the vocationally passive people are listed as "family members". The first group includes old age pensioners (group 8b), persons acquiring education (persons in educational establishments), and persons in alms-houses (group 8c "without a paid job"). According to present-day criteria they should be included in the group of vocationally passive people.

Table 5. Structure of Women's Employment in Warsaw in 1882 and 1897 by Branches of Occupation

Branches of occupation	1882		1897			
			Urban districts		suburbs	
	number	%	number	%	number	%
1. Agriculture	21	0.003	83	0.1	127	4.0
2. Industry & handicrafts	7,649	12.4	16,618	18.0	737	23.3
3. Trade, banks	4,180	6.7	6,905	7.5	232	7.3
4.Transport, communications	43	0.1	212	0.2	6	0.2
5. Administration, courts, of justice,professions	2,714	4.4	4,827	5.2	51	1.6

6. Domestic and personal services	31,597	51.5	41,946	45.4	974	30.8
of which:						
domestic service	29,918	48.8	39,238	42.5	841	26.6
7. Casual laborers	5,309	8.6	5,376	5.8	634	20.0
8. Not engaged in work:						
a. rentier-capitalists	3,523	5.7	7,710	8.4	193	6.1
b. old age pensioners	1,669	2.7	2,518	2.7	24	0.8
c. persons w/o paid job	3,579	5.8	5,236	5.7	137	4.3
9. Undefined/unknown occupations	1,309	2.1	949	1.0	51	1.6
TOTAL:	61,593	100.0	92,580	100.0	3,166	100.0

x   Scholarship holders, persons living on charity, prisoners, beggars, etc.

Source: M. Nietyksza, Ludność Warszawy, Table 48, pp. 182-183

Table 5 shows the number of women employed in each branch, while Diagram 3 illustrates the structure of women's employment and–for the sake of comparison–the structure of men's employment. The 1897 census took into account the Warsaw suburbs, which were developing outside the administrative boundaries of the city, but were integrally linked with it, in particular economically.

In 1882, domestic servants were the largest group of women working in Warsaw, numbering 31,600 i.e. about half of the total number of gainfully employed women. Together with casual laborers (8.6%), blue-collar workwomen of the lowest rank accounted for 60% of working women. At the end of the century servants were still the largest group (41,900) but their share in the total number of working women had clearly dropped (to 45.4%). The percentage of women working casually also decreased (to 5.8%), their number having risen insignificantly. In 1897, servants and women doing casual work constituted just over 50% of all gainfully employed women.

Women employed in industry and handicrafts were the second largest group. These two branches must be taken jointly for the censuses do not provide a basis for separating industry from handicrafts. A certain indication is supplied by the division into branches, which can be compared with other sources. The employment of women in Section 2 rose more than twofold, from 7,649 to 16,618, i.e. from 12.4% to 18%. The production of clothes and fancy goods predominated, employing 79.4% of the women working in this section in 1882 and 70% in 1897. Other branches employed a few percentages each.

An increase, though not so great, also occurred in trade and administration, and an almost fivefold rise took place in transport and communications. Section 3 includes women working in trade, hotels, catering establishments and insurance institutions and as intermediaries. More than 80% of the women included in this section were engaged in trade in various goods (81.5% in 1882 and 85.3% in 1897) and more than 10% ran hotels and catering establishments or worked there.

Very few women were employed in transport and communications: only 43 in 1882 and 212 in 1897. The former census registered only 6 women working in post offices, the latter already 64. The number of women employed by other means of transport than railroads and tramways rose from 37 to 64 (cabs, horse-drawn transport). At the end of the century women started working on the railroads and tramways (84, of whom 79 worked on the railroads).[19]

It is worth taking a closer took at the administration section. The changes which took place between the two censuses point to shifts within this section (Table 6).

The 1882 census does not distinguish social institutions as a separate item, probably including the persons employed there in other groups, in particular–I think–in the health service, in education and child rearing, perhaps also in private administration. This somewhat obscures the picture, but the direction of the changes is clear. In 1882 women worked mainly in the occupations traditionally regarded as the most apt for them; teaching, the upbringing of children, health services (only lower functions, of course) employed over 78% of the women working in this section. A relatively large group was connected with the various fields of art, especially the theatre and music; women also made their appearance as white-collar-workers in private institutions and enterprises. Fifteen years later the previously most important fields continued to predominate, though less strongly, and an evident rise took place in the employment of women in administration.

Table 6. White-Collar Women Workers in Warsaw in 1882 and 1897

| | 1882 | | 1897 | |
	number	%	number	%
State admin, courts of justice, legal profession	3	0.1	80	1.7
Private administration	171	6.3	562	11.6
Social Institutions (mainly charitable)	-	-	289	6.0
Clergy, church functions	94	3.5	107	2.2
Health service	801	29.5	1,141	23.6
Education and child upbringing	1,325	48.8	2,149	44.6
Science, Literature, art	320	11.8	458	9.5
Other occupations (draftswomen, copists)	-	-	41	0.8
TOTAL:	2,714	100.0	4,827	100.0

SOURCE: M. Nietyksza, Ludność Warszawy..., data from Annex 7.

Women included in the category "rentiers-capitalists" were an important group and their percentage was growing. In 1882 this group comprised landowners, house owners and persons defined as "capitalists", most probably persons living on the interest from their capital, for the owners of industrial and trade enterprises were included in the respective sections. In 1897 this group included persons living on interest from capital and profits from realty as well as persons "living on means deriving from their parents and relatives."[20]

In the suburbs fewer women worked as domestic servants than in the city but many more were employed in casual work and also in industry and handicrafts. The employment structure of the population in the suburbs corresponded to the economic and social character of these suburban villages, then in the process of urbanization and industrialization. They were of a decisively proletarian character. Since the flats were cheaper there, they attracted many newcomers who often worked in the over-crowded city.

Finally, let us show the percentage of women within the total number of gainfully employed people in the individual sections (Table 7).

Women decidedly predominated only among domestic ser-vants (over 75% of the total number of persons employed in this section) and this predominance was growing. They accounted for about one-third of the casual laborers (but for less than 17% in the suburbs). Their share in trade, at the level of about 20% can be regarded as stable, since for reasons discussed above, the percentage of unlisted relations employed as helpers in family businesses must have grown. A marked increase in the percent-age of women took place in industry and handicrafts. The percentage of women was also high among old age pensioners, which was probably due to the growing predominance of women in the older age groups. Their percentage among rentiers was slightly lower.

Table 7.
The Percentage of Women in Gainfully
Employed Groups in 1882 and 1897 by Occupation

Branch of occupation	Percentage of women in each section in:		
	1882	1897	
		urban districts	suburbs
1. Agriculture	3.5	8.9	24.0
2. Industry and handicrafts	13.7	18.6	10.6
3. Trade and banks	20.8	19.2	21.4
4. Transport, communications	0.7	1.8	0.6
5. Administration,courts of justice, professions	15.4	19.4	11.0
6. Domestic/personal service	77.5	78.3	78.4
of which: domestic service	77.2	78.2	76.4
7. Casual workers	34.4	31.3	16.9
8. Performing no work			
a. rentiers-capitalists	54.4	57.5	29.2
b. old age pensioners	56.8	62.5	37.5
c. without a paid job[x]	47.3	54.4	26.8
9. Undefined/unknown occup.	55.5	41.9	19.7
Total:	35.1	35.1	19.1

x e.g. scholarship holders, persons living on charity, prisoners, beggars, etc.
Source: M. Nietyksza, Ludność Warszawy, table on p. 186.

On the basis of less precise information and approximate calculations this observation of the trends of changes in the employment of women in Warsaw can be extended to include the period from the 1860s until the First World War. Although the women's employment structure was undoubtedly unfavorable, some favorable changes did take place. What is most important is that the percentage of unskilled women or women with low qualifications was falling while at the same time an increase in the employment of women was noticed in industry and handicrafts, trade and administration (mainly private). This means that an increasing number of women were doing better paid work which required vocational training or education.

Notes to Chapter 7

1.   M. Nietyksza, Ludność Warszawy na przełomie XIX wieku (The Population of Warsaw at the Turn of the 19th Century), Warszawa 1971, pp. 26-28; idem, Rozwój miast i aglomeracji miejsko-przemysłowych w Królestwie Polskim, 1865-1914 (The Development of Towns and Urban-Industrial Agglomerations in the Polish Kingdom, 1865-1914), Warszawa 1986, pp. 126, 135
2.   M. Nietyksza, Ludność Warszawy, p. 30.
3.   M. Nietyksza, Rozwój miast, pp. 260-261. Basic literature on this subject is quoted in the footnotes.
4.   See in particular: M. Nietyksza, Ludność Warszawy, and W. Pruss, Skład wyznaniowo-narodowościowy ludności Warszawy w XIX i początkach XX w. (The Religious and Nationality Composition of the Population of Warsaw in the 19th and at the Beginning of the 20th Century), in: Społeczeństwo Warszawy w rozwoju historycznym, Warszawa 1977, pp. 372-392.
5.   The basic statistical publications concerning Warsaw are discussed in M. Nietyksza, Ludność Warszawy, annexes 1 and 2.
6.   M. Nietyksza, Ludność Warszawy, p. 81.
7.   The army, both its active and passive members, have been left out in all tables concerning occupation.
8.   M. Nietyksza, Ludność Warszawy, p. 141.
9.   The census publications use slightly different age groups in tables concerning occupations. The working out of common categories has necessitated re-calcuations, some of which are estimates. The possible errors are of no statistical importance.
10.   M. Nietyksza, Ludność Warszawy, pp. 100, 105, 117-118.
11.   Ten-year age groups are used in the diagram in accordance with the grouping adopted in the 1897 census in the table showing the sex and age groups of religious denominations. The evident deformation of both pyramids of the Orthodox population results from the fact that it was impossible to exclude the numerous military garrison, which was greatly increased in the

years between the two censuses. The presence of the garrison can also be seen in the pyramid of the Protestants in 1897.

12. For a detailed analysis of the employment structure of youth in Warsaw (including minors) see M. Nietyksza, Struktura zatrudnienia młodzieży Warszawy w świetle spisów z lat 1882 i 1897 (The Employment Structure of the Youth of Warsaw in the Light of the Censuses of 1882 and 1897), Pokolenia 1966, No. 3/15, pp. 40-56.

13. I do not give the actual indices, for their comparison might be misleading without a detailed explanation of how the incorporation of suburbs affected vocational relations in the city. What is important is the markedly lower level of the vocational activeness of Jews in comparison with the other inhabitants of Warsaw.

14. M. Nietyksza, Ludność Warszawy, pp. 185-186.

15. J. Leskiewiczowa, Warszawa i jej inteligencja po powstaniu styczniowym 1864-1870 (Warsaw and Its Intelligentsia after the January Insurrection 1864-1870), Warszawa 1961, pp. 157-161.

16. S. Kieniewicz, Warszawa w latach 1795-1914 (Warsaw in the Years 1795-1914), Warszawa 1976, pp. 262-267; B. Cywiński, Rodowody niepokornych (The Genealogies of the Unsubmissive), Warszawa 1971, p. 53 ff.; H. Kiepurska, Wykładowcy Towarzystwa Kursów Naukowych/1906-1915/ (The Lecturers of the Society of Scientific Courses/1906-1915/) /in:/ Inteligencja polska pod zaborami. Studia (The Polish Intelligentsia under the Partitions. Studies), Warszawa 1987, pp. 269-270.

17. S. Kowalska-Glikman, Drobnomieszczaństwo w dziewiętnastowiecznej Warszawie (The Petty Bourgeoisie in 19th Century Warsaw), Warszawa 1987, pp. 81-85.

18. A. Żarnowska, Robotnicy Warszawy na przełomie XIX i XX wieku (The Workers of Warsaw at the Turn of the 19th Century), Warszawa 1985, pp. 29-32.

19. For date on the composition of the individual sections see: M. Nietyksza, Ludność Warszawy, annex 7.

20. M. Nietyksza, Ludność Warszawy, pp. 134-135.

Anna Żarnowska

8
Women in Working Class Families in the Congress Kingdom (the Russian Zone of Poland) at the Turn of the Nineteenth Century

Changes in the conditions of working class families and the large-scale entry of women onto the labor market in the last thirty years of the 19th century were the most important causes of the change in the social position of working class women milieu during the period of industrialization. Among the factors shaping the social status of proletarian women, having a family was undoubtedly the most important one. The role of a wife and mother to a large extent determined their economic situation and the prestige they enjoyed in their own social class. This is indirectly confirmed by such cases of social pathology as the increasing number of foundlings and infanticides in industrial towns in the 19th century.[1]

The social status and prosperity of a women's parents seem to have had a much smaller influence on her social position among urban workers; of much greater importance were the social status of her actual or prospective husband, and, above all his vocational qualifications (artisans' qualifications were held in special esteem) and possibly also the magnitude of his property (ownership of a workshop, a flat, a shop). The women's vocational qualifications were of much lesser importance in the working class. To begin with, few women had them in the period under review. As late as the end of the 19th century, vocational and educational aspirations were hardly noticeable among proletarian women. A radical change in women's attitudes in this respect occurred during the revolutionary years of 1905, 1906 and 1907.

The present state of research does not yet make it possible to ascertain to what extent involvement in parish life–which was widespread at that time, especially among Catholic women, and was fostered by the parish priest's prestige–influenced the social position of women; I think that it enhanced a working women's prestige in her own milieu, just as artisans' (vocational) qualifications contributed to that of her husband.

Let us revert to what I think was the most important factor determining a women's position in the working class, namely, her family status. At the end of the 19th and the be-ginning of the 20th century the family status of workers and workwomen, and the chances for family stability differed greatly, depending on their trade and branch of employment.[2]

At the end of the 19th century, the family situation of workers not employed in agriculture in the Congress Kingdom–and not only there–was determined by two opposing trends. One was the lack of stability and even the disintegration of the family, caused by the industrial revolution and mass migrations from the countryside to the towns. The lack of a family was then frequently a favorable factor on the labor market for workers as well as workwomen. The other trend was the gradual stabilization of working class families and the emergence of their specific characteristics. This process was connected with the progress of industrialization and urbanization (including the urbanization of the working class population) and with the growing stabilization of workers in industry, transport, the building trade, etc.

Both trends developed side by side, intersecting each other. They were strongest among industrial workers, but were also evident among workers employed in other branches (e.g., on the railways) which were developing in connection with industrialization.

I. A basic question arises: what chance did members of the working class in the Congress Kingdom have to establish a family and secure its stability at the end of the 19th century? And in particular, what chances did women have in this respect?

Table 1. Family Status of Workers and Domestic Servants in the Congress Kingdom in the Basic Branches of Employment
(percentage of the total number of workers and workwomen according to the 1897 Census)

Workers and Workwomen

Branch of employment	men	women	Heads of family			Family members			Single persons and persons		
			men	women	joint	men	women	joint	men	women	joint
Industry	53.5	23.6	50.6	8.6	40.5	22.0	63.5	32.0	27.3	27.8	27.3
Handicrafts/small scale industry	32.2	9.4	39.7	22.2	38.2	19.5	35.3	21.0	40.8	42.4	41.0
Trade	38.3	12.7	94.0	47.0	53.0	9.2	9.8	9.3	37.6	43.0	37.7
Unskilled workers/ casual laborers	75.0	23.0	67.0	27.3	54.0	13.7	35.0	20.6	19.3	37.7	25.4
Services	32.0	17.7	46.0	49.9	49.1	8.8	12.1	11.4	45.2	38.0	39.5
Domestic servants	46.5	0.5	37.3	0.5	6.2	4.8	4.3	4.4	57.8	95.5	89.4

Source: The author's own compilations on the basis of Chislennost' i sostav rabochikh i prislugi v Rossii (1897), St. Petersburg 1906, vol. II, table. 2.

The most significant indicator of the first of the two trends mentioned above was the relatively large number of workers and workwomen who, because of economic migrations, were unable to establish a family or were separated from it for a long time. This assumed exceptionally large proportions in central Russia during the development of industrialization. In 1897, more than half of all those employed in Russian industry, handicrafts, trade and transport lived a solitary life. In the Congress Kingdom this phenomenon had much smaller dimensions but even here about one-third of the workers and workwomen had no family. However, whereas in central Russia the development of industrialization complicated first and foremost the family life of men looking for a job (many more men than women were separated from their families), in the Congress Kingdom the percentage of single persons and persons who were living apart from their families was no smaller among workwomen than among workers. On the contrary: among those people employed outside industry in the Congress Kingdom, the proportion of single persons was often higher among women than among men (e.g., in the clothing handicrafts it amounted to 47% among women/girls and to 44% among men/boys, in trade to 43% and 37.5%, respectively, among unskilled persons employed on a daily basis in various fields to 37.7% and 19%, and in domestic service to 95.5% and just under 58%).[3] This was one of the most important, specifically Polish factors determining the family status of workwomen.

The low wages and the working conditions in many fields of employment, especially in trade, services and in some branches of industry (e.g., the textile industry) and in handicrafts (e.g., the manufacture of clothing) frequently made it impossible for workers, and even more so for workwomen, to establish a family or forced them to postpone this. Workwomen were seriously handicapped as far as the establishment of a family and its normal development were concerned. This is attested to by the disproportion evident in Warsaw at the end of the 19th century between the family situation of proletarian women and that of women from other social classes. Whereas only 17% of the 20-

40 year old women employed in industry and handicrafts were married, the respective proportion for all the female inhabitants of Warsaw in this age group was over 50%.[4]

The establishment of a family depended, of course, not only on economic factors connected with a work place. Among the cultural factors an enormous role was played by customs, which in their turn depended on: 1. the workers' and workwomen's links with the countryside, with a definite region of the country, with the local customs; 2. their links with the town and the influence of the urban way of life; 3. ethnic and religious ties and the resulting patterns of behavior.

The family situation of persons employed in trade and handicrafts (including small-scale industry) had some very similar specific features. This applies to men as well as to the few women working in these branches. In addition to the similarity of working conditions in small work places, a by no means unimportant role must have been played by the fact that the people working in these two branches derived from similar social backgrounds and that the nationalities composing these workforces were similar, the Jewish proletariat accounting for as much as 22% to 40% at the turn of the century. Wages in trade, small-scale industry and handicrafts were so low that in practice most of the persons employed in these branches were unable to set up a family and support it, at least not until they had gained qualifications, which frequently took many years. Consequently, the percentage of married people was extremely low among persons employed in artisan workshops and trade. According to data available for 1897, only 9.5% of the women working in artisan workshops and 13% of those employed in trade were married. The specific family situation of the persons employed in these two fields is also illustrated by the fact that the percentage of single persons and persons separated from their families was higher there than in other branches of the economy. In spite of this, at the end of the century almost half of the women employed in trade and nearly one-quarter of those working in handicrafts were supporting a family, while this was done by less than 10% of the workwomen employed in industry (see Table 1).

Even at the end of the 19th century, nearly half of the women employed in trade and handicrafts led a solitary life, either having no family or separated from it. No other group of the proletariat in the Congress Kingdom had such a high percentage of single women. Persons forced to lead a single life for some time constituted a proportionately smaller group even among industrial workers: just over one-quarter (about 27%) of both men and women in 1897.[5] As industrialization developed, the proportion of single persons, men and women, decreased considerably.[6]

Generally speaking, the chances for men and women were not equal, the risk of being unable to lead a normal family life being much greater for women than for men. Let us add that in view of the mechanisms of the labor market and the working conditions, the factors ruining family life accumulated in the case of domestic servants. This category, which to an overwhelming extent consisted of women among whom married women conprised only a fraction, was almost completely devoid of the possibility of setting up a family and was thus forced to lead a solitary life. The situation of persons employed in other services, such as laundries and baths, where women also predominated, was not much different. Yet, nearly half of them had to support a family, which did not always consist of their own children, but usually of younger siblings and disabled parents, on their meager earnings.

The other trend determining the family status of workers employed outside agriculture in the Congress Kingdom at the end of the 19th century, that is the trend towards a relative stabilization of the working class family, was evident in particular among railwaymen and workers employed in the technically most modern branches of industry, concentrated in urban centers (the iron and steel, metal, textile and chemical industries). The most important element of this stabilization was the possibility of living together, and this depended on the stability of the family's earnings, that is, on the one hand, on the regular work and earnings of the head of the family and, on the other hand, on the increasingly frequent habit of family members, especially married women, to take up paid work.

Hence, under the Polish conditions the increase in the number of women employed in industry can be regarded as an indication of the growing stabilization of working class families. Another indirect indication of this process was the increase in the number of married women among the gainfully employed women.

It was first and foremost the manufacturing industry that made it possible for members of working class families, for juveniles and married women, to earn money, thus contributing to the stabilization of working class families. Work in handicrafts was less attractive, since it usually separated young people from their families, while married women had little opportunity of working in an artisan workshop, with the exception of those engaged in the manufacture of clothes. In 1897, married women accounted for only about 9% of the women employed in handicrafts and for nearly one-quarter of those working in factories.[7] The percentage of married women was highest in the textile, mineral, alcohol-distilling, sugar and timber industries (in the last three branches mainly as seasonal workers). Married women preferred to work as cottage workers rather than seek employment in artisan workshops. The entry of married women into the labor market was, however, determined by the development of the textile industry, in which women accounted for at least 40% of the labor force, over one-quarter of them being married women. At the end of the 19th century, more than 80% of all married workwomen in the industry of Congress Poland were employed in the textile industry.[8] It is characteristic that among the women employed in the textile industry the 20-40 year age group had the largest number of married women. This shows that contrary to widespread opinion, women employed in the textile industry did not stop working after marriage, not even when they were most encumbered by maternal duties.[9] The largest groups of married women were employed in the textile centers of Łódź, the Łódź area and the Warsaw region: at Żyrardów, Marki and other places. In Warsaw itself, which was a center of many branches of industry and handicrafts with a well developed production of clothing (making wide use of women's work), married women were infrequently found in factories and manufacturing work-shops, accounting for only some 10%.[10]

Owing to the lack of sources, it is impossible to precisely determine whether, and to what extent, the beginning of the 20th century brought a further increase in the employment of married women. An indirect indication that this did take place is the large increase in the employment of women over the age of 18 which occurred in industry in the first 15 years of this century. In the years 1900-1914, the proportion of women in industry rose from 25% to nearly 28%.

II. Another important factor determining the women's social position in the working class family and milieu was the attitude of this milieu to women's paid work.

The working class in the Congress Kingdom, both during the period under review and later, was prejudiced against married women taking up regular jobs, especially in industry. It is worth stressing that the Jewish proletariat was most opposed to mothers seeking employment, and even worked to counteract it.

Opposition to married women taking up work in industry was manifested by the entire working class in Warsaw. In Warsaw, women gave up work in industry after marriage and, in particular, after bearing a child, more frequently than in the other working class centers in the Congress Kingdom. It is interesting that decisions to this effect were taken in Warsaw in the families of workers of various trades and different earnings, not only in the families of the relatively well paid metal workers, but also in those of municipal and unskilled workers. This may have been due to the fact that Warsaw, being a large city, offered women greater opportunities for casual work, outside industry.

In a situation of necessity, the wives of Warsaw workers looked for the additional earnings, necessary to maintain their families, in casual work rather than in factories: in services, domestic service, trade and the catering business (especially in Jewish families). They tried to work at home as cottage workers, executing the orders of factories, various artisan workshops and clothing shops, or took in and served tenants. Such work did not undermine the position of the father as the chief bread-winner and did not therefore change the patriarchal system of the family. The father retained the decisive voice in basic family affairs; the mother had a subordinate position, but it was she who strengthened the emotional ties binding the family.[12]

The workers' animosity against married women taking up regular paid work, especially in industry, was fostered by the Catholic and national press (inspired by the National Union of Workers), which propagated among the workers the patriarchial family pattern, in which a woman was to be subordinate to the head of the family and to perform ancillary functions, those of a wife, mother and housewife.[13]

This is no place to evaluate what reach and influence the Catholic press had among the workers of the Congress Kingdom; we will confine ourselves to stating that even as late as the beginning of the 20th century, paid work, also in industry, did not enhance a woman's prestige among the working class.

III. As industrialization and urbanization developed in the Congress Kingdom, the structure of working class families showed a tendency to change: a two-generation family began gradually to predominate over the family composed of more generations; this greatly increased the burdens on the mothers, who at the same time more and more often took up paid work.

These changes in the structure of working class families were noticeable already at the end of the 19th century, in particular in large towns among workers employed in those branches of industry which forced them to sever their ties with the countryside and agriculture. This was also a sign of the families' increased stability in town and frequently led to their expansion, for stability meant, among other things, the decision to have more children.

In the regions which were being industrialized, the natural increase began to rise gradually in the first years of the 20th century, when industry in the Congress Kingdom had already passed through the stage of its most dynamic development. It was only then that these regions began to outstrip the agricultural areas in this respect. And this took place at a time when the employment of married women in industry was growing.

The medical and demographic studies carried out in the Congress Kingdom in the first years of the 20th century show that families of unskilled and semi-skilled (trained) workers had the greatest number of children. The poorest proletarian families in Warsaw after 25 years of marriage had 9.6 children on average, but almost half of them (45%) died in infancy or childhood.[14]

But the years preceding World War I witnessed a gradual reduction in the percentage of very large working class families, composed of 10 and more persons, families which had played quite an important role among railwaymen, iron and steel workers, building workers and also textile workers as late as the 1890s. This was due to both the drop in the birth rate (in the 19th century working class families did not restrict the number of their children) and to the growing disintegration of families made up of several generations. Gradually, these new developments began to influence the woman's position in working class families, all the more so as–and this is implied by indirect data–the first 15 years of the 20th century witnessed the growth of a new type of working class families, composing several gainfully employed persons, in which not only the father, but also the mother and adult children were gainfully employed.

IV. However, there were no egalitarian tendencies in inner-family relations, in relations between the husband and the wife, or the parents and the children in the Congress Kingdom at the end of the 19th century and the beginning of the 20th. They were non-existent in the norms of family life and in customs. One cannot however underestimate certain elements which, thanks to the women's entry onto the labor market paved the way to the economic equality of men and women in working class families.

Already at the end of the 19th century some of the women employed in industry and trade in the Congress Kingdom were heads of families (about 5%). This category was particularly important in Warsaw, where more than one-third of the women working in factories and manufacturing workshops maintained their families by their earnings. The number of women bread-winners was the largest among unskilled women working on a daily basis in industry, transport and trade. According to the census of 1897, the earnings of more than one-quarter of the workwomen in the Congress Kingdom were the main source of maintenance for their families. Not many women were employed in trade and handicrafts but the proportion of women who supported a family was higher in these branches than among the women employed in industry.

As a rule, women's earnings could provide maintenance (inadequate as it was) for only the smallest families composed of no more than 2-3 persons. In most cases these were families orphaned by the father; unmarried women accounted for a large percentage of women bread-winners. Such families could enjoy economic independence and remain in town–this applied, above all, to Warsaw–only because they were fully settled there and had loosened their ties with the countryside.

Thus, it was industry, the textile industry, to be precise, which gave proletarian women the widest possibilities for earning money and acquiring relative economic independence. This is confirmed by the fact that outside Warsaw women who were the chief break-winners were almost exclusively textile workers (if we are to believe the data of the 1897 census). It was the women textile worker that became the symbol of women's relative economic independence in working class milieus at the turn of the century. However, we must not forget that women became family heads in this milieu not because they gained full equality with their husbands but usually because they had no husbands.

We must also remember that in view of the material conditions of the average working class family, a wife's abstention from gainful employment meant the necessity of serious economies at home, even if the husband was earning relatively well. Moreover, the mother frequently had an additional, difficult duty, namely, to relentlessly exact the husband's earnings, for in working class families it was the mother who was responsible for the household budget. The situation was made difficult by the spread of alcoholism among workers (mainly men). In the families in which man was the head, the wife's contribution to the family budget, whether in the form of services performed by her for the benefit of the family members, housekeeping, etc. or in the form of casual earnings, was as a rule underestimated in working class milieus. A woman's earnings were regarded as an addition to the contribution made by the head of the family.

A permanent job in industry or some other branch of the economy did little to raise a wife's (mother's) prestige, for her family did not usually realize this was an excessive burden for her. Nor did it contribute in any signficant way to enhancing her prestige in the working class milieu.

Notes to Chapter 8

1. For instance, in the 1870s Warsaw had 18 illegitimate children per 1,000 inhabitants, while the respective figure for the whole of the Congress Kingdom was two. In the years 1871-1873 every ninth infant in Warsaw was born out of wedlock. Some 5,000 illegitimate children were registered in Warsaw during that time and some 3,000 babies were found deserted. These figures were in fact much higher, for the statistics of that period did not fully cover the Jewish population, which avoided registering newborn babies. As late as the beginning of the 1880s, the daily press reported that the number of foundings and cases of infanticide were growing. (Anna Żarnowska, Robotnicy Warszawy na przełomie XIX i XX wieku [The Workers of Warsaw at the Turn of the 19th Century], Warszawa 1985, p. 97).

2. Eadem, Klasa robotnicza Królestwa Polskiego, 1870-1914 (The Working Class in the Congress Kingdom, 1870-1914), Warszawa 1974, pp. 206-233. See table 1 in the appendix.

3. Ibid., pp. 206-207.

4. Żarnowska, Robotnicy Warszawy, p. 32.

5. Żarnowska, Klasa robotnicza, pp. 206-207.

6. Ibid., p. 236.

7. Ibid., pp. 206-207.

8. Industrialization led to a large-scale entry of women onto the labor market in all European countries; what is interesting is that in spite of great differences caused by the type and rate of the process of industrialization, the participation of women in the industrial proletariat did not differ greatly in Europe at the beginning of the 20th century, oscillating between 30% and 40%.

9. Żarnowska, Wielkoprzemysłowe skupisko robotników w Żyrardowie na przełomie XIX i XX w. (The Manufacturing Industry Working Class Center at Żyrardów at the Turn of the 19th Century), in: Klasa robotnicza i ruch robotniczy na Zachodnim Mazowszu (The Working Class and the Working Class Movement in Western Mazovia), Warszawa 1981, pp. 32-34.

10. Żarnowska, Robotnicy Warszawy, pp. 97-98 and table 5 on p. 124.

11. Compiled on the basis of Otchety fabrichnykh inspiektorov 1900-1913, St. Petersburg 1901-1914.

12. Żarnowska, Robotnicy Warszawy, p. 100.

13. Pracownik Polski No. 10, 22.11.1906; Życie Robotnicze No. 34, 29.2.1908.

14. W. Szenajch, Porównawcza statystyka urodzeń i śmiertelności dzieci wśród ubogiej ludności chrześcijańskiej i żydowskiej w Warszawie i Łodzi (Comparative Statistics of Children's Births and Death Rates among the Poor Christian and Jewish Populations of Warsaw and Lodz). Warszawa 1916.

Adam Winiarz

<h1 style="text-align:center">9</h1>

The Women Question in the Kingdom of Poland During the Nineteenth Century: A Bibliographical Essay

The emancipation movement of Polish women began in that portion of the Polish Noble Commonwealth which since 1815 was called the Kingdom of Poland. Remaining Polish lands, those under Austrian (Galicia) and Prussian (Poznań control, played a secondary role in this movement. The woman question assumed special social importance in the Kingdom because economic changes, especially in the second half of the nineteenth century, were greater there than those in Galicia and the Poznan areas. Warsaw was, throughout the nineteenth century, the liveliest center of discussion about women: the most prominent practitioners and sympathizers of emancipation appeared in Warsaw, as did its greatest opponents.

The origin of the woman question in the Kingdom of Poland is connected to the crisis in the traditional upbringing of Polish women. The role of woman based on the family and the home, her total dependence on men, her education, which was limited to the proper use of French along with some music, and at that only among enlightened circles, no longer suited the aspirations or the social needs of women living in changing economic conditions. Given this situation, demands arose for the reform of the existing model of female upbringing and education. The beginning of the Kingdom and demands for reform come so close together that it is appropriate to connect them historically. Already in 1818, when the Diet was debating over land laws, women publicly expressed views defending their interests.[1] Among those speaking out was Anna (née Krajewska) Nakwaska (1781-1851), wife of a onetime Warsaw department official. In her articles "O oziębłości mężczyzn w wieku naszym dla płci pięknej" (About the coldness of the men of our era toward the fair sex.)[2] and "Krótki rzut oka na teraźniejsze wychowanie Polek" (A short glance at the contemporary rearing of Polish women)[3] she criticized the way women were raised. She demanded change in the upbringing of girls and proposed a school to train governesses and teachers necessary for female education.

Further discussion of the need to change the education of Polish women occurred in "Myśl o wychowaniu kobiet" (A thought about the rearing of women) which appeared in the *Tygodnik Warszawski* (Warsaw Diary) in 1822.[4] The author, writing under the pseudonym "L"[4a] began by criticizing contemporary female education and proposed a new model. Her arguments were the same as those that would be used in the future.

Apart from the discussion waged in the *Tygodnik Warszawski,* another voice joined the debate. It was the young Klementyna Tańska (1798-1845). Using a popular work by Jakub Glatz *Vermächtniss Rosaliens an ihre Tochter Amanda* as her model, she wrote *Pamiątka po dobrej matce, czyli ostatnie jej rady dla córki* (In memory of a good mother, or her last bequest to her daughter).[5] She first castigated the prevailing style of domestic and public education based on French models and commonly entrusted to foreigners, and then described her ideal of a national education. Emphasizing the need to bond girls to their own nation by careful study of the Polish language, history, and literature, she stressed the need to shape throughts and feelings and concluded by calling for an education which fashioned not only salon ladies, but good housewives and citizens as well. Her program was modest and limited, but even in its moderation, it suited the thoughts and aspirations animating Polish society, which is why *Pamiątka...* was so favorably received.[6] Her subsequent works, *Amelia Matką* (Amelia as Mother) *Listy o wychowaniu kobiet* (Letters about female education), and *O powinnościach kobiet* (About the obligations of women)[7] which were ideologically a further development of her position in *Pamiątka,* were not as popular. Tańska's program, despite some shortcomings, was a signpost for future generations of Polish women.

After the failure of the November uprising, Tańska emigrated as did many other Poles. She settled in France. Emigration to the West and forced deportations to Siberia deprived the Polish Kingdom of most of its politically aware and intellectually vital people. Cultural and intellectual life stagnated. In that situation women, who were inspired by Romanticism on the one hand and patriotism on the other to aspire for personal and national freedom, filled the void in public social and cultural activities. In 1833 Eleanora (née Gagatkiewicz) Ziemięcka (1819-1869) published her "Myśli o wychowaniu kobiet" (Thoughts about female education) in the *Tygodnik Polski* (Polish Weekly).[8] Other women followed her example and publicly dared to present their literary and journalistic works. Growing activism by women in this sphere increasingly focused attention on the woman question. The most spectacular example of the trend was the doctoral dissertation published in 1836 by Antoni Czajkowski (1816-1873) who surveyed the history of women's rights.[9]

A consciousness of the need to propagate women's issues led Paulina (née Radziejowska) Krakowowa (1813-1882) to begin in 1838, publication of *Pierwiosnek* (Primrose).[10] Edited exclusively by women, it published only women's work, and continued to be published until 1843. Maintained in the spirit of Tańska's ideas, it promoted the notion of higher education for women, their greater access to cultural life, and the cause of the peasants. During its six year existence, fifty-three women published in the journal. Among them were prominents as Tańska, her pupil Narcyza Żmichowska, and the previously mentioned E. Ziemięcka. Ziemięcka was self-taught, particularly in philosophy. It was she who first introduced Hegel's philosophy in the Kingdom via the *Biblioteka Warszawska* (Warsaw Library). In an attempt to popularize her studies she started publication, in 1842, of *Pielgrzym* (Pilgrim)[11] a monthly journal focusing on philosopy and literature. A year later she published *Myśli o wychowaniu kobiet* (Thoughts about female education)[12] of which selected portions had earlier appeared in *Biblioteka Warszawska* and *Pierwiosnek*. Taking a firm Catholic position which she displayed most vividly in *Zarysy Filozofii Katolickiej* (Survey of Catholic Philosophy)[13] she demanded that girls receive a moral education as well as education in various disciplines. She issued an extensive *Kurs Nauk Wyższych dla Kobiet* (A Course in higher education for women).[14] She was convinced that in order to adequately raise future generations of Polish women as mothers, nurturers, and teachers, one could not solely rely upon their wonderful maternal instinct; they had to be also well versed in pedagogy, psychology and ethics.

Significant support for the movement came in the 1840s from the journal *Przegląd Naukowy* (Survey of Education) whose editors Edward Dembowski and Hipolit Skimborowicz supported women's emancipation. Many women were grouped around their editorial staff. Later these became known as "Enthusiasts." Beside Narcyza Żmichowska and Anna Skimborowicz twenty women belonged to the group. The best known were Tekla Dobrzyńska, Emilia Gosselin, Faustyna Morzycka, Bibianna Moraczewska, Wincenta Zabłocka and Kazimiera Ziemięcka (sister-in-law to Eleanora). Despite their varying views especially about religion and the Church, Enthusiasts shared the conviction that women had the right to emancipation. They were also united in their conspiratorial work preceeding the revolution of 1848 for which most of them were imprisoned.

Some of the women like N. Żmichowska, B. Moraczewska, and K.Ziemięcka carried on a two-fold activity. Beside their efforts on behalf of national independence, they were deeply involved in literature. The Enthusiasts must be allotted a primary position in the ranks of the emancipation movement because of their attempts to raise the social, legal and educational status of women. Due to their influence, the women's movement in the Kingdom broke through the barriers of Tańska's tradition by releasing a natural protest in women against limits upon their intellectual development and isolation from social and patriotic activity.

Unfortunately the meritorious program of the Enthusiasts was distorted and rendered farcical by the activities of "Lionesses." These were mainly women of fairly superficial intellect whose extravagant public behavior gave greater emphasis to the loosening of customs than the well-being of the women's movement which, it appears, they did not understand. Most people did not distinguish between the Enthusiasts and Lionesses and ridiculed both the serious and the superficial aspects of what conflated as the emancipation movement. Some used their pens to ridicule emancipation in works such as *Lwy i Lwice* (Lions and Lionesses)[15] by Stanisław Bogusławski and *Emancypacja Sabiny ze stanowiska absolutnego* (Sabina's emancipation from an absolute position).[16]

Despite denigrations, Enthusiasts played a singular role in the development of the Polish emancipation movement. With their activities and their stance they managed to win many contemporary writers and social activists to their cause. Among these were Karol Baliński, Franciszek Nowakowski, Hipolit Skimborowicz and Kazimierz Władysław Wójcicki. This last vigorously undertook the task of writing the history of Polish women and published *Niewiasty Polskie* (Polish women) in 1845.[17] Skimborowicz, in turn, was fascinated by the personalities of the most prominent Enthusiasts and wrote the article *Umysłowość kobiet polskich* (The mind of Polish women)[18] in which he mentioned that among contemporary writers there were one hundred women. In addition, Karol Estreicher, who was professor of bibliography at the Main Warsaw School gathered materials for a bibliography of creative Polish women. He published part of his materials in the Cracow weekly *Niewiasta* (Woman)[19] edited by the distinguished Kazimierz Józef Turkowski. Estreicher's entire bibliography of creative women appeared in *Bibliografia polskiego XIX stulecia*. (Polish Bibliography in the 19th century).[20]

A new generation of emancipators who developed under the influence of Żmichowska and her colleagues had to act under quite different social and economic circumstances. Many women participated in the January uprising of 1863 thereby proving their autonomy and limitless self-sacrifice. After the failure of the uprising, the nation experienced a shortage of the bravest, most resourceful, and intellectually most gifted men. Some had died on the field of battle, others were exiled to Siberia; many emigrated to the West. Women remained, and they had to manage under the particularly difficult circumstances caused by the confiscation of estates and the emancipation of the peasants, all of which caused a great economic upheaval and meant that women in the Kingdom could not longer seek to secure their future through marriage alone, but were forced to prepare for independent professional work. The emancipation movement in western nations, especially the USA, served as a source of encouragement and as a model to be followed. Information about the women's movement in the west came to Polish women in translations of T.H. Buckle,[21] J.S. Mills,[22] E. Legouve,[23] P. Leroy-Beaulieu,[24] and E. Reich.[25]

Under the influence of this literature, interest grew in the women question. As a result, a whole new slate of publications appeared in the 1860s and 1870s such as Teresa Dymidowiczowa's (1817-1865) *Listy moralne poświęcone młodszemu pokoleniu Polek* (Moral letters dedicated to the younger generation of Polish women),[26] Zofia Meller's *Słówko o kwestii moralności kobiecej* (A word about the morality of women)[27] and Józef Juszczyk's (he was a master tailor) "Czy kobiety mogą być u nas rzemieślnikami?" (Can women be artisans?).[28] He supported full admission of women to the trades and his views were shared by Adam Goltz who wrote "Reforma w wychowaniu kobiet i użyciu ich czasu i pracy," (Reform of female upbringing and utilization of their time and work).[29] While emphasizing the need of religious education for girls he wanted professional schools in which they could receive a practical education. His views were largely shared by Władysław Chomętowski, who in "Stanowisko praktyczne dawnych niewiast" (The practical situation of women in the past)[30] tried to prove that in earlier times Polish women had not only been good wives and mothers but competent administrators of their estates. At a time when following the January uprising, many noble estates were left without men, Chomętowski's book clearly had a didactic purpose. Taking a different perspective than Goltz and Chomętowski, Witold Jaroszyński in *Kobieta* (Woman)[31] criticized female convent schools and their educational program. He wanted them replaced by secular education and, in addition, demanded access for women to higher education.

The work of Goltz and Jaroszyński were a challenge to the critics of female emancipation. Fiercest among those was Antoni Nowosielski who attacked the feminist movement in his articles "O przeznaczeniu i zawodzie kobiety" (The destiny and the profession of woman),[32] and "O kwestji Kobiecej" (About the woman question)."[33] Beside frightening his readers with a vision of disintegrating families and lax public morality, he tried to discredit the movement by suggesting that it was the direct outcome of socialism and other radical tendencies. He was assisted in this alarmism by Roman Bierzyński, the author of a rather famous, though paradoxical *Sommatologie de la femme*.[34] In brochures such as "Jeszcze słówko o kobiecie" (Just one more word about woman) and "Nieco o prawie kobiety do nauki i pracy" (A bit about the rights of women to education and work),[35] he sought to trivialize and ridicule the ideals of the women's movement. Rancorously he claimed that "the legions of women striving for independence are made up of divorcees, separated women, widows, old maids, and childless wives."[36]

Despite the propaganda campaign by the opposition the movement continued to grow. It was supported by young Warsaw positivists, although Józef Stupiński, the first Polish advocate of August Comte, opposed emancipation. The chief herald of Warsaw positivism, Aleksander Świętochowski, paid much attention to the women's movement. In May 1872 he published an essay "W sprawie kobiet" (About the Women Question) in the magazine *Niwa*"[37] where, basing his ideas on the works of Mill, Buckle and Legouve, Despine, and Urlici he pondered the issue and sought solutions. He concluded that the best solution would come from schools and life itself. He took the same position in his article "Klauzurowe i swobodne wychowanie kobiet" (The controlled and the free education of women).[38] He went further in his views in a four part study entitled "Kwestia małżeńska: I. Geneza i zasady, II. Miłość i ugoda, III. Poligamia i poliandria, IV. Separacja i rozwód" (The question of marriage: I. Genesis and principles, II. Love and agreement, III. Polygamy and Polyandry, IV. Separation and divorce).[39] His thesis stressed marriage as a partnership between man and woman, united and maintained by physical drives, moral feelings, family and social aims. "For this partnership to attain a higher purpose, both sides need equal rights, and the partnership should be end as soon as its organic nature begins to dissolve. That is, husband and wife should have equal status in the family and should be free to separate when the harmony of the union undergoes change." This approach was not only novel but in light of Polish society's position, which was primarily Catholic and viewed marriage as indissoluble–revolutionary.

A major event of national proportion came with lectures by A. Świętochowski "O średnim wykształceniu kobiet" (About the secondary education of women) and "O wyższym wykształceniu kobiet" (About higher education for women) given at the Warsaw Social Club on the first of April and the thirteenth of December in 1873. An expanded version of the lectures was published in *Przegląd Tygodniowy* (Weekly Review).[40] He stressed unqualified equal educational rights for women. Further, he wanted educational programs adjusted to women's situation and responsibilities in society. Beside sketching the history of women's drive for education, Świętochowski discussed the educational situation of women in other nations. He went on to point out the suitable direction which women's education should follow and concluded by saying "women based on their own human as well as familial and social standing have the right to higher education; research, law, life and human events show nothing to counter this, in fact they sanction the right." The lectures caused a commotion. There was support but also opposition. The bi-weekly *Niwa* which recommended the lectures as a model for all those wanting to speak publicly, argued with supporters of secondary education for women, claiming that it was more suitable to give women professional training.[41] The conservative press, trying to discredit Świętochowski's position, claimed the lectures were devoid of merit both in their content and method. Nonetheless, the lectures brought increased support for the women's movement and success to the lecturer.

The Warsaw discussion about women's education crossed the borders of the Kingdom and elicited a response in Galicia. There the conservative position was expressed by Anastazja Dzieduszycka (1842-1890) in such works as *Kilka myśli o wychowaniu i wykształceniu niewiast naszych* (A few thoughts about the rearing and education of our women), *Gawędy matki* (A mother's tales), *Jeszcze o wychowaniu i powołaniu kobiet* (Once amore about the education and calling of woman), *Książka młodej kobiety* (The young woman's book).[42]

A more liberal and progressive position was taken by Józefa Dobieszewska (1820-1899) in her pamphlet "Wychowanie kobiet wobec dzisiejszych dążeń społecznych (Women's education in light of current social goals).[43] Leon Biliński treated the woman question as part of a larger social issue. He was a professor of political economy at Lvov and in 1874 gave a lecture "O pracy kobiet ze stanowiska ekonomicznego" (Women's work from an economic point of view).[44] He was an unqualified supporter of women's economic emancipation but opposed them on the subject of political rights.

In the Kingdom, in the meantime, discussion about women gained momentum and continued spreading into wider circles. Both men and women discussed it. Among the women, Eliza Orzeszkowa's voice was the loudest and most committed. In 1871 she published "Kilka słów o kobietach (A few words about women) in the *Tygodnik mód i powieści* (Fashion and story weekly);[45] two years later it appeared in book form. She described women's economic conditions and told them what they would have to do in the future. She said: "There is no better way to deprive someone embarking on life than by failing to give them the love and means to work; there is no way to do them greater harm than by narrowing their field of work and taking away their strength and means for it. In this way are all women deprived, except for the wealthy ones. It is time to discard the superstition which causes rich girls to be raised as dilettantes instead of preparing them for professional work. All women need to be prepared for professional work since the time of rentiers and those living on respect has passed and the time of workers has arrived."[46] She went on to say that all women should be learning "everything that men learn, and everything that makes women legitimate and intelligent beings; everything on which her moral and material existence rests."

Orzeszkowa illustrated her views by her stories. Some of them became famous outside of Poland, particularly *Marta*.[47] In it Orzeszkowa told the tragic tale of a young widow who perished along with her child because she had never been prepared to earn her own living. First published in serial form in 1872, it was translated into several languages including Esperanto. In German it appeared as *Ein Frauenschicksal* (A Woman's Fate).[48] It became a standard in the circulating mobile libraries, and part of the propaganda for the women's group Frauenbildung.

Orzeszkowa dealt with the social situation of women in other works such as *Ostatnia miłość* (Last Love), *Pamiętnik Wacławy* (The diary of Wacława) and *Panna Graba* (Miss Graba). She used these to protest against discrimination of women and to demand educational reform and equal rights in the economic sphere. In probing the inequality women experienced in marriage, she called for the right to divorce, moral reform of marital life, and the shaping of a new type of man who would view a wife as an equal partner.

The literary and journalistic activities of Orzszkowas rendered significant service for the women's movement. Under her it gained strength and won new adherents and sympathizers, resulting in many new publications, some supporting and some fighting the emancipation movement. Negative was Nowicki in his pamphlet "Kilka myśli o emancypacji kobiet ("A few thoughts about the emancipation of women).[49] Henryk N. argued with him in the journal *Bluszcz* (Ivy)[50] and so did August Jeske in the

journal *Wieniec* (Wreath).[51] The continually debated topic was
how to raise and educate women. Jadwiga Ochorowiczowa in
"Uwagi ogólne o wychowaniu i wykształceniu dziewcząt"
(General remarks about the rearing and education of girls)[52] and
Joanna Kuczyńska in "Mysli o edukacji kobiet" (Thoughts about
the education of women)[53] expressed their opinions but added
nothing new to the debate.

The discussion took a new direction with the appearance of
Edward Prądzyński's *O prawach kobiety* (Women's rights).[54]
The appearance of the book represented the conclusion of a
period of sometimes disorderly and sometimes dignified discussion on the topic of women's liberation. Being a lawyer, Prądzyński
took his views from law and economics. But he lacked the
courage to demand full rights for women. His vision of equality
meant primarily women's increased maternal influence. He
considered the husband's authority inviolable, insisting on rights
only for unmarried women, while viewing the marriage partnership as one requiring sacrifices only from women. Yet even this
tempered position provoked outrage in a large part of society.
The journal *Przegląd Katolicki* (Catholic Review) came out with
a criticism of those ladies who had handed Prądzyński an in-
scribed album as tribute. Editors of the journal expressed the
hope that those ladies had not read his book because if so one
would have to doubt their reason and virtue. A year after the
appearance of that book, Prądzyński published "Kobieta i wymiar
kary w społeczeństwie (Woman and the measure of punishment
in society)[55] in which he stated, among other things, that since
women are by nature milder than men they can help reduce the
crime rate and moderate penal laws by rendering them more
humane.

Prądzyński's work was seconded by Stanisław Przyborowski
in his *O prawach kobiety* (About the rights of women).[56] Analyz-
ing the differences, specifically the physical and psychological
ones between men and men, he concluded that it was only the
absence of rights and cultural conditioning which pushed women
into a subsidiary position. He said in the introduction "Give
women an education, and she will match men in politics, in her

desire to solve social and educational problems. The proof lies in the fact that among outstanding individuals in human history there have been women." In conclusion he insisted that "If we raise women to be good workers, if we stimulate their autonomy by assuring them economic security, it will be easier for us in the future to make of them resourceful mothers, and also citizenesses when that time comes, as well as wives, guardians of future generations and human welfare in general, not to mention companions to men in the field of learning."[57] This faith in women's abilities and intellectual competence was shared, though not fully, by Tymoteusz Stępniewski in his pamphlet "Kobieta, jej udział w rzeczach miłosierdzia, lecznictwa i nieżaleznej pracy (Woman, her participation in acts of mercy, healing, and independent work).[58] But a critical opinion of women's intellectual resources came from Ludwik Dziankowski in *O charakterze kobiet podług Spencera* (About the nature of women according to Spencer).[59] As is evident from this title, the feminist movement in Poland came, for sometime, under the influence of Herbert Spencer.

The Warsaw supporters of the women's movement were attacked by Stanisław Bronkowski of Posen. In *Emancypacja i równouprawnienie kobiety* (Emancipation and equal rights for woman)[60] he insisted that Polish women did not need emancipation which was created by the unhealthy and iconoclastic spirit of the USA. He considered the journalistic efforts of such women as Orzeszkowa highly dangerous and countered the ideal of the emancipated woman with an ideal of the picous woman.

But the views of such as Bronkowski did not halt the women's emancipation movement in the Kingdom of Poland. For the movement was supported by leading journalists and writers. The previously mentioned K.W. Wójciki published, in 1875, *Niewiasta Polska w początkach naszego stulecia (1800-1830)* (The Polish woman at the beginning of our century [1800-1830])[61] while H. Skimborowicz, a few years later came out with a series of articles on N. Żmichowska and the Enthusiasts as well as other prominent women artists and writers.[62] Piotr Chmielewski worked on similar topics. In the introduction to his

Autorki polskie XIX w. (Polish women writers of the nineteenth century)[63] published in 1885, he discussed contemporary literature and the state of research on Polish women.

Aside from these works which appeared in the 1880s others also analyzed the situation of women but from different perspectives. The *Przegląd Pedagogiczny* (Pedagogical Review) ran some articles on the working and social situation of teachers; this occurred mainly while Jan Władysław Dawid was its editor. Zofia Kowerska also focused on the plight of teachers. Her "O wychowaniu macierzynskim" (On maternal upbringing)[64] written for a contest advertised by *Bluszcz* easily served as concise psychological text on the theory of child-rearing. Romania Kamieńska published *Przyczyny i skutki kobiecej niewoli* (The cause and consequences of women's slavery)[65] while Józef Gajnert's "Kobieta w gospodarstwie i rodzinie" (Woman in the home and in the family),[66] written in a conservatively liberal spirit was intended as an advice book for rural housewives. E. Orzeszkowa continued to voice her opinions as she had done in the previous decade. Not only did she publish in the journal *Świt* (Dawn) but her concise survey of the woman question and movement in the Kingdom of Poland appeared in the collective work *The Woman Question in Europe* by Theodore Stanton.[67]

In the 1880s socialism gained momentum in the Kingdom. The attitude of Polish socialists toward the women's movement was defined in its general program which called for "total freedom of the individual, without consideration of gender, race or nationality." Socialists appreciated the women's fight for their rights and understood the need to support it. They especially respected those women whose strong will and determination overcame the opposition and outrage of society as well as those who sought learning and independence. The unknown author of the article "Wyzwolenie kobiet i socjalizm" (The Liberation of women and socialism) in 1886 wrote "How much ridicule and insult is heaped everywhere upon those who instead of twinkling their eyes and frequenting balls....have engaged in difficult slow study and spend their entire days over books, thereby winning for themselves and their comrades the right to work."[68]

In 1891 on the twenty-fifth anniversary of E. Orzeszkowa's literary activity, Paulina Kuczalska-Reinschmit's hope to arrange a convention of Polish women including the author failed, so instead, she settled for the publication of a commemorative book *Upominek* (A Keepsake).[69] Among others, the book contained Kuczalska-Reinschmit's essay "Trzy doby kwestii kobiecej u nas (Our three days of the women's question). German women also contributed and Orzeszkowa replied with "List otwarty do kobiet niemieckich" (An open letter to German women).[70] Here she expanded her ideas about contemporary women. She considered demands for professional education as too meagre a program and insisted that after twenty years of successful efforts for education women ought to have reached the second phase of their development, paying attention to moral issues. She defined herself as opposed to ruthless phrases such as "Force before law" or "exterminate"; women should instead "create a better world by spreading ideas of harmony in all aspects of life such as home, school, associations;[71] if they were to assist the cause of peace, they, themselves, had to attain a high moral level of existence. "The fighting women of the 19th century should be followed by the apostles and reformers of the twentieth." The right education would create just such a woman according to Orzeszkowa's proposal in the *Związek Cnoty* (Association of Virtue). Her program extended far beyond Polish pedagogical thought of the positivist era. Her eager heart outstripped current pedagogy but not only on the question of women. Her new work *Gloria Victis* was a hymn of love and praise over the graves of the insurrectionists of 1863. In 1891 she published *O kobiecie* (On woman)[72] consisting of three parts: 1. Polish Women 2. Indian Women 3. Letters about women.

Journalism and literature helped deepen the ideological basis and consolidated the emancipation movement of women in the Kingdom and created incentives to activate and radicalize their demands. Aside from Orzeszkowa the women's movement was greatly supported by the pen of Bolesław Prus. Yet in his novel *Emancypantki* (Emancipated Women)[73] he took a fairly conservative position.

The natural character of women, as one deduces from his novel, limits women's life in social and political spheres. Similar views were held by the author of "O emancypacji i równouprawnieniu kobiet" (About emancipation) in his *Kobieta w społeczeństwie ze stanowiska przyrodniczego* (Woman in society from a biological point of view).[74] Progressive journalists who in their desire to promote the movement unmasked and criticized all signs of retrogression, attempts to split the movement, and distortions of its nature, pointed out to the public that the movement was not developing linearly and also that its aim and nature was different for the bourgeoisie than it was for the proletariat. Bronisław Darski in *Emancypacja i macierzyństwo* (Emancipation and motherhood) wrote that "the woman question appears in those spheres where women suffer from excess free time, and promotes issues which are far removed from the majority of women...their point is, can women love three or four more times than they did before?(...) they demand equal rights with men with respect to free love (...) Meanwhile the serious side of this painful issue: to return to women their social significance which they have lost on the one hand because of luxury and on the other because of poverty (...) to return to the family those children seduced by the market (..) all this has lain fallow."[75] The majority of those concerned with the woman issue, and especially progressive journalists, emphasized above all the injustice of the socio-economic conditions for women, and the social distance which made the solution of the problem impossible. Stanisław Gall in his article "Emancypacja kobiet" (Emancipation of women) wrote "What is the situation of proletarian women with respect to the emancipation movement of middle class women? First of all, for proletarians, there is no conflict with men since that is not necessary. This is so because in this group the interests of the women are the interests of the men.(...) the demands of women emancipators are without meaning for workers. What use is it, to a working woman, to demand higher education or female high schools? (...) what does she care for reforms in the civil code, in commercial or family law, when she has no wealth, and the married conditions for working women have a different character than bourgeois ones which reflect the fact that the new codes were intended for the bourgeoisie.[76] Progressive journalists clearly stressed their conviction that economic conditions and unequal social conditions condemned women to be exploited and that it was the change in those conditions that would determine their future role in society. Social equality for women was tied, according to them, to abolition of class exploitation. The vision of new social conditions carried with it the vision of future family relations. These projected new family relations were egalitarian in nature. They promised much greater emotional ties as well as similarity of interests. According to this vision, marriage was increasingly becoming an expression of individual inclinations and its function was to make the union of man and woman happier and more successful than had hitherto been possible. The condition for fulfilment of these expectations was to be the acknowledgement of woman as being entitled to equal decisions in marital relationships.

Along with the vision of the new family model came the propaganda for conscious motherhood, forming an integral element of healthy family relations. Regulation of the number of children and family planning were factors, which according to progressives, would permit women to escape from narrow domestic duties and therefore put them in the position of being autonomous beings. This issue was analyzed among others by Zofia Daszyńska-Golińska in *Krytyka* (Criticism),[77] who expressed the most current views on the question of relations between husbands and wives and within the family. Her perspective was largely shared by Zenon Pietkiewicz in *Szkice Społeczne* (Social Sketches).[78] In a large section of his work entitled "Woman" he analyzed such issues as education, social life, the education of girls, motherhood, and marriage.

Apart from publications dealing with the contemporary emancipation issues toward the end of the century, others appeared which took the prominent Polish Kingdom women into consideration. First of all there was a new edition of Felicja (née Wasilewska) Boberska's (1825-1889) brief biographies of women such as Tańska-Hoffmanowa, Żmichowska, Emilia Plater, Klaudyna (née Działyńska) Potocka, Anna Nakwaska, Emilia Sczaniecka, Maria (née Czartoryska) Wirtemberg.[79] Tańska-Hoffmanowa provoked the most interest from among this group because of the centenary of her birth in 1898. Piotr Chmielewski[80] and Antonia Machczyńska[81] specifically focused on her pedagogy.

Particularly noteworthy are memoirs of the 1863 uprising of which a large number appeared at the turn of the century. Among them are numerous and previously unknown accounts the most interesting of which are Sewryna Duchińska,[82] Jan Stella Sawicki,[83] Marian Rogiński,[84] Franciszek Rawita Gawroński.[85] Those of Emilia Heurichowa and Teodora Kiślańska are the outstanding ones in this group.[86] On the fourtieth anniversary of the uprising a collection containing selections by various participants came out.[87] Józef Kościesza-Orzegalski made the provocative observation that women "were greater patriots than the men. Many a young man would not have participated had he not feared the ridicule and derision of women."[88] Russians also wrote about the women of the uprising in Nicholas Berg's *Zapiski o polskich spiskach i powstaniach* (Notes on Polish conspiracies and uprisings)[89] and W. Nostitz's *Wospominania iz wriemion polskogo miatieża.*[90] Many valuable details are also to be found in the correspondence of three participants of the uprising: Ewa Horyniec, Marta Rogala, and Małgorzata Bianiasówna published in 1908 by Bronisław Laskownicki in *Nasz Kraj* (Our Nation).[91] Numerous, although slight, references to the participation of women in the uprising exist also in the source works of Stanisław Zieliński *Bitwy i potyczki 1863-1864* (Battles and skirmishes 1863-1864)[92] and Henryk Cederbaum's *Powstanie styczniowe. Wyroki Audytoriatu Polowego* (January Uprising. The judgements of the Field Court).[93] This latter cites the names of eighty-nine women who appeared in Russian courts because of their various actions during the uprising. Among them were noble, urban, and peasant women. Given this fact the fixed stereotype of the Polish woman of that era, portrayed in literature as either the brave noblewoman–"amazon" on the one hand, or the mournful sufferer on the other, (as portrayed by Artur Grottger for example), misses the truth and needs correction. F.R. Gawroński described one such "amazon," namely, Henryka Pustowójtówna.[94] Henryk Wierciński also wrote about her in *Ziemia Lubelska*.[95] He was the author of *Polki w 1863 r.* (Polish women in 1863).[96]

The movement entered a new phase at the beginning of the twentieth century when the ideological gains and organizational skills of the earlier period helped foster a wide social program and necessary propaganda. The most spectacular example of this was the planned publication in 1903 of *Głos kobiet w kwestji kobiecej* (Women's voices on the women's question)[97] containing articles by the most prominent leaders of the women's movement in the Kingdom and Galicia, members of the Polish Socialist Party, the Polish Social Democratic Party, and other non-party radicals. The theme dominating all the articles was the demand for equal rights in view of equal obligations, equal pay for the same work, and access to all forms of education and new professions. This agenda was developed in the 1904 Warsaw issue of a collection entitled *Kobieta współczesna* (Contemporary Woman).[98] This was an important publication illustrating the accomplishments of women especially in the field of learning and education, yet it was far removed from the radicalism of the articles appearing in *Women's voices on the women's question.* Some of the issues presented in these collections were concurrently discussed in popular periodicals. For example Paulina Kuczalska-Reinschmit published in *Ogniwo* (Link) the article "Emancypacja a miłość" (Emancipation and love),[99] while Izabela Moszczeńska announced in *Głos* (Voice) an interesting cycle of articles, "Kwestia kobieca w chwili obecnej" (The Women's Question at this moment).[100] She severely criticized women's accomplishments to date. She pointed out that neither the paid work for which they fought, and which made women "work cattle" and appendages of machines, nor the ability to become educated made for a true liberation of women, just the opposite: they enslaved her and made her dependent. She also concluded that educated women were not contributing to learning, and that all they did is become like men: "they go forward, but in the crowd of a general procession, while men are the standard-bearers who proceed them.[101] In the opinion of I. Moszczeńska women needed above all to concentrate on the issues of female hygiene, physical labor, prostitution, and the general problems of women's lives. She claimed that the women's movement needed new ideas which would allow women to release their full potential, so that they would not be treated simply as a doctor or teacher, but as a complete human being entitled to unconditional development. Waleria Marrené Morzkowska in *Kobieta czasów obecnych* (The contemporary woman)[102] added to this discussion by examining the upbringing of women and their preparation for professional work.

The revolution of 1905 had a significant impact on the women's movement. One of its social effects was the easing of political repression by Tsarist authorities. Taking advantage of, as it turned out, a short-lived thaw, conspiratorial organizations of women (from Poland and Lithuania, the Women's Association for the promotion of peasant education, the Flying University etc.) immediately transformed into open organizations and associations, and in some instances even changed their names and altered the nature of their work. It is here we find the source of the rich literature devoted to various aspects of the woman question. In this atmosphere Jadwiga Szczawińska-Dawidowa wrote her article criticizing female pensions for *Głos* (Voice)[103] while Teodora Męczkowska in "Służące i prostytucja" (Servants and prostitution)[104] portrayed the social standing and the moral conditions of women employed as servants in well-to-do houses. In turn, P. Kuczalska-Reinschmit published: "Młodzież żenska a sprawa kobieca" (Young women and the woman question)[105] and "Wyborcze prawa kobiet" (Elective rights of women)[106] while Maria Turzyma wrote *Wyzwalająca się kobieta* (The self-liberating woman).[107] The appearance of several other publications was tied to the Warsaw Congress of Polish Women which occurred in June 1907 and which was tied to the fortieth anniversary of Orzeszkowa's literary activity. Before the celebration Kuczalska-Reinschmit published, in 1906, "Orzeszkowa w ruchu kobiecym" (Orzeszkowa in the women's movement),[108] and

Maria Czesława Przewóska wrote "Eliza Orzeszkowa w literaturze i w ruchu kobiecym" (Eliza Orzeszkowa in literature and in the women's movement).[109] Also echoing the celebration was I. Moszczeńska's *O życiu i pracach Orzeszkowej* (About the life and works of Orzeszkowa).[110] She also, along with Julia Dickstein and Cecylia Walewska, edited a poll which sought to assess Orzeszkowa's influence on the social views of women. Aside from that the main organizors of the Women's Congress, among them M. Rajchmanowa (Orka), suggested the publication of *Kobieta polska w życiu społecznym* (Polish woman in social life) as a way of honoring Grzeszkowa. Very soon, in 1907, T. Męczkowska published *Ruch kobiecy. Ideały etyczno-społeczne* (The Women's movement. Ethical and Social Ideals).[111] In the next two years the following publications appeared: Aniela Szycówna's *Kobieta w pedagogice* (Women in Pedagogy),[112] and C. Walewska's *Ruch kobiecy w Polsce* (The Women's Movement in Poland).[113] In the latter, the author hoped to make a survey of the Polish women's movement. Unfortunately, hastily written, it contains many generalizations and oversimplifications.

Simultaneously, but independently of the enterprise *Kobieta polska w życiu społecznym,* a series appeared which was sponsored by the Polish Association for Women's Equal Rights. Just in one year, 1908, they came published: "Ekonomiczne czynniki ruchu kobiecego" (The economic factors in the women's movement)[114] by Edward Chwalewik, Ludwika Jahołowska-Koszutska's "Herezje w ruchu kobiecym" (Heresies in the women's movement),[115] Witold Koszutski's "Kobieta i polityka" (Woman and Politics),[116] Józef Lange's "O prawach kobiety jako żony i matki" (About the rights of woman as wife and mother),[117] and C. Walewska's "Z dziejów krzywdy kobiet" (From the history of women's wrongs).[118] Aside from the Polish Association for the Equal Rights of women and its publications, other groups also published that year. Until the outbreak of World War I about a total of twenty brochures and special publications appeared with some of them focusing on very narrow or very specific issues affecting the women's movement. A sampler of their variety is

illustrated by Maria Dulębianka's *Polityczne stanowisko kobiety*
(The Political situation of woman),[119] Justyna Budzińska-
Tylicka's *Higiena kobiety i kwestji z nią związane* (Women's
hygiene and connected issues),[120] Józefa Kodisowa's *Kwestja
Rodziny w sprawie kobiecej* (The family and the woman question),[121] Anna Leśniewska's *Nowe drogi pracy kobiet* (Newo
ways for women's work),[122] and the collective work *Kobieta
polska jako autorka pedagogiczna* (Polish woman as a pedagogical author).[123]

During those several years preceeding World War I, aside
from publications dealing with contemporary issues of the
women's movement, others dealt with prominent women in the
Kingdom during the nineteenth century. Biographies of figures
such as K. Tańska, I. Czartoryska, M. Wirtemberska, P.
Krakowowa, E. Ziemięcka, and N. Żmichowska appeared in the
monumental *Album biograficzny zasłużonych Polaków i Polek
wieku XIX* (Biographical album of worthy Polish men and
women in the nineteenth century).[124] It was Tańska and N.
Żmichowska, from among these women, who excited the greatest interest of historians. Separate historical sketches about their
activities were penned by Aleksander Kraushar[125] and Maksymil-
ian Bienenstock.[126] A. Machczyńska[127] also devoted time to
these women in her works as did Jadwiga Petrażycka-Tomicka.[128]
The work of these two authors represents the first attempt to
synthesize the history of Polish women.

The women's movement in the Kingdom found itself in a
difficult situation at the outbreak of the war. Nonetheless,
women not only did not cease their activity, but did a spectacular
job of organizing the 1917 Congress of Polish Women in
Warsaw. Its lectures, opinions, and public proposals were published in a memoir,[129] which contains very interesting source
material. That same year, A. Kraushar published a small item
"Generałowa Sowińska i Klementyna Hoffmanowa w czasach
powstania listopadowego i po kapitulacji Warszawy" (The wife
of General Sowiński and Klementyna Hoffmanowa during the
November uprising and after the surrender of Warsaw).[130] A very
popular work, by Irena Kosmowska, "Polska w życiorysach i

charakterystykach" (Poland through lives and characteristics)[131] appeared, in Warsaw, almost simultaneously. Kosmowska dwelt on the activities of Żmichowska and the Enthusiasts.

The social and legal situation of Polish women underwent marked change after independence in 1918. New political conditions provoked novel agendas giving rise to new organizations and associations. Despite the many difficulties for women in the Second Commonwealth they did become full citizens. One would expect that, as a result, a rapid development of women's historiography would have followed. But research on women did not develop and the situation was even worse with respect to historical studies on the women's movement in the Kingdom of Poland despite the apparent need for such studies. The Women's Progressive Political club issued a resolution in 1921 about the historical documentation of the Polish Women's movement.

Just as before independence, all research initiatives and all publication attempts with respect to the survey of the women's movement were born in Warsaw, Lwów or Kraków. In 1919 Józef Białynia-Chołodecki published, in Lwów, the lecture he had given at the Women's Volunteer League: "Kobieta polska w obronie ojczyzny" (Polish woman in defense of the fatherland).[132] He synthesized women's imput into national defense beginning with the legendary Wanda[133] and ending with World War I. In his discussion of the nineteenth century he paid particular attention to the participation of women in the January uprising. Other historians tackled the topic as well. During the first decade of independence Marian Dubiecki,[134] Franciszek Białokur,[135] Karolina Bielańska,[136] and Ludwik Zembrzuski[137] all wrote on the topic. Józef Kajetan Janowski, in his memoirs, referred to women's activities prior to and during the uprising.[138] Historians were also interested in the conspiratorial activity of Żmichowska and the Enthusiasts during the revolutionary era of 1848. Anna Minkowska treated this topic in broader historical perspective in "Organizacja spiskowa 1848r. w Królestwie Polskim" (Conspiratorial activity in the Kingdom of Poland during 1848)[139] as well as in another article "Tragizm entuzjastek" (The tragedy of the Enthusiasts).[140] Tadeusz Fiutowski focused on just one of the Enthusiasts, Izabela Zbigniewska.[141] The publication of Żmichowska's correspondence expanded the field of knowledge about her.[142] Krausbar's "Polki twórcze czasów nowszych" (Creative Polish women of our time)[143] was a expanded and corrected version of previously published items. In the 1920s studies dedicated to the literary and scholarly activities of women appeared. In 1922 The Society for the Advancement of Professional Training of Women sponsored the publication of Walewska's *Kobieta polska w nauce* (The Polish woman in academe).[144] After discussing the beginning of the women's educational movement in the nineteenth century, the author traced women's accomplishments in philosophy, history, economics, medicine and other areas. J. Petrażycka-Tomicka's *Kobieta w piśmiennictwie polskim* (Women as authors in Poland)[145] lauded the authorship of thirty-two Polish women, beginning with Queen Elizabeth and ending with Narcyza Żmichowska.

New publications explaining the woman question in the Kingdom appeared in the 1930s. C. Walewska's *W walce o równe prawa. Nasze bojownice* (The fight for equal rights. Our warriors).[146] came out in 1930 but it was essentially a collection of articles which had been published earlier by *Kobieta Współczesna* (Contemporary Woman) and consisted of brief accounts of prominent women in the movement with a last chapter dedicated to their activities. Also in 1930 the collection *Na straży praw kobiety* (On guard for women's rights)[147] appeared, intended as a memoir by the Women's Progressive Political Club of the first decade of the organization's activity. Among articles, which varied in their scholarly merit, the *Rys historyczny ruchu kobiecego w Polsce* (Historical survey of the women's movement in Poland) covered the activities of women in the Kingdom, albeit greatly condensed, beginning with the November Uprising. Women's activism in the uprising continued to interest researchers as witnessed by Maria Złotorzycka's "Warsztat pracy społecznej kobiet w 1831r." ("The workshop of women's social activism in 1831"),[148] A. Minkowska's "Kobiety w powstaniu styczniowym" (Women in the January Uprising)[149]

"Ostania Entuzjastka" (The last Enthusiast),[150] and Maria Bruchnalska's *Ciche Bohaterki* (Quiet Heroines).[151] This last work, despite many imprecisions and the absence of indexes which makes it difficult to use, is very important with respect to the women's participation in the uprising of 1863. Aside from portrayals of women in 1863 other publications appeared in the early 1930s showing women's contribution to various areas of human knowledge. In 1932 Dr. Melanie Lipińska's *Kobieta i rozwój nauk lekarskich* (Woman and the development of medical knowledge),[152] published earlier in France, came out in Warsaw. She surveyed women in medicine from antiquity to the present. She pointed out the significance of women in European medicine, as well as in the Near and Far East and both of the Americas, not forgetting to mention Warsaw women doctors at the turn of the century. Łucja Charewiczowa, who at the VII International Congress on Historical Studies of 1933 in Poland, gave a lecture "Czy należy opracować specjalną historię kobiet" (Should there be a separate history of women)[153] published an interesting article "Stanowisko kobiet polskich w popularyzatorskiej i naukowej pracy historycznej" (The position of Polish women in popular and scholarly historical work).[154] Her essay is important because of its focus on the contribution of Polish women to knowledge. It came out in 1939 under the editorship of Maria Loriowa in *Materiały do bibliografii piśmiennictwa kobiet polskich* (Materials for the bibliography of the writings of Polish women).[155]

The question of research on Polish women, aside from the forementioned L. Charewiczowa, was also raised in 1935 at the VI Historical Congress in Vilnus. During Anna Strzelecka's session on "Kobieta w polityce dynastycznej i w życiu dworskim za panowania Władysława Jagiełły" (Polish woman in dynastic politics and court life during the reign of Władysław Jagiełło) Professors Stanisław Zakrzewski and Stanisław Kutrzeba pointed out the absence, in Polish historigraphy, of works on the role and place of women in the history and culture of the Polish nation. Sharing this opinion the Association of Polish University Women made a special appeal to the participants of the Congress to undertake research on the women's movement in Poland.[156]

The appeal did not get much response among Polish historians. Of the few items dedicated to the history of women which appeared until World War II only three dealt with women in the Kingdom. In 1936 in *Przegląd Współczesny* (Contemporary Review) Jan Hulewicz published his interesting "Walka kobiet polskich o dostęp no uniwersytety" (The fight by Polish women for access to universities).[157] This historian, who had studied in Cracow with Stanisław Kot, continued this direction and in 1939 published *Sprawa wyższego wykształcenia kobiet w Polsce w XIX wieku* (The question of higher education for women in nineteenth century Poland).[158] He portrayed the aspirations and the direction those took, along with a brief sketch of the education of girls in the Kingdom of Poland. In the meantime Zofia Zaleska's *Czasopisma kobiece w Polsce. (Materjały do historii czasopism 1818-1937)* (Women's magazines in Poland [Materials for the history of magazines 1818-1937]).[159] This was the first and only thorough survey of Polish women's magazines. In her discussion of magazines in the Kingdom the author covered the major trends of the women's movement.

The war years, the period of occupation, along with the social and political changes following 1949, created a totally different perspective for research on the fate of Polish women in general, but particularly the women's movement in the Kingdom. Despite the difficulties caused by the unprecedented destruction of Polish libraries and archives during the war years, historians continued their work and as personal and institutional means of scholarly research were rebuilt the topic and chronological dimensions of the research widened, but simultaneously the communist authorities installed in Poland increased their political indoctrination of the academic world and determined paramenters and topics for scholarly research. The direction of historical studies was also shaped by the politics of publication, namely the preferences were for progressive topics and Marxist-Leninist methodology. That situation, among others, made it impossible for the unit called into existence by the board of University Women to issue the two volume *Encyklopedia ruchu kobiecego* (Encyclopedia of the Women's Movement). In 1948, a year before the organization was disbanded by the authorities, T. Męczkowska still managed to publish "Problemy ruchu kobiecego" (Problems of the Women's Movement)[160] in which she introduced, among others, a brief version of the women's movement in the Kingdom of Poland. In that same year, Zofia Żarnecka published *Działalność oświatowa Faustyny Morzyckiej na tle epoki* (Scholarly activity of Faustyna Morzycka in the context of the epoch)[161] and Adam Próchnik, *Kobieta w polskim ruchu socjalistycznym* (The Polish Woman in the Socialist Movement).[162] But this last was only a republished fragment of the author's ealier prewar work *Kobieta w walce o niepodległość i socjalizm w Polsce* (Woman in the fight for indepedence and Socialism in Poland).[163] Mieczysława Romankówna also published a biography of Orzeszkowa which she had researched before the war.[164]

The early 1950s was a period of increasing oppression and political persecution. In this difficult time few publications appeared dealing with women's activities in the Kingdom of Poland. Those that were published were ideologically the same. It is enough to mention from among this group Leon Kaltenbergh's "W służbie siermięgi przeciw kontuszowi" (In service to the peasant coat and against the noble coat), "O kobietach w rewolucji 1905-1907 r." ("About women and the revolution of 1905-07)[165] or Dionizja Wawrzywkowska-Wierciochowa's "Maria Bohuszewiczówna, ostatnia działaczka 'Proletariatu' (Maria Bohuszewiczówna, the last activist of the "Proletariat").[166] In 1955 the same author published the diary of Bohuszewiczówna.[167] In the following year she published one article "Tajny Uniwersytet Kobiecy—duma postępowej Warszawy" (The Flying University for Women—pride of progressive Warsaw).[168]

The partial liberalization of social life after October 1956 enabled historians and researchers on women's issues to increase and widen their scope. In 1956 K. Lutyńska published "Ideologia czasopism rodzinnych Królestwa Polskiego w latach 1860-1880" (The ideology of family magazines in the Kingdom of Poland during 1860-1888)[169] and in its wake came Stanisław Jedlewski's article about Jadwiga Szczawińska-Dawidówa,[170] M. Romankówna's about Enthusiasts,[171] Helena Olszewska's about Helena Kuczalska, the founder of the Warsaw school of Swedish Gymnastics,[172] and Wawrzykowska-Wierciochowa's about the conspiratorial activities of women and women's associations at the end of the nineteenth and beginning of the twentieth century.[173] Along with these articles came memoirs and correspondence of prominent women such as Żmichowska,[174] Jadwiga Prendowska,[175] Paulina Wilkońska,[176] Jadwiga Sikorska-Klemensiewicz,[177] Jadwiga Łuszczewska,[178] and Romana Pachucka.[179] This epistolary and memoir literature represents an interesting and rich source of information about the life and activities of Polish women in the nineteenth century Kingdom of Poland but even more. Its additional importance is due to a penetrating analysis of the aims and tasks of the Polish women's movement especially at the end of the nineteenth and start of twentieth century. R. Pachucka's memoirs make this point most vividly: she was one of the most active women in the movement at the turn of the century and cooperated with other activists such as Józefa Bojanowska and P. Kuczalska-Reinschmit. As a result, her diaries are a mine of information on the subject of the fight for the franchise, the right to work in various professions, and increasing gains in university education.

Growing interest in women's history and the women's movement resulted in a whole series of monographs at the end of the 1950s and 1960s as well as the first attempts at synthesis. In 1959 Zbigniew Filar's *Anna Tomaszewicz-Dobrska. Karta z dziejów polskich lekarek* (Anna-Tomaszewicz-Dobrska. A chapter from the history of Polish women doctors).[180] She studied medicine at Zurich and became the first woman to practice medicine in Warsaw, 1878-1918. Filar depicts her life and work against the background of women's attempts to gain entry to higher education and the study of medicine. Also in 1959 Bożena Krzywobłocka published *O czarnej sukience i powstańczej dwururce* (About a black dress and the revolutionary double barrel)[181] in which she fictionalized the best known participants of the 1863 uprising. In the next few years there followed: Regina Kociowa on Irena Kosmowska,[182] Hanna Mortkowicz-Olaczakowa on Stefania Sempołowska,[183] Krystyna Jabłońska on Faustyna Morzycka,[184] Edmund Jankowski on Orzeszkowa,[185] and Martian Stępień on Żmichowska[186] and a few more works by Wawrzykowska-Wierciochowa[187] of which *Z dziejów kobiety wiejskiej* (The history of village women) and *Od prządki do austronautki* (From spinner to astronaut) are most worthy of mention. In the book on village women Wawrzykowska-Wierciochowa discusses them from the 1860s to post World War II. She presents village organizations, both social and educational. She also gives considerable attention to the single conspiratorial group which spanned all three partitioned areas of Poland: the Women's Association of the Crown and Lithuania.[188]

In the second book she cites the various contributions women made to national culture covering by one thousand years of activities by Polish women (from the tenth century till 1939). She undertakes the discussion within a European context and pays particular attention to the fight for independence. She covers the legal situation of women in Poland from the beginning of its statehood, women's role in the medieval urban family, and the effect on women of the progressive currents during the sixteenth and seventeenth century. She shows the beginning of the emancipation movement and the participation of women in the November and January uprisings. Furthermore, she discusses the numerous women's organizations of the late nineteenth century as well as the prominent women activists. Both of Wawrzykowska-Wierciochowa's books, despite some shortcomings with respect to merit and methodology represent, a significant contribution to Polish women's historiography. Stanisław Wasylewski's *Życie polskie w XIX w* (Polish life in the nineteenth century)[189] and Helena Duninowna's *Kobieto puchu marny* (Woman you worthless fluff)[190] must be included in that category, too. The last one is a collection of popular historical sketches whose common topic is the Polish woman, mainly in the nineteenth century. Both are written in lively contemporary style and contain significant information about women in the Kingdom of Poland.

A whole new spate of publications dedicated to the history and activism of Polish women appeared in the 1970s and 1980s. For the most part, however, these were popular or literary items in the form of biographical sketches, biographies and monographs. Within this group there are publications which to a lesser or greater sense touch on the woman question in the Kingdom of Poland. Among these are the works of B. Krzywobłocka,[191] M. Romankówna,[192] Jan Detko,[193] Bogdan Nowroczyński,[194] Gabriela Pauszer-Klonowksa,[195] Jadwiga Dackiewicz,[196] D. Wawrzykowska-Wierciochowa,[197] and Stefan Król.[198] Król's work covers the lives of one hundred and one prominent Polish women from antiquity to the present. Written for popular consumption, these works do not contribute anything new to scholarship. Among women from the time of the Kingdom we find Tańska-Hoffmanowa, I. Czartoryska, N. Żmichowska, M. Konopnicka and H. Pustwojtowna. The activities of Pustwojtowna before the uprising of January are the topic of an article by Ryszard Bender.[199] M. Złotorzycka also writes about her and other participants in another popular work.[200] Wiktoria Śliwowska in "Polskie drogi do emancypacji" (Polish roads to emancipation)[201] discusses the activities of women in the Polish independence movement during 1833-1856. Women's role in the cultural life of Warsaw during that period is documented by Helena Michałowska in *Salony artystyczno-literackie w Warszawie 1832-1860* (Artistic and literary salons in Warsaw 1832-1860)[202] and Zofia Chyra-Rolicz deals with the associations of the women's movement at the turn of the century.[203] Maria Zawalska, absorbed by the journalistic and editorial activities of Maria Konopnicka put together an article on a peripheral issue "Spór Marii Konopnickiej z Czesławem Jankowskim o poglądy na kwestję kobiecą" (The Quarrel between Maria Konopnicka and Czesław Jankowski about the woman question).[204]

Historians were also interested in the participation of women in education and learning. Kamila Mrozowska undertook this problem in "Sto lat działalności kobiet polskich w nauce i oświacie" (One hundred years of activities by women in learning and education).[205] Extending the chronological framework of this topic (from XIV-XX), her article "Kobiety polskie w nauce i oświacie" (Polish women in learning and education) was included in a collective work *Kobiety Polskie* (Polish Women).[206] In this same publication there was also a group of articles with a single ideological cast: Irena Koberdowa's "Kobiety w ruchu robotniczym" (Women in the workers movement), Wawrzykowska-Wierciochowa's "idział kobiet polskich w ruchu robotniczo-rewolucyjnym" (The participation of Polish women in the workers revolutionary movement), Michał Szyszko's "Kwestia kobieca w polskim ruchu robotniczym" (The woman question in the worker's movement) and Maria Mioduchowska's "Kobiety w ruchu ludowym (Women in the people's movement) as well as others which did not deal with the women's movement in the Kingdom of Poland.

This bibliographical survey of works and publications concerning the woman question in the Kingdom of Poland leads me to conclude that this broad issue still lacks a synthesis. The existing studies usually concentrate on only one of the aspects of their activities. The personalities representing the women's movement are limited to factual data, nothing has been done to delve into their attitudes or goals, that is, to present them as real people. Instead they are grouped around goals such as the struggle to gain access to university education, for example. So far nothing has been written showing the views of feminists about their issues. Researchers have mainly selected those who contributed to various aspects of national culture or those who actively participated in political or conspiratorial activity, but who often treated their participation in the women's movement as a secondary, or one just artificially connected with it, because they simply were women living in an era when emancipation activity occurred. Those activists whose leading task and aim in life was the fight to give to the "fair sex" their proper standing in social, cultural and economic life have been mostly ignored. Therefore the history of the women's movement in the Kingdom of Poland and, even more so, the history of the entire Polish women's movement await their historian.

Notes to Chapter 9

1. Plea by the future wives of the inhabitants of Poland to the employers in the Kingdom of Poland. In: "Pamiętnik Warszawski," 1818, vol. 12, pp. 109-113.

2. Translator's Note: It is customary, to this day, to give women's maiden names as a way of identifying their family of origin. The reasons for this are described in Bogna Lorence-Kot's "Child-Rearing and Reform: A Study of the Nobility in Eighteenth-Century Poland." Westport, Conn.: 1985.

3. "Pamiętnik Warszawski," 1819, vol. 13, pp. 325-328. This article must have provoked the interest of readers because the next edition of "Warsaw Diary" published an article "Some remarks about the article: About the indifference of men toward women." In addition, the growing interest in the activities of women is attested to by the work of Jan Sowiński "About Learned Polish Women". Warsaw and Krzemieniec 1821, which was favorably received by women of the upper social spheres. The author discussed the literary contributions of fifty-six pre-modern Polish women. The announced second edition did not appear.

4. "Pamiętnik Warszawski," 1820, vol. 16, pp. 238-252.

4a. Ibid., 1822, vol.3, pp. 348-373.

5. K. Tańska, Pamiątka po dobrej matce, czyli ostatnie jej rady dla córki. Przez młodą Polkę. Warszawa 1819. Cf. the review by K. Brodziński, in: "Pamiętnik Warszawski," 1819, vol. 15, pp. 311-319. I. Kotowa, Pierwsze dzieło Klementyny Tańskiej, in: "Pamiętnik Literacki," 1925/1026. vol. XXII and XXIII, p. 206 and passim. The author changed her name into Hoffmanowa when marrying Karol Hoffman in 1829.

6. Tańska's book became so popular that a second edition came out in 1819. Between 1819 and 1898 followed ten more editions and two in form of her collected works.

7. K. Tańska, Amelia matką. Warszawa 1822-1824, vol. 1-3. Vol. 4 never came to publication. Listy o wychowaniu kobiet. Wrocław 1849, vol. 1-3, 2nd ed. Berlin 1851, 3rd ed. Berlin-Poznań 1866.

8. E. Ziemięcka, Myśli o wychowaniu kobiet nadesłane przez młodą Polkę, in: "Tygodnik Polski," 1833, vol. 1, pp. 24-27, vol. 2, pp. 116-126.

9. A. Czajkowski, O prawach kobiet. Kraków 1836.

10. "Pierwiosnek. Noworocznik obejmujący pisma samych dam!." Warszawa 1838-1843.

11. "Pielgrzym. Pismo poświęcone filozofii, historii i literaturze." Warszawa 1842-1846.

12. E. Ziemięcka, Myśli o wychowaniu kobiet. Warszawa 1843.

13. E. Ziemięcka, Zarysy filozofii katolickiej w czterech poglądach zawarte. Warszawa 1857.

14. E. Ziemięcka, Kurs nauk wyższych dla kobiet, obejmujący psychologię, estetykę, pedagogikę i moralność. Vol. 1-4, Warszawa 1863-1864.

15. S. Bogusławski, Lwy i lwice. Komedia w 3 aktach wierszem, in: Komedie oryginalne. Warszawa 1848, vol. 2, pp. 126-158.

16. A. Wilkoński, Emancypacja Sabiny ze stanowiska absolutnego. Komedia w dwóch aktach, in: Ramoty i ramotki literackie. Warszawa 1845, vol. 2, pp. 8-91.

17. K. W. Wójcicki, Niewiasty polskie. Zarys historyczny. Warszawa 1845.

18. H. Skimborowicz, Umysłowość kobiet w Polsce, in: "Kalendarzyk Damski" na rok 1844. Warszawa 1843, pp. 9-40.

19. "Niewiasta," 1860, No. 7, pp. 2-4, No. 8, pp. 2-4, 1861, No. 1, pp. 2-4, No. 2, pp. 2-4 and No. 4, pp. 2-4, 1862, No. 2, pp. 15-16, No. 3, p. 24, No. 4, pp. 31-32, No. 5, p. 40, No. 6, pp. 47-48, No. 8, p. 64, No. 10, p. 80, No. 12, pp. 95-96.

20. K. Estreicher, Bibliografia Polska XIX stulecia. Kraków 1873, vol. 1, pp. 48-52 and vol. 6, p. 24.

21. T. H. Buckle, Wpływ kobiet na postęp wiedzy. Warszawa 1867.

22. J. S. Mill, O poddaństwie kobiet. Toruń 1870, 2nd ed. Kraków 1886 and 3rd ed. Kraków 1887.

23. E. Legouvé, Dzieje moralne kobiet. Warszawa 1873, vol. 1-3.

24. P. Leroy-Beaulieu, Praca kobiet w XIX w. Warszawa 1875.

25. E. Reich, Studia nad kobietą. Warszawa 1876.

26. T. Dymidowiczowa, Listy moralne poświęcone młodszemu pokoleniu Polek. Warszawa 1863.

27. Z. Meller, Słówko w kwestii moralności kobiecej, in: "Przegląd Tygodniowy," 1867, No. 9, pp. 65-67.

28. J. Juszczyk, Czy kobiety mogą być u nas rzemieślnikami? In: "Przegląd Tygodniowy," 1867, No. 39, pp. 305-306, No. 40, pp. 313-314.

29. A. Goltz, Reforma w wychowaniu kobiet i użyciu ich czasu i pracy. Warszawa 1869.

30. W. Chomętowski, Stanowisko praktyczne dawnych niewiast. Warszawa 1872.

31. W. Jaroszyński, Kobieta. Warszawa 1869.

32. A. Nowosielski, O przeznaczeniu i zawodzie kobiet, in: "Tygodnik Ilustrowany," 1862, No. 166, pp. 215-218.

33. A. Nowosielski, O kwestii kobiecej, in: "Gazeta Polska," 1870, No. 126, pp. 1-3, No. 127, pp. 1-3.

34. R. Bierzyński, Somatologie de la femme, études physiologiques. Paris 1869.

35. R. Bierzyński, Jeszcze słówko o kobiecie. Warszawa 1870; Nieco o prawie kobiety do nauki i pracy. Warszawa 1871.

36. Ibid., p. 37.

37. A. Świętochowski, W sprawie kobiet, in: "Niwa," 1872, No. 10, pp. 231-235.

38. A. Świętochowski, Klauzurowe i swobodne wychowanie kobiet, in: "Niwa," 1872, No. 44, pp. 972-976.

39. A. Świętochowski, Kwestia małżeńska: I. Geneza i zasady, II. Miłość i ugoda, III. Poligamia i poliandria, IV. Separacja i rozwód, in: "Przegląd Tygodniowy," 1872, No. 46, pp. 361-362, No. 48, pp. 377-378, No. 50, pp. 393-394, 1873, No. 3, pp. 17-18.

40. A. Świętochowski, O średnim wykształceniu kobiet, in: "Przegląd Tygodniowy," 1873, No. 14, pp. 107-108, No. 15, pp. 114-115, No. 16, pp. 124-125, No. 17, pp. 131-132, No. 18, pp. 139-140, No. 19, pp. 146-147. O wyższym wykształceniu kobiet, ibid., 1874, No. 1, pp. 9-10, No. 2, pp. 17-18, No. 3, pp. 25-26, No. 4, pp. 32-33, No. 5, pp. 41-42, No. 6, p. 49, No. 7, pp. 56-57, No. 8, pp. 65-66, No. 9, pp. 73-74.

41. Cf. "Niwa," 1875, No. 32, pp. 517-518.

42. A. Dzieduszycka, Kilka myśli o wychowaniu i wykształceniu niewiast naszych. Lwów 1871, 2nd ed. Warszawa 1874. Gawędy matki. Lwów 1872. Jeszcze o wychowaniu i powołaniu kobiety. Warszawa 1878. Książka młodej kobiety. Warszawa 1881.

43. J. Dobieszewska, Wychowanie kobiet wobec dzisiejszych dążeń społecznych. Lwów 1871. Review by A. Świętochowski, in: "Przegląd Tygodniowy," 1871, No. 41, pp. 333-336. Dobieszewska's husband, a physician, was a great supporter of women's higher education.

44. L. Biliński, O pracy kobiet ze stanowiska ekonomicznego. Lwów 1874.

45. E. Orzeszkowa, Kilka słów o kobietach. Lwów 1873, 2nd ed. Warszawa 1874, 3rd ed. Warszawa 1893. Cf. Tanie zbiorowe wydanie powieści E. Orzeszkowej. Warszawa 1886, vol. 36. Tanie zbiorowe wydanie pism E. Orzeszkowej. Warszawa 1893, vol. 42. E. Orzeszkowa, Wybór pism. Warszawa 1952.

46. E. Orzeszkowa, Marta. Warszawa 1873.

47. "Marta" was published in Germany three years later. The last German edition appeared in East Berlin, 1984.

48. Complete title: Kilka myśli wstępnych o emancypacji kobiet przez N(owickiego), Warszawa 1872.

49. Słowo w kwestii reformy społecznego stanowiska kobiety przez Henryka N. Warszawa 1872.

50. A. Jeske, Wychowanie kobiet, in: "Wieniec," 1872, No. 28, pp. 255-257.

51. J. Ocherowiczowa, Uwagi ogólne o wychowaniu i wykształceniu dziewcząt. Warszawa 1873.

52. J. Kuczyńska, Myśli o edukacji kobiet. Warszawa 1874.

53. E. Prądzyński, O prawach kobiety. Warszawa 1873.

54. E. Prądzyński, Kobieta i wymiar kary w społeczeństwie. Warszawa 1874. (Published lecture from 29th of March 1874, given in Warsaw.)

55. S. Przyborowski, O prawach kobiety. Radom 1876.

56. Ibid., pp. 7 and 62.

57. T. Stępniewski, Kobieta, jej udział w rzeczach miłosierdzia, lecznictwie i niezależnej pracy. Warszawa 1876.

58. L. Dziankowski, O charakterze kobiet podług Spencera. Warszawa 1877.

59. S. Bronikowski, Emancypacja i równouprawnienie kobiety. Poznań 1877.

60. K. W. Wójcicki, Niewiasta polska w początkach naszego stulecia (1800-1830). Warszawa 1875.

61. H. Skimborowicz, Gabriella i Entuzjastki (przez Sfinxa), in: "Bluszcz," 1880, No. 10, pp. 73-74, No. 11, pp. 81-82, No. 12, pp. 89-90, No. 13, pp. 97-98, No. 14, pp. 106-108, No. 15, pp. 113-114, No. 16, pp. 121-122, No. 18, pp. 137-138, No. 19, pp. 145-146, No. 21, pp. 163-164, No. 27, pp. 209-210, No. 28, pp. 217-219, No. 29, pp. 227-229, No. 30, pp. 233-234 and

No. 32, pp. 249-250. Polki autorki, artystki i w dziejach krajowych sławne, ibid., 1880, No. 2, pp. 9-10, No. 3, pp. 17-18, No. 5, pp. 33-34, No. 6, pp. 43-44 and No. 7, p. 50. Polki autorki i artystki, ibid., 1879, No. 8, pp. 65-66, No. 9, pp. 75-76, No. 10, pp. 81-82, No. 13, pp. 108-109, No. 14, pp. 116-117, No. 15, pp. 125-126 and No. 16, pp. 134-135.

62. P. Chmielowski, Autorki polskie XIX w. Studium literacko-obyczajowe. Warszawa 1885.

63. Z. Kowerska, O wychowaniu macierzyńskim. Warszawa 1881, 2nd ed. Warszawa 1894.

64. R. Kamieńska, Przyczyny i skutku kobiecej niewoli. Warszawa 1884.

65. J. Grajnert, Kobieta w gospodarstwie i rodzinie. Warszawa 1888.

66. E. Orzeszkowa, Polki, in: T. Stanton, The Women Question in Europe. Przekład K. Sosnowskiego. Warszawa 1885, pp. 282-292.

67. "Przedświt. Czasopismo socjalistyczne," 1886, No. 9-12, p. 3.

68. Upominek. Książka zbiorowa na cześć Elizy Orzeszkowej (1866-1891). Kraków-Petersburg 1893. Due to difficulties with Tsarist censorship publication was delayed by two years so that Orzeszkowa did not receive the volume until autumn of 1893. The commemorative volume contained over two hundred authors.

69. E. Orzeszkowa, List otwarty do kobiet niemieckich w kwestii równouprawnienia kobiet. Warszawa 1900.

70. E. Orzeszkowa, List otwarty, ibid., p. 37.

71. E. Orzeszkowa, O kobiecie. Warszawa 1891. The first part of this work "O kobiecie polskiej" was mainly the same Orzeszkowa had prepared for T. Stanton's publication.

72. B. Prus (legal name: Aleksander Głowacki), Emancypantki, Warszawa 1894.

73. O emancypacji i równouprawnieniu kobiet, przez Przyjackiółkę młodzieży. Warszawa 1893. Bronisław Chlebowski is supposed to be the author.

74. H. Nussbaum, Kobieta w społeczeństwie ze stanowiska przyrodniczego. Warszawa 1897.

75. B. Darski, Emancypacja i macierzyństwo, in: "Głos," 1896, No. 20, p. 461.

76. S. Gall, Emancypacja kobiet, in: "Krytyka," 1896, vol. 1, p. 17.

77. Z. Daszyńska-Golińska, Znaczenie studiów ekonomicznych dla

ruchu kobiecego, in: "Krytyka," 1896, vol. 1, pp. 154-160 and 225-231.
78. Z. Pietkiewicz, Szkice społeczne. Warszawa 1898, pp. 105-223.
79. F. Boberska, Klementyna z Tańskich Hoffmanowa, Lwów 1893; Narcyza Żmichowska. Lwów 1893; O Polkach, które się szczególniej zasłużyły ojczyźnie w powstaniu listopadowym. Lwów 1893.
80. P. Chmielowski, Klementyna z Tańskich Hoffmanowa. Zarys biograficzno-pedagogiczny. Petersburg 1898.
81. A. Machczyńska, O życiu, pismach i wpływie Klementyny z Tańskich Hoffmanowej, Lwów 1899.
82. S. Duchińska, Wspomnienia moje z roku 1863, Lwów 1890.
83. J. S. Sawicki (płk. Struś), Wspomnienia. Kraków 1909. Cf. Ludzie i wypadki z 1861-1865. Obrazki z powstania. Lwów 1894, pt. 1-2.
84. M. Rogiński, Zapiski z czasów walki. Lwów 1910.
85. F. R. Gawroński, Pamiętniki czasów niedawnych. Kraków 1909.
86. E. Heurichowa i T. Kiślańska, Wspomnienia matki i córki z powstania 1863 r. Warszawa 1918.
87. W 40-tą rocznicę powstania. Wybór wspomnień. Lwów 1903. Cf. Księga Pamiątkowa, opracowana staraniem Komitetu Obywatelskiego w czterdziestą rocznicę roku 1863-1864 przez Józefa Białynię Chołodeckiego. Lwów 1904.
88. J. Kościesza-Ozegalski, Wspomnienia z krwawych dni. Kraków 1893, p. 282.
89. M. Berg, Zapiski o polskich spiskach i powstaniach. Warszawa 1906, pt. 1-10. Zapiski o powstaniu polskim 1863 i 1864 roku i poprzedzającej powstanie epoce demonstracji od 1856 r. Kraków 1899, pt. 1-3.
90. W. Nostitz, Wospominania iz wriemion polskogo miateża. Petersburg 1898.
91. B. Laskownicki, Polki w powstaniu styczniowym, in: "Nasz Kraj," 1908, vol. 3, pp. 32-34.
92. S. Zieliński, Bitwy i potyczki 1863-1864. Raperswill 1913.
93. H. Cederbaum, Powstanie styczniowe. Wyroki Audytoriatu Polowego z lat 1863, 1864, 1865 and 1866. Warszawa 1917.
94. F. R. Gawroński, Henryka Pustowojtówna. Sylwetka biograficzna 1838-1861, Lwów 1911. 2nd ed. in: Monografie z powstania styczniowego. Warszawa 1928.
95. H. Wiercieński, Henryka Pustowojtówna, in: "Ziemia Lubelska," 1916, No. 32, pp. 28-34.

96. H. Wiercieński, Polki w 1863 r. Lublin 1916.

97. Głos kobiet w kwestii kobiecej. Kraków 1903.

98. Kobieta współczesna. Praca zbiorowa. Warszawa 1904.

99. P. Kuczalska-Reinschmit, Emancypacja a miłość, in: "Ogniwo," 1904, No. 48, pp. 1142-1144.

100. I. Moszczeńska, Kwestia kobieca w chwili obecnej, in: "Głos," 1903, No. 26, p. 406 and No. 27, p. 422.

101. I. Moszczeńska, ibid., No. 25, p. 390.

102. W. Marrené-Morzkowska, Kobieta czasów obecnych. Warszawa 1903.

103. J. Szczawińska-Dawidowa, Pensje żeńskie, in: "Głos," 1905, No. 34, pp. 513-514 and No. 35, pp. 528-529.

104. T. Męczkowska, Służące a prostytucja. Warszawa 1905.

105. P. Kuczalska-Reinschmit, Młodzież żeńska a sprawa kobieca. Warszawa 1906.

106. P. Kuczalska-Reinschmit, Wyborcze prawa kobiet. Warszawa 1907.

107. M. Turzyma (właściwe nazwisko Wiśniewska), Wyzwalająca się kobieta. Kraków 1906.

108. P. Kuczalska-Reinschmit, Orzeszkowa w ruchu kobiecym, in: "Wędrowiec," 1906, No. 11, pp. 207-210.

109. M. Cz. Przewóska, Eliza Orzeszkowa w literaturze i ruchu kobiecym. Zarys syntetyczny. List jubilatki. Lwów 1906. 2nd ed. Kraków 1909.

110. I. Moszczeńska, O życiu i pracach Orzeszkowej. Warszawa 1910. Cf. Ich spowiedź. Wyniki ankiety dla uczczenia Orzeszkowej. Z przedmową Julii Dicksteinowej, objaśnieniami Cecylii Walewskiej. Warszawa 1912.

111. T. Męczkowska, Ruch kobiecy. Ideały etyczno-społeczne ruchu kobiecego. Warszawa 1907.

112. A. Szycówna, Kobieta w pedagogice. Matka, Warszawa 1908.

113. C. Walewska, Ruch kobiecy w Polsce. Warszawa 1909, pt. 1-2.

114. E. Chwalewik, Ekonomiczne czynniki ruchu kobiecego. Warszawa 1908.

115. L. Jahołkowska-Koszutska, Herezje w ruchu kobiecym. Warszawa 1908.

116. W. Koszutski, Kobieta i polityka. O potrzebie praw politycznych dla kobiet. Warszawa 1908.

117. J. Lange, O prawach kobiety jako żony i matki według przepisów obowiązujących w Królestwie Polskim. Warszawa 1908.

118. C. Walewska, Z dziejów krzywdy kobiet, Warszawa 1908.

119. M. Dulębianka, Polityczne stanowisko kobiety. Warszawa 1908.

120. J. Budzińska-Tylicka, Higiena kobiety i kwestie z nią związane. Warszawa 1909.

121. J. Kodisowa, Kwestia rodziny w sprawie kobiecej. Warszawa 1909.

122. A. Leśniewska, Nowe drogi pracy kobiet. Warszawa 1909.

123. J. Kosmowska, D. Milkuszyc, A. Szycówna, Kobieta polska jako autorka pedagogiczna. Warszawa 1912.

124. Album biograficzne zasłużonych Polaków i Polek XIX wieku, wydane staraniem i nakładem Marii Chełmońskiej. vol. 1, Warszawa 1901 (contains the biographies of I. Czartoryska, K. Hoffmanowa, E. Jaraczewska, P. Krakowowa, K. Potocka, M. Wirtemberska). Vol. 2, Warszawa 1903 (deals with the biographies of E. Sczaniecka, K. Sowińska, E. Ziemięcka, N. Żmichowska).

125. A. Kraushar, Kartka z życia Narcyzy Żmichowskiej (1844-1850), Warszawa 1909. (Miscellanea historyczne No. 35).

126. M. Bienenstock, Ze studiów nad historią oświaty w Polsce (Klementyna z Tańskich Hoffmanowa). Stryj 1913.

127. A. Machczyńska, Kobieta polska. Szkic historyczny na wystawę w Pradze w roku 1912. Lwów 1912.

128. J. Petrażycka-Tomicka, Z dziejów kobiety polskiej. Lwów 1914.

129. Pamiętnik Zjazdu Kobiet Polskich w Warszawie w roku 1917, pod redakcją J. Budzińskiej-Tylickiej. Warszawa 1918. Cf. Pamiętnik Zjazdu Kobiet Polskich 11 i 12 maja 1913 r. Kraków 1913.

130. A. Kraushar, Generałowa Sowińska i Klementyna Hoffmanowa w czasach powstania listopadowego i po kapitulacji Warszawy. Lwów 1917. (Miscellanea historyczne No. 67.) Cf. Warsztat pracy społecznej kobiet w 1831 r. Drobiazgi historyczne. Warszawa 1909.

131. I. Kosmowska, Polska w życiorysach i charakterystykach. Warszawa 1917.

132. J. Białynia Chołodecki, Kobieta polska w obronie ojczyzny. Słowo wstępne Marii Mazurkowej. Lwów 1919.

133. Translator's Note: The legendary Princes Wanda preferred death to marriage with a German.

134. M. Dubiecki, Udział kobiet naszych w powstaniu styczniowym, in: "Bluszcz," 1922, No. 5, pp. 35-37.

135. F. Białokur, Praca samarytańska i społeczna kobiet w powstaniu

styczaniowym 1863-1864 r. Warszawa 1928. Polski Czerwony Krzyż. Warszawa 1926.

136. K. Bielańska, Weteranki, in: "Bluszcz," 1924, No. 11, p. 129.

Kobieta polska w 1863 r., in: "Kobieta Współczesna," 1928, No. 46, pp. 5-6.

137. L. Zembrzuski, Rola kobiety w dziejach obcej i polskiej wojskowej służby zdrowia, in: "Lekarz Wojskowy," 1927, No. 6, pp. 681-688.

138. J. K. Janowski, Pamiętniki o powstaniu styczniowym. Lwów 1923-1931, pt. 1-3.

139. A. Minkowska, Organizacja spiskowa 1848 roku w Królestwie Polskim, Warszawa 1923.

140. A. Minkowska, Tragizm "entuzjastów," in: "Wiedza i Życie," 1929, vol. 3, s. 145-152.

141. T. Fiutowski, Izabela Zbiegniewska. (Przyczynek do historii Entuzjastek). Włocławek 1929.

142. Narcyssa i Wanda. Listy Narcyzy Żmichowskiej. Kraków 1929.

143. A. Kraushar, Polki twórcze czasów nowszych. Warszawa 1929. The book deals with the lives and works of Deotyma, Maria Ilnicka, Generałowa Sowińska, Klementyna Hoffmanowa, Gabriela Żmichowska and Klaudyna Potocka.

144. C. Walewska, Kobieta polska w nauce. Warszawa 1922.

145. J. Petrażycka-Tomicka, Kobieta w piśmiennictwie polskim (po roku 1863). Kraków 1927.

146. C. Walewska, W walce o równe prawa. Nasze bojownice. Warszawa 1930.

147. Na straży praw kobiety. Pamiętnik Klubu Politycznego Kobiet Postępowych 1919-1930, w opracowaniu Sylwii Bujak-Boguskiej. Warszawa 1930.

148. M. Złotorzycka, Warsztat pracy społecznej kobiet w 1831 r., in: "Kobieta Współczesna," 1931, No. 6, pp. 4-5.

149. A. Minkowska, Kobiety w powstaniu styczniowym, in: "Dla przyszłości," 1931, No. 1, pp. 3-5.

150. I. Zbiegniewska–Ostatnia entuzjastka. Warszawa 1931.

151. M. Bruchnalska, Ciche bohaterki. Udział kobiet w powstaniu styczniowym (materiały). Miejsce Piastowe 1933.

152. M. Lipińska, Kobieta i rozwój nauk lekarskich. Warszawa 1932.

153. Cf. Ł. Charewiczowa, Est–il fondé d'écrire une histoire spéciale de

la femmé? Part from: La Pologne au VII-e Congrés International des Sciences Historiques. Varsovie 1933, pp. 1-5.

154. Ł. Charewiczowa, Stanowisko kobiet polskich w popularyzatorskiej i naukowej pracy historycznej, in: "Kwartalnik Historyczny," 1933, vol. XLVII, pp. 3-26.

155. Materiały do piśmiennictwa kobiet polskich (do roku 1929). Nauki matematyczno-przyrodnicze i nauki stosowane. (ed.) M. Loriowa, Warszawa 1934.

156. Pamiętnik VI Powszechnego Zjazdu Historyków Polskich w Wilnie 17-20 września 1935. Lwów 1935, p. 572. Cf. H. Witkowska, Kobieta w przeszłości dziejowej (Z VI Zjazdu Historyków Polskich w Wilnie), in: "Kurier Warszawski," 1935, No. 273, p. 14.

157. J. Hulewicz, Walka kobiet polskich o dostęp na uniwersytety. Warszawa 1936.

158. J. Hulewicz, Sprawa wyższego wykształcenia kobiet w Polsce w XIX wieku. Kraków 1939.

159. Z. Zaleska, Czasopisma kobiece w Polsce. (Materiały do historii czasopism). Rok 1818-1937. Warszawa 1938.

160. T. Męczkowska, Problemy ruchu kobiecego, in: "Komunikat nr. 14 Zarządu Głównego Polskiego Stowarzyszenia Kobiet z Wyższym Wykształceniem," Warszawa 1948.

161. Z. Żarnecka, Działalność oświatowa Faustyny Morzyckiej na tle epoki 1864-1910. Warszawa 1948.

162. A. Próchnik, Kobieta w polskim ruchu socjalistycznym. Warszawa 1948.

163. A. Próchnik, Kobieta w walce o niepodległość i socjalizm w Polsce. Warszawa 1938.

164. M. Romankówna, Na nowych drogach–studia o Elizie Orzeszkowej. Kraków 1948.

165. L. Kaltenbergh, W służbie siermięgi przeciw kontuszowi, in: "Służba Zdrowia," 1950, No. 12, pp. 7-8. O kobietach w rewolucji 1905-1907, ibid., No. 18, pp. 6-7.

166. D. Wawrzykowska-Wierciochowa, Maria Bohuszewiczówna, ostatnia działaczka "Proletariatu," in: "Wiedza i Życie," 1954, No. 1, pp. 43-47. Kobieta polska w zaraniu ruchu wyzwoleńczego, ibid., No. 3, pp. 152-157. Zapomniana bojownica sprzed 100 lat, in: "Za wolność i lud," 1954, No. 6, pp.

8-9. Kobiety polskie pod sztandarem rewolucji, in: "Wiedza i Życie," 1955, No. 3, pp. 166-168.

167. M. Bohuszewiczówna, Pamiętnik. Opracowała D. Wawrzykowska-Wierciochowa. Wrocław 1954. 2nd ed., Warszawa 1984.

168. D. Wawrzykowska-Wierciochowa, Tajny Uniwersytet Kobiecyduma postępowej Warszawy, in: "Problemy," 1956, No. 12, pp. 891-893.

169. K. Lutyńska, Ideologia czasopism rodzinnych Królestwa Polskiego w latach 1860-1880, in: "Przegląd Nauk Historycznych i Społecznych," 1956, vol. 7, pp. 289-329.

170. S. Jedlewski, Jadwiga Szczawińska-Dawidowa, postępowa działaczka oświatowa przełomu XIX i XX w., in: "Studia Pedagogiczne," 1956, vol. 3, pp. 264-318.

171. M. Romankówna, Sprawa entuzjastek, in: "Pamiętnik Literacki," 1957, No. XLVIII, pp. 516-537.

172. H. Olszewska, Helena Kuczalska–pionierka wychowania fizycznego w Polsce, in: "Wychowanie fizyczne w szkole," 1958, No. 4, pp 6-22.

173. D. Wawrzykowska-Wierciochowa, Kobiece Koło Oświaty Ludowej (1883-1894), in: "Przegląd Historyczno-Oświatowy," 1960, No. 3, pp. 49-66. Udział kobiet w tajnym i jawnym ruchu społeczno-kulturalnym w Warszawie. Praca zbiorowa pod redakcją S. Tazbira. Warszawa 1961, pp. 283-319. Aldona Grużewska w rewolucyjnym ruchu młodzieży polskiej i rosyjskiej, in: "Przegląd Historyczny," 1962, No. 1, pp. 128-141.

174. N. Żmichowska, Listy, vol. 1. W kręgu najbliższych. Do druku przygotowała i komentarzem opatrzyła M. Romankówna. Pod redakcją S. Pigonia. Wrocław 1957. N. Żmichowska, J. Baranowska, Ścieżki przez życie. Wspomnienia. Opracowała m. Romankówna. Wstęp Z. Kossak, Wrocław 1961.

175. J. Prendowska, Moje wspomnienia. Kraków 1962.

176. P. Wilkońska, Moje wspomnienia o życiu towarzyskim w Warszawie. Warszawa 1959.

177. J. Sikorska-Klemensiewicz, Przebojom ku wiedzy, Wrocław 1960.

178. J. Łuszczewska (Deotyma), Pamiętnik 1843-1897, Warszawa 1968.

179. R. Pachucka, Pamiętnik z lat 1886-1914, Wrocław 1958.

180. Z. Pilar, Anna Tomaszewicz-Dobrska. Karta z dziejów polskich lekarek. Warszawa 1959.

181. B. Krzywobłocka, O czarnej sukience i powstańczej dwururce.

Warszawa 1959, 3rd ed. Warszawa 1964. Cf. Biografie nietypowe. Warszawa 1960 (concerning J. Woykowska, M. Ilnicka, K. Bujwidowa, J. Dawidowa, F. Morzycka).

182.　R. Kociowa, Irena Kosmowska. Warszawa 1960.

183.　H. Mertkowicz-Olczakowa, Panna Stefania. Dzieje życia i pracy Stefani Sempołowskiej. Warszawa 1961. Cf. Stefania Sempołowska, Pisma, vol. 1-4. Warszawa 1960.

184.　K. Jabłońska, Płomień na wietrze. Opowieść o Faustynie Morzyckiej. Lublin 1964.

185.　E. Jankowski, Eliza Orzeszkowa. Warszawa 1964 (with editions in the following years 1966, 1973, 1980 and 1987).

186.　M. Stępień, Narcyza Żmichowska. Warszawa 1968.

187.　D. Wawrzykowska-Wierciochowa, Z dziejów kobiety wiejskiej. Szkice historyczne 1861-1945. Warszawa 1961. Od prządki do astronautki. Z dziejów kobiety polskiej, jej pracy i osiągnięć. Warszawa 1963. W kręgu miłości i bohaterstwa. (Z dziejów humanitaryzmu polskiego i prakursorów Polskiego Czerwonego Krzyża). Warszawa 1965. Maria Bohuszewiczówna. Warszawa 1967. Nieznana karta działalności Marii Konopnickiej. Warszawa 1967. Z dziejów tajnych pensji żeńskich w Królestwie Polskim, in: "Rozprawy z Dziejów Oświaty," 1967, vol. 10, pp. 109-159. Pani Maria Jankowska-Mendelsohn. Warszawa 1968. Najdziwniejszy z adiutantów. Opowieść o Anieli Henryce Pustowojtównie. Warszawa 1968.

188.　Translator's Note: The term "Crown" refers to Poland and is a holdover of the Noble Commonwealth which was a union of Poland and Lithuania.

189.　S. Wasylewski, Życie polskie w XIX w. Kraków 1962.

190.　H. Duninówna, Kobieto puchu marny. Łódź 1965.

191.　B. Krzywobłocka, Delfina i inne. Warszawa 1988, 4th ed. Cf. Cezaryna Wojnarowska. Warszawa 1979. Towarzyszki tamtych dni. Opowieść o kobietach związanych z ruchem robotniczym i pierwszych polskich socjaliatkach. Poznań 1982.

192.　M. Romankówna, Narcyza Żmichowska. Kraków 1970.

193.　J. Detko, Eliza Orzeszkowa. Warszawa 1971.

194.　B. Nawroczyński, Cecylia Niewiadomska-tajna nauczycielka (1855-1925), in: "Przegląd Historyczno-Oświatowy," 1978, No. 4, pp. 505-508.

195.　G. Pauszer-Klonowska, Pani na Puławach. Warszawa 1980.

196. J. Dackiewicz, Paryż zdradzony czyli Izabela Czartoryska. Lublin 1975.

197. D. Wawrzykowska-Wierciochowa, Emilia Sczaniecka. Opowieść biograficzna. Warszawa 1970. Z umiłowania. Opowieść biograficzna o Wandzie z Wolskich-Umińskiej (1841-1926), Lublin 1973. Wysłouchowa. Opowieść biograficzna. Warszawa 1975. Płaskowicka. Opowieść biograficzna. Warszawa 1979. Stefania Sempołowska, Warszawa 1981. Sercem i orężem ojczyźnie służyły. Emilia Plater i inne uczestniczki powstania listopadowego 1830-1831. Warszawa 1982. Nie po kwiatach los je prowadził...Kobiety polskie w ruchu rewolucyjnym. Warszawa 1987. By dla wszystkich świeciło słońce...Opowieść o prawdziwym życiu niezwykłych kobiet. Lublin 1989.

198. S. Król, 101 kobiet polskich. Ślad w historii. Warszawa 1988.

199. R. Bender, Henryka Pustowojtów w manifestacjach przedpowstaniowych 1861 r., in: Losy Polaków w XIX-XX w. Warszawa 1987, pp. 576-597.

200. M. Złotorzycka, O kobietach żołnierzach w powstaniu styczniowym. Warszawa 1972.

201. Polskie drogi do emancypacji (O udziale kobiet w ruchu niepodległościowym w okresie międzypowstaniowym 1833-1856), in: Losy Polaków, ibid., pp. 210-246.

202. H. Michałowska, Salony artystyczne-literackie w Warszawie 1832-1860. Warszawa 1974.

203. Z. Chyra-Rolicz, O związkach ruchu emancypacji kobiet ze spółdzielczością przed odzyskaniem niepodległości, in: "Spółdzielczy Kwartalnik Naukowy," 1983, No. 3, pp. 119-130.

204. M. Zawialska, Spór Marii Konopnickiej z Czesławem Jankowskim o poglądy na kwestię kobiecą, in: "Rocznik Zakładu Narodowego im. Ossolińskich," 1975, vol. 11, pp. 115-127. Cf. "Świt" Marii Konopnickiej. Zarys monograficzny tygodnika dla kobiet, Wrocław 1978.

205. K. Mrozowska, Sto lat działalności kobiet polskich w nauce i oświacie. Kraków 1971.

206. Kobiety polskie. Praca zbiorowa. Warszawa 1986.

DATE DUE